The Native Speaker: M ⌐ ....y

BILINGUAL EDUCATION AND BILINGUALISM

Series Editors: Professor Colin Baker, *University of Wales, Bangor, Wales, Great Britain* and Professor Nancy H. Hornberger, *University of Pennsylvania, Philadelphia, USA*

Other Books in the Series
At War With Diversity: US Language Policy in an Age of Anxiety
James Crawford
Cross-linguistic Influence in Third Language Acquisition
J. Cenoz, B. Hufeisen and U. Jessner (eds)
Curriculum Related Assessment, Cummins and Bilingual Children
Tony Cline and Norah Frederickson (eds)
Dual Language Education
Kathryn J. Lindholm-Leary
English in Europe: The Acquisition of a Third Language
Jasone Cenoz and Ulrike Jessner (eds)
Foundations of Bilingual Education and Bilingualism
Colin Baker
Identity and the English Language Learner
Elaine Mellen Day
An Introductory Reader to the Writings of Jim Cummins
Colin Baker and Nancy Hornberger (eds)
Language and Literacy Teaching for Indigenous Education: A Bilingual Approach
Norbert Francis and Jon Reyhner
Languages in America: A Pluralist View
Susan J. Dicker
Language, Power and Pedagogy: Bilingual Children in the Crossfire
Jim Cummins
Language Revitalization Processes and Prospects
Kendall A. King
Language Use in Interlingual Families: A Japanese-English Sociolinguistic Study
Masayo Yamamoto
The Languages of Israel: Policy, Ideology and Practice
Bernard Spolsky and Elana Shohamy
Learning English at School: Identity, Social Relations and Classroom Practice
Kelleen Toohey
Learners' Experiences of Immersion Education: Case Studies of French and Chinese
Michèle de Courcy
Multicultural Children in the Early Years
P. Woods, M. Boyle and N. Hubbard
Power, Prestige and Bilingualism: International Perspectives on Elite Bilingual Education
Anne-Marie de Mejía
Reflections on Multiliterate Lives
Diane Belcher and Ulla Connor (eds)
The Sociopolitics of English Language Teaching
Joan Kelly Hall and William G. Eggington (eds)
World English: A Study of its Development
Janina Brutt-Griffler

Please contact us for the latest book information:
Multilingual Matters, Frankfurt Lodge, Clevedon Hall,
Victoria Road, Clevedon, BS21 7HH, England
http://www.multilingual-matters.com

BILINGUAL EDUCATION AND BILINGUALISM 38
Series Editors: Colin Baker and Nancy H. Hornberger

The Native Speaker: Myth and Reality

Alan Davies

MULTILINGUAL MATTERS LTD
Clevedon • Buffalo • Toronto • Sydney

Library of Congress Cataloging in Publication Data
Davies, Alan
The Native Speaker: Myth and Reality/Alan Davies
Bilingual Education and Bilingualism: 38
Includes bibliographical references and index.
1. Native language. 2. Applied linguistics. I. Title. II. Series.
P120.N37.D38 2002
418--dc21   2002014538

British Library Cataloguing in Publication Data
A catalogue entry for this book is available from the British Library.

ISBN 1-85359-623-X (hbk)
ISBN 1-85359-622-1 (pbk)

Multilingual Matters Ltd
UK: Frankfurt Lodge, Clevedon Hall, Victoria Road, Clevedon BS21 7HH.
USA: UTP, 2250 Military Road, Tonawanda, NY 14150, USA.
Canada: UTP, 5201 Dufferin Street, North York, Ontario M3H 5T8, Canada.
Australia: Footprint Books, PO Box 418, Church Point, NSW 2103, Australia.

Typeset by Aarontype Ltd.
Printed and bound in Great Britain by the Cromwell Press Ltd.

Contents

Preface

I grew up in South Wales in what had once been a Norman town and long before that a Roman settlement. Like so many of the world's habitations it had never been completely taken over, always the place of walls, built by the conqueror and inhabited by those the conqueror left behind, never fully native and, as such, always a place attracting anger and envy, contempt as well as imitation. Such places can lose out entirely to the locals who come to settle, first around and then within. But some, it is surprising how many, remain still as symbols and traditions of the faded past they once had. Dublin is still to some extent an Imperial city, Vienna still the centre of the Hapsburg empire and in Granada the Moorish past remains.

My South Wales had been part of what in Ireland was called the Pale. It included most of Southern Glamorgan and southern Pembroke and had been settled by Normans, later by Flemings and Hugenots and always by English speakers. The place names from Milford Haven through Gower to Newport still show this and the local language has always been English. These English speakers lived in the fertile vales and later in the industrial valleys. Above them on the hills and in the mountains were the old Britons, the Welsh speakers.

Over time the Welsh learnt English, very rarely the other way round. The Welsh and English speaking groups intermarried and Welsh declined as all languages have in the path of a juggernaut like English. It is sometimes claimed that this was deliberate, a policy of language genocide or linguicism (Skutnab Kangas & Phillipson, 1994). But there is another view. In schools where Welsh was marginalized in favour of English, it is possible to interpret this promotion of English as a way of providing access for the minority children to the majority culture, language and society. The argument would have been that since these children already had Welsh what they needed was exposure to English, and the only setting for that was, in Welsh-speaking areas, the classroom. It is, of course, the same argument that is everywhere used in the English, French (and so on) medium schools, the argument too that is used in support of language immersion schemes in Canada and elsewhere. True there is criticism of such policies on the grounds of the restriction on personal and cognitive development which, it is argued, may well need the channel of the first language for full development. But even if such arguments about cognitive development through the first language are correct, they were not in vogue in the 19th century when Welsh children were first being taught entirely through the medium of English.

The native English of the non-Welsh-speaking South Walians was a stigmatised variety, stigmatised by themselves as much as by others. They were not Welsh speakers (therefore di-Cymraeg) neither were they speakers of a prestige English. This led some to hyper-correct in English and others to attempt to learn Welsh as a second language. In both cases, what was at issue was a feeling of uneasy identity.

In my own case, as a non-Welsh-speaking South Walian, after many years living outside Wales, I decided when already in my forties that I had to test my Welshness by learning Welsh. Over the years I had made some desultory attempts and, of course, when I was at school, in Wales we had Welsh language lessons on the timetable every day: Welsh taught as if a foreign language. My mother was a Welsh speaker but since my father did not speak Welsh, the language of our home had always been English. But that is itself too glib an explanation. Even if he had been a Welsh speaker, I guess that we would still have made English our home language since English for my parents' generation (whether Welsh speakers or not) represented modernity, openness, new ideas and emancipation. Welsh for them was marked for the tightness of the closed communities of the valleys and the isolated farms, the chapel and the past.

So in the mid-1970s I spent a summer in Aberystwyth where I found that learning Welsh in the right context and with the right mental set was easy and quick. In 12 weeks I had gone far beyond all those years of primary and secondary school Welsh classes where like most of my class-mates I had found Welsh boring and old-fashioned. Welsh has not stuck. Easy come, easy go, last in first out. But that doesn't matter because I now have the satisfaction of having learnt it easily and the knowledge that I could do so again. Proof of Welshness? Perhaps. More important for our present purposes is the appeal to the common human experience of feeling and asserting identity through language. We all want to belong, we all want to be native speakers, we all choose groups to which we aspire even though we may change our minds and leave, as I left, quite promptly, my adult Welsh-speaking group because I found its nationalism and exclusiveness oppressive and proselytising.

As a proselyte I was expected to choose my identity. I had always vaguely assumed that, like masks, identities could be added on. It seemed possible in the USA to be black and American, so why not Welsh and British (even indeed Welsh and English)? But among the teachers and learners of Welsh as a second language such dual identity was not acceptable to those who were *gryf yn yr achos* (strong in the cause). You had to be either Welsh or English, either Welsh or British. Not both. Such a choice I found meaningless. My wife was English, our children had never lived in Wales. It was of course a no-win situation since for those activists among whom I had learnt my Welsh my refusal to choose was in itself a choice, a choice against Welsh. If to be Welsh meant making such a choice then I decided that was a Welsh identity I did not wish to have. Was that what being a native speaker of Welsh really meant?

The native speaker is for a start one who can lay claim to being a speaker of a language by virtue of place or country of birth. But birth place alone as a defining characteristic seems too restricting since children can be moved very quickly after birth from one country to another. We need to add the notion of adoption as an alternative; the definition then becomes: by place or country of birth or adoption. There is the further sense of ascription − a person does not choose to be, can't help being a native speaker.

The cognate of *native* is *naif* (both through Old French) meaning natural, with the sense of not being able to help it. Together they comfortably cover the sociolinguistic (country of birth or adoption) and the psycholinguistic (not being able to help oneself) attributes of the native speaker. But the native and the natural can be in conflict when one wishes to change identity, to adopt a new group, because what one then has to demonstrate both to the old and the new groups is that the natural and the naïf are in harmony, that as well as consciously adopting the new group, at the same time one can't help it, that the adoption is without apparent effort.

What I try to show in this book is that being a native speaker is only partly about naïve naturalness, that is about not being able to help what you are. It is also, and in my view more importantly, about groups and identity: the point is that while we do not choose where we come from we do have some measure of choice of where we go to. Difficult as it is, we can change identities (even the most basic ethnicity, that of gender), we can join new groups.

In my years teaching English, first (and briefly as a mother tongue), then as a foreign language and then the long period teaching applied linguistics in Edinburgh, I have always been interested in the social aspects of language learning and language use. In my teaching of sociolinguistics I have increasingly found the native speaker to be a kind of icon to which discussions about language teaching and learning return. The native-speaker concept appears to be both the process and the product to which we appeal. Process because native-speaker-like behaviours are used in the preparation and investigations of learners, product because it is the native-speaker criterion that is appealed to as a measure of success in learning, teaching and research. As such it is useful but it is also useless in that by being both process and product it provides only its own circular definition.

I have found myself speculating that the native speaker is like the healthy person in medicine (or indeed any such state of assumed perfection) where the only definition seems to be negative, a lack of malfunction: thus the native speaker would be someone who is not a learner (etc.) rather than someone who is something positive. Why is it that such an apparently fundamental idea should be so elusive? Why is it that as a notion it appears to have come into prominence so recently? When was the first use of the term? I cannot find anything earlier than Bloomfield's *Language* (1933).

Hence this book. What it turns out to be is a kind of introduction to aspects of sociolinguistics using the concept of the native speaker as a focal point. No harm in that, since what I think I manage to do (certainly what I have tried to do) is to tackle some of the recurring issues and problems as they may appear to a beginner interested in applied linguistics. I hope that readers will also see the book in this way. Not for any answers it may have, not even for catching up with the native speaker, but for the issues it addresses and the questions it asks.

The book is dedicated to the memory of my father, a very Welsh (non-Welsh-speaking) Welshman. I want to thank Mary Ann Julian for patient critiques of successive drafts as well as well as for helping me understand why the native and the naïf do not have to be in conflict. I would also like to mention the encouragement I had in completing the book from Terry Quinn, Tim McNamara, Cathie Elder and other friends in Australia as well as the detailed comments by a number of anonymous reviewers. I have tried to take both the encouragements and the critiques into account in revising my manuscript.

Preface to Second Edition

The *Native Speaker in Applied Linguistics* was published in 1991. Ten years later the topic continues to excite and to tantalise. In at least two areas, that of second language acquisition research and post-colonialism, interest in the topic has grown, showing the robustness of the concept as both myth and reality. For this edition I have made small adjustments to the original text. The main changes are the title which takes account of this double role of native speaker, and the addition of two new chapters: one (Chapter 8) on the challenge to the native speaker by World Englishes, post-modernism and post-colonialism; and the other on the connection between second language acquisition research (SLA research) and assessment (Chapter 9).

My thanks to Mike Grover of Multilingual Matters for recognising the need for this update and for his patience in waiting for it, to John Maher for his insightful comments, to my four children Ben, Sara, Megan and Hester for their love and confidence and to my students in Edinburgh, Melbourne and elsewhere for allowing me to pursue the snark.

I dedicate this volume to the memory of my Welsh parents, my mother, Anne Jane Lewis, a native speaker of Welsh (Cymraes Cymreig) and my father. Wiliam Irfonwy Davies, a native speaker of English (Cymro di-Cymreig). The mismatch of their given names reveals the ambiguity of the Welsh English identity.

Chapter 1

Introduction

Linguistics should acknowledge once and for all that its true object of study is people, the human individual and the human group, Native Speaker and his namesakes. (Yngve, 1981: 43)

The Native Speaker in Applied Linguistics

Applied linguistics makes constant appeal to the concept of the native speaker. This appeal is necessary because of the need applied linguistics has for models, norms and goals, whether the concern is with teaching or testing a first, second or foreign language, with the treatment of a language pathology, with stylistic discourse and rhetorical analysis or with some other deliberate language use. But when we look for a definition of the native speaker which will act as an applied linguistic benchmark, the concept slips away and we wonder whether after all Lewis Carroll's snark is only a boojum.

The concept of a native speaker seems clear enough, doesn't it? It is surely a common sense idea, referring to people who have a special control over a language, insider knowledge about 'their' language. They are the models we appeal to for the 'truth' about the language, they know what the language is ('Yes, you can say that') and what the language isn't ('No, that's not English, Japanese, Swahili ...'). They are the stakeholders of the language, they control its maintenance and shape its direction. A language without native speakers, whether a dying language (for example Australian aboriginal languages, Celtic languages), the language of an isolated group (for example immigrant communities several generations old) or an artificial language (for example Esperanto), such languages we say are non-viable precisely because they lack sufficient native speakers. But just how special is the native speaker?

This common-sense view is important and has practical implications, as I show later, but the common-sense view alone is inadequate and needs the support and explanation given by a thorough theoretical discussion. Such a thorough theoretical discussion is lacking. True, there are the various comments made by well-known linguists and it is with these that I want to begin. These comments are all helpful but they are also quite partial and do not make sense of the complexity of the native speaker. That complexity is what this book is about. It is written with the interests and background of post-experience graduate students in applied linguistics particularly in mind and it is hoped that undergraduate students following courses in sociolinguistics and language teachers in training may also find the discussion of value.

Referring to the Native Speaker

The need for such an extended discussion of the native speaker is explained by Ferguson's comment: 'Linguists ... have long given a special place to the native speaker as the only true and reliable source of language data' (Ferguson, 1983: vii). The argument I present explores and agrees with the view Ferguson puts forward:

> much of the world's verbal communication takes place by means of languages which are not the users' mother tongue, but their second, third or *n*th language, acquired one way or another and used when appropriate. This kind of language use merits the attention of linguists as much as do the more traditional objects of their research. (ibid.)

I do, however, put a query against Ferguson's eventual conclusion: 'In fact the whole mystique of native speaker and mother tongue should preferably be quietly dropped from the linguist's set of professional myths about language' (ibid.). As my discussion shows there is no doubt about the myth-like properties of the native-speaker idea. The question remains, however, of whether it is also a reality. I attempt to answer that question.

Theoretically, as we shall see, the native-speaker concept is rich in ambiguity. It raises, quite centrally, the issue of the relation between the particular and the universal. Chomsky, as a protagonist of the universalist position, conveys to Paikeday's questioning approach about the status of the native speaker (Paikeday, 1985) the strongest possible sense of the genetic determinants of speech acquisition which, as he sees it, must mean that to be human is to be a native speaker.

What Chomsky does is to equate language development with other normal development, finding no interest in questions about developmental states or stages which he regards as contingent and essentially of no theoretical interest. In the same vein Chomsky finds distinctions between synchronic states of language or languages and dialects uninteresting, 'the question of what are the "languages" or "dialects" attained, and what is the difference between "native" and "non-native" is just pointless' (Chomsky quoted in Paikeday, 1985: 57). Chomsky's whole argument depends on a rationalist opposition to 'incorrect metaphysical assumptions: in particular the assumption that among the things in the world there are languages or dialects, and that individuals come to acquire them' (p. 49).

And so Chomsky must conclude that 'everyone is a Native Speaker of the particular language states that the person has "grown" in his/her mind/brain. In the real world, that is all there is to say' (p. 58). This is a major thread in the range of views on the native speaker and we return to it later. Chomsky's view is uninfluenced by any social factor or contextual constraint. Variety and context, he seems to argue, are trivial. This is a thoroughgoing unitary competence view of language in which language use is contingent and the native speaker is only a realisation of that competence at a linguistic and not a language level. For Chomsky, like many theoretical linguists, is not interested in languages: what he studies is language.

For our present purpose, however, we note that Chomsky does bring to our attention the real individual, living, as he says, in the real world, whose speech repertoire is multiple. His view may take no account of social or sociolinguistic analysis or parameters but he is not unaware that the real word consists of complex variation.

Next, two comments on the importance of the mother tongue in education. (We turn shortly to the vexed issued of terminology.) The British/Australian linguist, Michael Halliday, does not use the term native speaker; however what he says about the mother tongue is very relevant. He comments:

> Opinions differ regarding the uniqueness of the mother tongue for very many people ... no language ever completely re-places the mother tongue. Certain kinds of ability seem to be particularly difficult to acquire in a second language. Among these, the following are perhaps most important in an educational context:
>
> (1) saying the same thing in different ways,
> (2) hesitating, and saying nothing very much
> (3) predicting what the other person is going to say
> (4) adding new verbal skills (learning new words and new meanings) when talking and listening.
>
> It is not being suggested that we can never learn to do these things in a second language ... Nevertheless, there are vast numbers of children being educated through the medium of a second language, and of

teachers trying to teach them, who have not mastered these essential abilities. (Halliday 1978: 199–200)

The position taken up in this book is generally sympathetic to Halliday's conclusion that it is possible but difficult for an adult second language learner to become a native speaker of the target language. The issue of disadvantage, which Halliday raises in connection with education in a second language, is taken up in Chapters 5 and 7. To what extent educational disadvantage can be attributed to not being a native speaker is debatable, especially since a similar argument of lacking adequate language resources is made for certain groups of native speakers who, it has been claimed (Bereiter & Englemann, 1966), suffer from a language deficit. For our discussion in this book, this raises acutely the question of what it is one is supposed to be a native speaker of.

A contrary view to Halliday's is given by the American linguist, Leonard Bloomfield, author of *Language* (1933) and a student in the anthropological tradition of early 20th century American linguistics of American Indian languages. Like Halliday, Bloomfield does not use the term native speaker but writes instead of 'the native language'.

The child growing up in the province, say, in some mountain village, learns to speak in the local dialect. In time, to be sure, this local dialect will take in more and more forms from the standard language ... The child, then, does not speak the standard language as his native tongue. It is only after he reaches school, long after his speech-habits are formed, that he is taught the standard language. No language is like the native language that one learned at one's mother's knee; no-one is ever perfectly sure in a language afterwards acquired. 'Mistakes' in language are simply dialect forms carried into the standard language'. (Bloomfield, 1927: 151)

Bloomfield is less accommodating than Halliday. In his view. second language learners of target languages do not become native speakers of those languages. Native speakers need to get started at their mother's knee. We should note that Bloomfield does not comment here on the simultaneous acquisition of two languages at the mother's/father's knee.

In another context Bloomfield does refer to the native speaker: 'The first language a human being learns to speak is his native language; he is a native speaker of this language' (Bloomfield, 1933: 43). Here, he makes the obvious point that children learn to speak as they learn to do everything else, by observation and participation and interaction with the people around them.

Katz and Fodor (1962: 218), later American linguists, less interested in descriptions than Bloomfield and more concerned with the relation between language and the mind, opined: 'The goal of a theory of a particular language must be the explication of the abilities and skills involved in the linguistic performance of a fluent native speaker'.

In this way the native speaker becomes central to the interests and concerns of linguistics, with the native speaker being the relevant example of natural phenomena for scientific study. Noam Chomsky (1965: 24) refers to the native speaker as being both the arbiter of a grammar and (when idealised) as somehow being the model for the grammar: 'A grammar is . . . descriptively adequate to the extent that it correctly describes the intrinsic competence of the idealised native speaker'.

Chomsky thereby neatly compounds one of the central ambiguities of the native-speaker idea, using it to refer to both a person and ideal. Or, as Coulmas (1981: 10) states: 'The native speaker leads a double life in Chomsky's work, (1) as a creature of flesh and blood, that is the linguist himself, (2) an idealisation'.

Richards *et al.* in their *Dictionary of Applied Linguistics* (1985) and Crystal in his *Dictionary of Linguistics* (1997) emphasise the importance of intuition in defining the native speaker, Crystal helpfully pointing to the need to take account of bilinguals who are native speakers of more than one language. This relation between bilingualism and the native speaker is a major topic in Chapter 5.

Mary Tay's contribution to the discussion is original in that she comments on the status of the native speaker in relation to the so-called New Englishes, that is the English of Singapore, India and so on. She refers to the lack of clarity of most definitions and notes that the two factors usually appealed to are first, priority of learning and second, an unbroken oral tradition. She comments that both are unsafe criteria; the first because of bilingualism, the second because an adult may have shifted dominance from one first language to another or because a second learned language may have had as much influence on a first learned as the other way around. Tay therefore proposes that a native speaker of English who is not from one of the traditionally native-speaking countries (for example the United States, the United Kingdom) is:

one who learns English in childhood and continues to use it as his dominant language and has reached a certain level of fluency. All three conditions are important. If a person learns English late in life, he is unlikely to attain native fluency in it; if he learns it as a child, but does not use it as his dominant language in adult life, his native fluency in the language is also questionable; if he is fluent in the language, he is more likely one who has learned it as a child (not necessarily before the age of formal education but soon after that) and has continued to use it as his dominant language'. (Tay, 1982: 67–8)

What these views indicate is the accuracy of Coulmas' statement that a tension exists between the flesh and blood and the idealisation definitions. I shall argue that in applied linguistics both definitions are necessary and that there is no necessary contradiction between them. This book sets out to examine the native-speaker concept from various points of view and attempts to develop more precise criteria for its definition. In particular the book considers the relevant question of the relation between being a native speaker and being a second language learner, raising the question of whether the latter can become the former.

The Practical Importance of the Native Speaker

The practical importance of the term is emphasised by Paikeday (1985), who points to the employment discrimination against those who lack the 'ideal' native-peaker attributes: 'native speakership should not be used as a criterion for excluding certain categories of people from language teaching, dictionary editing, and similar functions' (Paikeday, 1985: 88).

Paikeday's own solution seems to be to separate the ideal and the operative meanings of native speaker, making proficiency the criterion for employment, and personal history the criterion for ideal membership. As we shall see such a rigid distinction is difficult to maintain when it comes to judgements of grammaticality which Paikeday wants to associate with the proficient-user meaning of native speaker rather than with the ideal-member use: 'the people we refer to as arbiters of grammaticality are not really so because true arbiters of grammaticality are proficient users of languages, not just native speakers' (Paikeday, 1985: 53). As we have already noted, it is not clear how much attention we should give to such judgements of grammaticality. That, too, is an issue to be dealt with later.

In using a native speaker as model for its language plans, curriculum design and remedial schedules, applied linguistics has to take up the Paikeday challenge, which is essentially which native speaker to choose and lurking behind all such choices is undoubtedly the Paikeday dilemma of whether a new model (which can be supported by acknowledged proficiency) outweighs a distant 'historically authentic' model; for example Indian English models or Nigerian English models versus British or American models (see Chapter 8). But this dilemma is, in fact, just one example of the more general case. There is equally a dispute between the British and American models just as there is among other metropolitan models, and just also as there is between any Standard and other dialects. The important choice of a model, therefore, raises issues of acceptability, of currency and of intelligibility. It is in part for this reason, as we shall see, that Paikeday's distinction between the ideal-native-speaker definition and the operative one is not finally tenable.

Nevertheless, it remains of practical importance. Consider the institutionalised activities of publishing and examining in the written language and of selecting radio and television newsreaders/casters in the spoken language. In such cases there is compelling social consensus in favour of the use of a model type. It is also the case that a particular type of native speaker (or native-speaker-like non-native speaker) is chosen, the prestige model.

The term native speaker is used in two distinct (but related) senses in relation to this consensus. The first is that in some way the native speaker is taken, as we shall see, to represent an idealised model. The second is that an individual native speaker is him/herself used as an exemplar of such a model. And while general or theoretical linguistics may be content to take any individual as an exemplar of his/her native speech (one of our uses of the term native speaker) applied linguistics cannot afford to be so generous and so unconcerned with sampling importance.

The everyday use of the term native speaker can cause offence. University departments where linguistics and applied linguistics are taught commonly make use in their daily discussions of the terms native speaker and non-native speaker. Such use is not intended to be exact, rather it is an appeal to commonsense, to use a difficult and uncertain concept which is at the same time a useful piece of shorthand. Appeals of the following kind are frequently made in academic settings in the UK:

We need 10 native speakers for a test on Friday

I am looking for three non-native speakers to help with a questionnaire

What do the native speakers think about this (piece of discourse, stylistics exercise and so on?)

I've posted a job vacancy for a native-speaking teacher on the noticeboard.

What is clear is that such shorthand requests cause a good deal of offence. In the first place what is not stated is that what is typically being referred to is a native speaker of English; in the second place the fact that everyone is a native speaker of something is ignored (as in the case of 'innocent' sexist remarks); and in the third place it is denied that a highly proficient non-native speaker may also have acquired both linguistic and communicative competence and be, therefore, in terms of what is required in formal higher education and in intuitions about Standard English, indistinguishable from a native speaker.

What is also ignored, though it is very obviously there underneath the surface, is the racism of such remarks. What is so often meant by native speaker in this context is the deliberate exclusion of those who are, in fact, in with a chance of being one. A Singaporean, a Nigerian or an Indian might see him/herself as a native speaker of English but feel a lack of confidence in his/her native speakerness. An unmarked message in the UK context ('... native speaker ...') is therefore not reassuring without the addition 'including Singaporeans, Nigerians, Indians and so on ...'. Alternatively the notice might state: 'We need three native speakers of British English ...'.

There is the counter argument which needs to be stated and that is, that in all such cases it is really up to the individual to identify him/herself; no-one else can do it. That is to say that where there is doubt we define ourselves as native speakers or as non-native speakers of particular languages. The problem here is peculiarly one for those who belong to the post-colonial communities, such as Singapore, Nigeria, India, where the New Englishes are in use (see Chapter 8). The hard-line approach to this would be to say that yes indeed they are native speakers if they so decide, either of British/American English or of Singaporean/Nigerian/Indian English. The question is one that is likely to be thought about seriously only by educated Singaporeans, Nigerians, Indians and so on. Membership, as I see it, is largely a matter of self-ascription not of something being given; it is in this sense that members decide for themselves.

In spite of what I have argued about membership coming first it must be the case that those who claim native-speaker status then have responsibilities in terms of confidence and identity. They must be confident as native speakers and identify with other native speakers and be accepted by them. That is exactly what is required in acquiring any new ethnicity.

The Argument of the Book

This book is about the native speaker. Its purpose is twofold: first, to detail the complexity of the knowledge and skills possessed by the native speaker of any language; and second, to make that complexity seem less exclusive, more ordinary and attainable by non-native speakers. In so doing I hope to illustrate just how difficult are the problems of the second language learner and, at the same time and paradoxically, help learners (and their teachers) feel more confidence about their knowledge, their communicative ability and their intuitions. The native-speaker boundary is, as we shall see, one as much created by non-native speakers as by native speakers themselves.

The concept of native speaker will be examined, its uses in the field of applied linguistics discussed and a way of coming to terms with its ambiguities offered. The approach is more speculative than experimental, the intention being to try to make sense of the idea rather than to provide empirical evidence for the distinctive features of native speakerness. Such an experimental approach, necessary as it is, properly follows this attempt to set parameters and uncover uses of the term. The discussion ranges widely across linguistics, psycholinguistics and sociolinguistics.

However, the bulk of the discussion is given to sociolinguistic ideas and research. I hope to show that by basing ourselves in sociolinguistic argument and evidence an understanding reconciliation of the different uses of the native speaker idea can be achieved.

Chapter 1: Introduction

The theoretical question raised in Chapter 1 is whether a definition of native speaker is readily available. The corresponding applied topic is that of the model of choice for language teaching and other institutionalised language uses. The native speaker, it is proposed, is important both as an ideal (the 'myth') of the title and as model (the 'reality' of the title).

Chapter 2: Psycholinguistic Aspects of the Native Speaker

Do non native speakers use a separate cognitive system from that used by native speakers as their language develops? That is the theoretical question. The applied issue, which is now at the heart of applied linguistics, is that of second language acquisition. The basis for my argument in Chapter 2 is that in a non-trivial sense native speakers and non native speakers behave differently linguistically. This difference appears to reflect not one complete and one incomplete system, but rather two systems. This is the case however inadequately the non-native speaker may make him/ herself understood (Loveday, 1982) − for example when s/he is making one of the typical errors described by Burt and Kiparsky (1972), such as:

'was a riot last night' (p. 13);
'the girls was decided to play the piano' (p. 53)

or when talking normally as described by Richards (in Crewe, 1977a: 73)

> From there step by step I promoted okay. From there I go where I
> said cannot do night duty. So do change office. Now then the one
> work with me, together with me, we rotate shift. He said you always
> do morning while I alway pao (Hokkien borrowing) night How can?
> Cannot. So they transfer me. Transfer me where are OC office clerk.
> about how to type. Nothing boy. Go down there and sit and then I
> do writing only. No ned to learn. There one clerk to do work. I am
> MP vocation. They just only clerk. So I higher rank la. Then I work in
> the reservist.

This is a Singapore youth whose English is at the lower end of the speech
continuum. Here he is describing his experiences during his military
service. The low form, Richards (p. 72) tells us, is fairly widely used as a
medium of informal communication by those with limited education and
of lower social or economic status.

Chapter 3: Linguistic Aspects of the Native Speaker

Here the theoretical question is the sort of grammar a native speaker
has and whether native speakers and non-native speakers have different
grammars. The corresponding applied question concerns the nature and
scope of pedagogic grammars which are typically concerned with the
deliberate shaping of a learner's current grammar so as to match that of a
native speaker.

Rutherford (1987: Chapter 12) provides a number of sample pedagogic
grammar exercises. One good example is the following: referential relations serving cohesion for example are fairly easy to verify and for these
the learner might simply be asked to verbally identify in a given text what
the highlighted referent corresponds to, as in:

> After they saved a little money, Howard and Ellen wanted to buy a
> house. So they did. The floor plan was almost exactly the same as that
> of Ellen's parents' home, where she was reared. Buying it was not easy
> for the young couple, but Ellen was determined to go through with it.
> She could not stand living in their small apartment any longer. She
> wanted the kind of space that she had always lived with. Howard
> couldn't quite understand his wife's insistence on moving to more
> spacious quarters. Their small apartment was big enough for him.

In fact it was almost like the one he had lived in as a child. But he could remember his mother saying almost daily, 'If only I had more room'. (Rutherford, 1987: 164)

Exercises of this kind link the practical proficiency aspect of understanding the meaning with metalinguistic knowledge of the grammar; thus the mechanics and the control are bracketed and internalised.

The discussion in Chapters 1, 2 and 3 provides the necessary underpinning and background for the main argument of the book which examines the native-speaker concept as a sociolinguistic construct from a variety of points of view.

Chapter 4: Sociolinguistic Aspects of the Native Speaker

The theoretical question I address in Chapter 4 is the extent to which being a native speaker is a social construct, a choice of identity and a membership determined as much by attitude and symbolically as by language ability and knowledge. The applied topic is that of the role and development of language in dynamic multilingual situations especially those of high migrant mobility.

Cross-cultural communication research has shown that communicative breakdown is common in such situations and can be attributed to a range of factors (Gumperz, 1982). A common breakdown in an encounter such as a job interview is where the non-native speaker applicant has low proficiency and is, at the same time, anxious and defensive. An interesting example is cited by Williams (1985: 165):

The monolingual Australian interviewer (I), an officer with the Commonwealth Employment Service, is interviewing an immigrant woman (J) who is a recent arrival from Cuba, for a job as hospital attendant at a senior citizens' hostel in Perth.

I: Also the hospital is a psychiatric hospital. Er ... so, I don't know if that's going to cause any bother to you ... or any problems at all. Are you familiar with the term 'psychiatric hospital'?

J: [repeats slowly in Spanish] Psiquiatri ... (people with psycho logical problems)

J: [incredulously] In my family?

I: No ... No ... No! No ... No!'

One of the less obvious causes of breakdown is that of culturally-tied conventions (Gumperz, 1982; Pride, 1985). Several researchers have suggested that misunderstandings may arise because of the differing ways in which discourse is organised in different languages, the parallel, circular and digressive described by Clyne (1982) for example in contrast with the linear of English. Misunderstandings are frequently interpersonal but they can also be related to tasks as, for example, Kaplan (1966) suggested in connection with a lack of progress in learning to write in a second language.

This topic, that of the boundary problem between the non-native speaker and the native speaker, is taken up again in Chapter 5 in two special senses, those of bilingualism and semilingualism.

Chapter 5: Lingualism and the Knowledges of the Native Speaker

Is it possible to be a native speaker of more than one language or of no language at all? That is the theoretical question I discuss in this chapter. I also examine the kinds of language knowledge possessed by the native speaker. The applied topic I look at is that of disadvantage, in particular educational disadvantage, which has been explained as the outcome of a language deficit (Bereiter & Englemann, 1966). The question of linguistic inadequacy can be shown in the comparison between the Black English sentence analysed by Labov (1972):

It ain't no cat can't get in no coop.

which though heavily stigmatised because of its negative repetition is also totally systematic, and the semilingual stereotype of the

Him plenty rice

type. The argument which we accept is that the first of these is not linguistically crippling, though it may be so socially in contexts where Standard English matters. The latter may be linguistically crippling but is never, we maintain, the sole linguistic resource available to a speaker.

What is evident, however, is that non native speakers can, in principle, achieve levels of proficiency equal to native speakers. But can the same be said for their competence? I now therefore turn to the special claim of the native speaker to communicative competence (and see later).

Chapter 6: Communicative Competence Aspects of the Native Speaker

The theoretical question of this chapter is whether the native speaker is privileged in terms of communicative competence. Arising out of this discussion is the applied question of the validity of communicative language teaching and whether the term 'communicative' implies a method or a content.

The cutting edge of the communicative movement in language teaching has been to emphasise the priority of meaning before form, that is to say that the language acquirer gains linguistic form by seeking situational meaning. This is generally accepted as the chief way in which the child learns his/her own first language (Donaldson, 1978) and is increasingly accepted as the major positive motivation for learning a second language. At the same time, as researchers such as Hatch *et al.* (1986) have pointed out, the second language acquirer is also concerned to come to terms with and master the forms of the target language — if only because his/her first language already gives access to a wide range of situational meanings.

Work directly related to emphasising and presenting meaning to the second language acquirer right from the start of second language acquisition is that of Prabhu (1987) who has recorded his experience in South India with a task-based syllabus according to which young Tamil-speaking learners of English are exposed to tasks (rather like games or puzzles) which require the use of English for their completion or solution. Prabhu's evidence of the ways in which the search for meaning can promote the development of control over linguistic form is impressive. Doubts have, however, been expressed about the amount of language support actually given to the learners (Brumfit, 1984; Beretta, 1986).

The communicative competence discussion in Chapter 6 raises centrally the issue of the involvement of culture in language and of the acquisition of culture as an analogue to the learning of language (Kramsch, in press). In Chapter 7 I develop this theme by considering the ways in which different ethnicities and social institutions establish membership (and therefore validate participation as well as authority) in comparable terms to language.

Chapter 7: Intelligibility and the Speech Community

The theoretical question for this chapter concerns norms and intelligibility: does intelligibility depend on there being agreed language norms and what status do they have? The relevant applied question here is that of the role of correctness, linguistically and pedagogically, in the use of a standard language in society, in general, and in education, in particular. Ryan and Giles (1982) have collected research evidence on the importance of attitudes in informing our reactions to language, including our own, and have argued that attitudes can best be represented in terms of two sociostructural determinants, standardisation and vitality. What is badly needed and so often lacking is a clear and steady examination of the real language in use and an adequate analysis of what it represents and what it means. That is as true of the British Black English example (Sutcliffe, 1982)

mi asks di man fi put mi moni iina him pakit

as it is of the multiple negative Black English example already discussed. It is also true of the ways in which native speakers actually talk to one another when speaking colloquially, and not how they are supposed to talk – or how they talk when they are on their best behaviour. That is precisely the problem with notions about norms rather than the actual norms themselves. The following brief extract (starting with Utterance 10) from a family of native speakers of English breakfasting together shows a number of features which might well be corrected and/or stigmatised if the speakers were known/thought to be non native speakers. We draw attention here particularly to the 'poetic' learning of the term 'yawn' and use of the non-occurring term 'yawn out' (in this excerpt only two speakers are quoted, Anne, mother and Hester, aged 5):

10.	Hester:	I was … up watching television at 10 o'clock, Mum
11.	Anne:	Mm no you weren't
12.	Hester:	yes I was
13.	Anne:	(now listen) you were very (COUGH) naughty to come down again … (?) (it means) you just get worn out
14.	Hester:	I didn't yawn
15.	Anne:	I said worn out
16.	Hester:	I didn't yawn out
17.	Anne:	I didn't say yawn out I said worn out
18.	Hester:	what's that mean
19.	Anne:	tired
20.	Hester:	I'm not tired didn't (??) that wasn't tired. (Davies, 1990b)

An ill-informed language view assumes that certain forms are correct, always so, and certain forms incorrect, again always so. This cannot be so; correctness if it exists depends on context, as shown in this extract.

Chapter 8: Losing One's Language

Chapter 8 evaluates the challenge to the concept of the native speaker from post-modernism and, in particular, post-colonialism. The question is raised of the centrality of language to a sense of loss of identity, expressed powerfully in the 1960s and 1970s, in the appeal among francophone writers to the concept of négritude.

How to cope with the intrusion of the new imperial world language is the applied problem, found in all sorts of societies wishing to participate in the global economy. How they do so ranges from the insistence in New Varieties of English (NVE) contexts on the status of a local standard to the valorisation in foreign language contexts of the non-native speaker teacher. What matters in all cases, it is argued, is that the community should be confident in choosing its own solution.

Chapter 9: Assessment and Second Language Acquisition Research

In Chapter 9 we discuss the contribution of language assessment to our understanding of the native speaker and then examine evidence of second language acquisition research (SLAR) into the idea of the exceptional learner. What is at issue here is how far we must rely on the critical period hypotheses (CPH) and indeed on maturation as crucial distinguishers of native speaker (NS) and non-native speaker (NNS). Recent evidence suggests that there is no discrete borderline and that the NS–NNS connection is a continuum.

Chapter 10: Conclusion: Who is the Native Speaker?

In Chapter 10 we draw the discussion to a conclusion, clarifying our own view of the native speaker and linking the native speaker to the earlier discussion of identity to the idea of the standard language and to proficiency. The major theoretical question discussed in Chapter 10 is whether an adult non-native speaker can become (cross over, pass as) a native speaker of a target language. The applied question which arises naturally out of a theoretical discussion on the relative status of language varieties is just which (version of a) target language it is appropriate to use for international purposes and so our applied question in this chapter is that of the validity of international English.

When Kachru (1985: 13) can write of the 'claims of English as an international or universal language' he is explicitly drawing our attention to the seemingly inexorable growth of English as the most widespread second language ever. But there is also behind his and similar remarks the implicit question of what if anything can be done to promote the situation in which some version of English would be Haugen's 'world language'

(Graddol, 1997; van Els, 2000). Such a proposition was very much in mind in the 1940s in the concern with and promotion of Basic English by C.K. Ogden and I.A. Richards, and even by Winston Churchill.

What Basic English does is to focus our minds on the question of simplification in language. It raises both the fact of simplification actually happening, as of course it does as a common language strategy and of the uncertainty as to whether deliberate simplification is ever possible.

Terms of the Argument

To be the native speaker of a language means to speak it 'from your mother's knee' (Bloomfield), as your mother tongue or first language (L1). Or so it seems. As we shall see such a definition is not straightforward and is difficult to uphold. It is not wholly clear, for example, what is meant by mother tongue and by first language. Other terms used to indicate a claim to a language by an individual are: dominant language, home language. Let us examine each in turn.

Mother tongue

The mother tongue is literally just that, the language of the mother and is based on the normal enough view that children's first significant other is the mother. Of course there are situations in which that caretaking person is not the biological mother but instead the father, grandparent or nurse. But in most cases it probably is the mother and therefore it is the mother who provides most of the spoken input for the child and with whom the child identifies and wishes to exchange meanings. If language learning is indeed learning how to mean (Halliday, 1975) then for the child it is the mother that s/he wishes to mean to and be found meaningful by. As we have just noted, it is not always straightforward in that the role of 'mother' may be taken by some other adult; similarly the mother, biological or not, may provid bi- or multi-lingual input for the child either because the 'mother' is herself bilingual or because the role of mother is shared by several adults who use more than one language in speaking to the child. It is therefore not inappropriate that the term mother tongue is used rather than mother language because what is meant is that the child's first input is that of the mother. To what extent the child's own developing idiolect is identified as that of the mother rather than that of the child's own peer group is a matter for empirical investigation (Ochs, 1982).

First language

'First language' refers to the language which was learned first. Again this seems straightforward. Your first language is the language ('tongue') you learned from your mother, biological or not. This however, is, straightforward for only a small group of people and may reflect the monolingual nature of much anglo-centric society. Many people live in multilingual societies and we all live in multidialectal societies. The mother tongue and the first language may be different because, first, the mother tongue is, as we have seen, influenced by peers as well as by parents, it may be more than one language and then it is not easy to decide which one is first. Second, what is the first language may change over time so that, for example, a young child for whom Welsh is the mother tongue or 'first language' in the sense of time of learning, may gradually come to use English more and more and relegate Welsh to a childhood experience. It may not be completely forgotten but is, in some sense, no longer as useful, no longer generative or creative and therefore no longer 'first'.

For the large number of people in this category the mother tongue is no longer the first or dominant language. Equally it can be the case that such people would claim to have more than one first language and this raises what is in some sense a philosophical question of whether it is possible to have more than one first language at the same time. As we shall see later, it cannot be only a philosophical question since there may be certain criteria (in addition to an individual's own self-identification) determining one's claim to a first language which enables us to distinguish first from second language and being a first language speaker from being labelled semilingual (that is having no first or adequate language).

Naturally this takes us back to the relation between mother tongue and first language because in the case of the bi (or multi) dialectal mother, if we accept that one's mother tongue is the code of the individual mother and is not isomorphic with any one or more language, then we may be led into surmising that what mothers speak is either an interlanguage or a set of semilingual codes.

Dominant language

The term 'dominant' language links in here because of the underlying assumption that what was one's first language can change over time and another code take its place as one's first language. This must be the case of the Welsh child mentioned earlier (or the African or Singaporean child and so on) who moves through education or some other major life change into a situation in which s/he uses English or other language of wider communication (LWC) for most if not all purposes; in such cases it can happen that not only the child but the whole family shifts in this way, leaving behind the child's so-called first language. But in most cases it is the child who shifts alone and then for him/her it is English, French or some other LWC which is now dominant. Or perhaps it is safer to say that it is English or French which is dominant in domains outside the home while it is still the mother tongue which is dominant at home. In other words the child has more than one dominant language, each language being dominant in certain areas of life.

Home language

'Home language' (rather like mother tongue) refers to some factor outside the speaker, in this case the home and is, for that reason, easier to distinguish. The home language is the language of the home (and may, as we have seen with mother tongue, in reality be a mixed language or a set of languages/dialects). In a certain sense, home language is defined negatively in terms of what it is not (rather as the other terms are) since it is perhaps easier to define the public code which is often a recognised (and described) standard: English, French and so on. The home language then is — for many children — what is left after the public, standard code has been removed. At the same time, for some children the public standard code is also the home language. Thus in the case of middle-class native English speakers the home language may well be largely identical with the Standard English that is used as a medium in schools and taught to foreigners (and this applies whether we are talking of England, the USA, Australia or other metropolitan native English speaking country). I say 'largely' because there may be another language in use (one parent may be the first language user of another language) or one or more non-standard dialects may be in use some of the time or we may wish to claim that there is in use some kind of unique family variety. For present purposes it is helpful to note that these terms can be defined in relation to what they are not: first language in relation to second language, dominant language in relation to the language it has superseded, home language in relation to the public official code, and mother tongue in relation to what one's peers are speaking.

Native speaker tends to be used in each of these ways: native speaker means having language X as one's mother tongue, as one's first language, as one's dominant language, as one's home language.

Langue

There are other terms which we also need to consider since they too are invoked as being relevant to the native speaker: they are competence – both linguistic and communicative – and langue. Let us take langue first since that is the older term. Saussure's use of langue (de Saussure, 1966) was an attempt to define not the native speaker but what it is that is shared by a language community. In putting forward his trinity of categories:

- langage (everything going on linguistically in the speech community),
- langue (the system employed and
- parole (the utterances actually used by people)

Saussure was, in my judgement, more interested in the atypical, monolingual community than in multilingual communities. For him langue is what people share, the average of their individual speech differences. Langue for Saussure is therefore the linguist's object of attention.

The question Saussure addressed is important theoretically and practically. It has already come up implicitly in our earlier discussion in terms of mother tongue, although we have not yet mentioned it explicitly. The argument goes as follows: if it is indeed the case that the mother tongue is what the 'mother' has as her own idiosyncratic idiolect then although that is the chief source of what the child acquires it cannot be identical with what the child acquires. Otherwise it would not make sense to speak of the mother tongue as being the mother's own idiolect. There must be certain differences between the mother's own code and that of her child, and if that is the case then the differences both between adults and between the child on becoming adult and the child's own mother must be even greater. And yet, as Saussure pointed out, the members of a community, including the mother and child, understand one another. They must therefore share something which enables them to understand one another – to be mutually intelligible and which they acquire as they acquire the mother tongue, first or dominant language.

Of course they do not all speak the same way – indeed it does not disturb Saussure's case if we accept, as we have already, that everyone speaks differently. That is allowed for under Saussure's term of parole. Nevertheless the point that he makes – and it is a valid one worth repeating – is that all members of a community do share the set of rules which make up langue. As will be observed, this is a circular definition since it is not clear what that community is except in terms of the very thing it is set up itself to define, the rules of its langue. In spite of this it remains a valuable heuristic to recognise that speakers of English possess a language different from that of French: equally that speakers of British English and speakers of American English have somewhat different languages. But that is precisely the point at which the argument becomes difficult because it is not clear how big such differences have to be in order for them to imply a different language. The point is that the differences of dialect and indeed the differences between subdialects (such as in family uses) can, given fine enough descriptions, be viewed as systematic and not just as differences at the parole level and therefore — however minuscule — differences of langue. Should such family differences then be regarded as different languages? The langue solution also raises the serious question of just who it is that has access to a langue and whether a special type of experience is necessary. In other words it raises the question of whether or not late acquisition of a first language is possible. Do second language speakers have access to a second language langue? And if so is it the same langue as the langue of first language speakers? Or to put the issue another way does one need to be a mother tongue/first language speaker in order to have its langue? As will be observed, this raises the same sort of issue as our earlier discussion of being a mother-tongue speaker of more than one language and of being semilingual. Langue then appears to be a useful attempt to label that which so-called native speakers have in common (for the moment we will avoid having to decide whether one can become a late native speaker) but in the event a vain attempt since it remains circular and does not help us define exactly what it is that language means. It labels membership of the community who claim to speak a language without defining what it is that they have. Nevertheless, as a social definition, for that is what it is, it is very powerful since as with all social definitions it recognises that membership is largely self-defined, a matter of self-ascription. What it also does is to recognise that speakers necessarily share community membership. In the same way that members of a community share a culture so members who speak a language share langue. Although that definition is circular, at least it gets us over the dangerous solipsism which insists that languages do not exist (Le Page & Tabouret-Keller, 1985) and that they are mere social or linguistic artefacts. This is not the case, surely: languages are both social facts and human reality in that people can communicate with others who 'speak the same language'. This is the problem that language addresses and for which it provides an explanation.

Why is it that members of a community can communicate with one another remains unclear. Do they share attitudes, norms, etc., or do they somehow have the same linguistic system, or both? According to Renate

Bartsch, Saussure never made his own position clear, wanting language somehow to include both norms and system:

> Saussure seems to have made a distinction betweem norm and system – as two aspects of the whole which he calls language ... [he] assumes that applying the method of classification by the two kinds of relationship will result in one language system with only small deviances between language uses. This is an assumption the truth of which is by no means obvious. (Bartsch, 1988: 152)

Competence

The related notion of competence was introduced by Chomsky (1965) to specify both the knowledge ability of an individual which enables language acquisition to take place and represents that mature ability and also to signify the goal of linguistic theory, that is to explain and describe competence. Language evidence for competence is provided by performance which, like competence, is subject to systematic idealisation. Thus competence is the system (both the linguist's and the native speaker's), performance the processing of the system and language use (combining performance and competence), the data which we use to test our theory

The notion of linguistic competence moves the argument on one stage in that it seeks to answer the question of what it is that the members of the langue community possess. It appears to address precisely the problem that we claimed earlier langue does not solve, the question of defining what the label langue means. Why do we say 'appears to address' the problem? The question can be put another way: does competence need to assume langue in order to consider meaningfully what it is that language speakers do or know?

There are two answers to this question. The first is that we can assume that a different description will be needed for all idiolects; that seems a possible way of establishing the competence enterprise and is in line with such possible statements as: linguistics seeks to define the properties of grammars, whether or not they have anything to do with human beings; or linguistics is not about human communication.

What this view is really saying is that competence is about idealised speakers: indeed Chomsky's definition of linguistics as being about the idealised native speaker in a homogeneous speech community is of obvious relevance. Such an approach is not a social one; it takes no account of situation, purpose, domain or variety. It is psycholinguistic or cognitive-scientific and linked to the computer analogue for the brain. It raises the interesting question of what systems must underlie human communication but it ignores all aspects of social concern. It also assumes different languages as given, because its main focus of interest is in what all individuals possess, both the assumed general language faculty and the idiolect.

Within this view different languages are not important; but what is of interest is the individual's idiolect, not because it is different from other idiolects but because it must, according to the theory, provide evidence for the universal code we are all supposed to share.

However, even so extreme and rigorous a view must take some account of limited social aspects since any elicitation of data, and even the concept of the idealised native speaker, must mean there is some account being taken of the speaking world. Otherwise it would be possible for someone who does not know the language or whose speech is full of performance errors of a severe kind or who is aphasic to be used for elicitation and clearly that is not what happens. So that even here there is a tacit assumption that the world is made up of speech communities of more than one person. Or, to use Coulmas's terms, the double life of the native speaker does come together on occasion, the idealisation can put on flesh and blood (Coulmas, 1981: 10).

The second answer to the question as to whether competence needs to assume langue is that competence does need to assume langue on the grounds that langue itself needs an explanation as to how it is that (native) speakers understand one another. In other words what competence sets out to do is to provide a description of langue. So far we have been discussing linguistic competence; one of the debates which the interest in competence stimulated was precisely what should be done about the social aspects of language which linguistic competence refused to take account of and which can be subsumed under language appropriateness. Interests in these social aspects is not new, indeed they have always been thought important, as Saussure's appeal to langue (itself a 'social fact') shows. Saussure seems to have borrowed the notion of langue from the sociological ideas of Durkheim. British linguistics, influenced in part by the Prague School, was also concerned to reflect the social context of language in its descriptions, as Malinowski's (1923) and Firth's (1950) discussions of the context of situation remind us.

Chomsky's insistence on examining competence without social factors was deliberate since the task of linguistics in his view has been to consider only the underlying systems. There is a counter argument which states that what is linguistics is never totally separate, even at the abstract level, from what is cultural or social. This is a view usually put forward by anthropologically minded linguists such as Halliday (1978) and Hymes (1970).

Communicative competence

As a consequence, Hymes (1970) proposed the term communicative competence in order to point to the learned knowledge of cultural norms which is crucial to language use. The position taken up by communicative competence is that knowing what to say is never enough; it is also necessary to know how to say it. And by 'how' is not meant the performing of the speech that is getting the words out; rather what is meant is using the appropriate register, variety, code, script, formula, tone and formality. Once again the issue for our consideration is to what extent such cultural knowledge can be acquired late; and to what extent getting it right, that is using the appropriate forms, only comes to those who acquire the language as their 'mother tongue'. It is commonly assumed that communicative competence may be harder to acquire than linguistic competence – if we put aside those well-known cases of fossilisation in foreign accents. We consider this question in Chapters 6 and 8.

Whether or not it is conceptually helpful to treat commumcative and linguistic competence as separate remains an open question, as we have noted earlier.

Second language, foreign language and bilingual

The topics second and foreign language are also relevant to our consideration of the native speaker. We have already noted that defining the mother tongue and the first and dominant language is done in opposition to, for example, the second language. This suggests that we might hope to define in separate and perhaps rigorous ways the second language and the foreign language. Alas! that is not the case. A second language is, in fact, defined in term of a language which is learned after the first language (or the mother tongue) – not of course that it is inferior in any way, just that it comes after the first in time of learning (Stern, 1983). And so we are back at finding ourselves unable to define the first language except in terms of what is earliest acquired.

A distinction is perhaps useful between the language of a bilingual (or multilingual) child acquired in a home or environment where more than one input is available) and the child who acquires a non-home or non-intimate language in a more public setting (Romaine, 1989; Hamers & Blanc, 1989). Such a setting is often education and the second language is sometimes used to define a situation in which the child is being educated in a language medium which is not the home language; but the second language does not have to be the language of education – it may be the lingua franca of the public environment in which the child begins to grow (for example Nepal). What seems to underlie the use of the term second language is that it indicates a command which is less than that of the first language, but stronger than that of the foreign language.

Foreign languages then seem to be acquired in order to interact with foreigners, that is groups outside one's native environment.

This also seems to imply that a foreign language does not carry with it the kind of automatic grasp of its systems that are appealed to in terms of the first language and are suggested in some areas of the second language. A foreign language has not been, it can be surmised, internalised in the same way that a first (and perhaps a second) language has. A foreign language speaker cannot be appealed to for authoritative pronouncements about the language's rules and its use. First language speakers, of course, can be; and, as we shall see, this is the problematic and very interesting issue about second languages: whether control of a second language, which, as we have seen, is by definition learned after the first, can become as internalised as the first; whether being a native speaker and being a first language speaker (or a mother tongue speaker) are synonymous and whether a second language speaker can be a native speaker of that second language.

Summary

In this chapter we have considered the role of the native speaker in applied linguistics, set out our argument, provided a plan for the book as a whole chapter by chapter and noted the range of views in the literature. We examined the commonsense view of the term, noting the set of terms which the concept of native speaker implies: mother tongue, first language, dominant language, home language, linguistic competence, communicative competence, second language, foreign language. In the chapters which follow we tease out the distinctions among these terms further, seeking an answer to the question of whether being a native speaker is, in fact, a matter only of self-ascription or whether it is also (or instead) a matter of objective definition. The commonsense view alone is inadequate. It needs support which is available in the central linguistic disciplines. We turn now in Chapters 2 and 3 to brief considerations of the native speaker from a psycholinguistic and a linguistic point of view.

Chapter 2
Psycholinguistic Aspects of the Native Speaker

In this chapter I deal with a number of matters already raised in Chapter 1. My purpose in raising them again (as will be the case in later chapters) is to add to our understanding by bringing in information in the case of Chapter 2 from the field of psycholinguistics.

First, however, by way of illustration, I will quote an example of one important difference between the language of a learner and that of a native speaker. This comes from a paper by Faerch and Kasper dealing with the interlanguage of request modification. They are here discussing internal syntactic and lexical phrasal modifiers:

> From a psycholinguistic point of view, one can assume that native speakers use them with little conscious attention, precisely because they are void routines ... that do not contribute to the propositional development of the discourse ... hearers (do not) consciously attend to them when interpreting incoming speech. What hearers do notice, however, is their absence, as is evident from the following conversational exchange between a German learner (L) and a native speaker of English (N):

> (N has taken L's library seat)
> **L:** hey what did you do
> **N:** pardon
> **L:** you put my books on the other side and it's my seat now (a bit later)
> **L:** you wouldn't be angry if you er come back and you see that there's something er that there's somebody other
> **N:** well at least I would ask them the other person if they er if they needed long to complete their work or or if if I could possibly have my seat back but I wouldn't come up and say hey what are you doing with my seat. (Kasper, 1981, quoted in Faerch and Kasper, 1989: 243)

Growth of Psycholinguistics

Psycholinguistics, the empirical and theoretical study of the mental faculty that underpins our consummate linguistic ability (Altmann, 2001), has shown considerable development in the last 40 years, drawing in part on earlier studies in psychology and language where the concern was with such topics as word association and language attitudes, but more considerably and increasingly on the particular interests in cognition and language acquisition which were always central to the transformational generative (TG) linguistic paradigm. Psycholinguistics continues today to be of importance in linguistics, though perhaps less so than formerly, and it also continues to interest psychologists. What is perhaps more important is that psycholinguistics has become increasingly important in the development of the new discipline of Cognitive Science. From a psycholinguistic point of view to say that an individual is a native speaker is of course redundant. Surely, everybody is a native speaker. Now is that indeed the case?

Is Everybody a Native Speaker?

Let me suggest four possibilities. I can say:

(1) that every individual is a native speaker of all his/her linguistic behaviour, that is that underlying all one's normal linguistic behaviour is a system or set of systems (allowing, of course, as all descriptions, however wide ranging, must, for randomness and happenstance);
(2) that every individual is a native speaker of one language, but only one, the one that he/she acquired as a mother tongue;
(3) that some individuals are native speakers of more than one language whether or not acquired early; and
(4) that some individuals never achieve native speaker status in any language and may be regarded as semilingual.

The First Approach: Idiolectal Native Speaker

The first approach states that one is a native speaker of the whole of one's repertoire, that is that everything one says (or presumably writes and understands) can be accounted for in terms of the set of linguistic rules that are under one's control which together make up a coherent system. Now in one sense, rather a trivial sense, this must be true in that everything one does is done by one's self and is therefore one's own responsibility and therefore, in some sense, under one's own systematic control; that is it would not happen unless one allowed it to happen.

The trouble with this argument is that it is self-defeating; it cannot be refuted because it is self-evident. Such an approach is probably a pseudo-procedure, that is a proposal never realisable in practice; it is also formidably non-theoretical since it provides no explanation of what human beings do or have since it is quite ungeneralisable. In addition, it does not make much sense since it does not mark randomness, whether accidental (errors, nonsense and so on) or imitations, that is slabs of language borrowed in from others' use. For example, if I use a quotation or a non English sentence, or if I use two forms of the same verb (dived, dove), they would all have to be accommodated within the description of my repertoire and rules would need to be provided to account for all such evidence. Furthermore, and more importantly, it does not allow for language switching and therefore requires that we devise different systems for monolinguals and for bi/multilinguals, one system in each case; and that while one person is a native speaker of, say, English, another is a native speaker of, say, English and Japanese (plus all the other bits of language use that occur in everybody's speech). As for example, if I switch from, say, English to Japanese with different interlocutors during a day's conversation, then all the texts of all my encounters, English and Japanese, would need to be accommodated within one grammatical description.

It is indeed the case that merged systems are possible (Gumperz, 1964; Fasold, 1984). What is at issue here is the impossibility of providing a linguistic description to take systematic account of all data in every idiolect. Such an undertaking would be a collection rather than an analysis. So for both practical and theoretical reasons this first approach seems to be a non starter. It also interestingly raises the question of the opposition between the two traditional types of bilingual – the coordinate and the subtractive (de Houwer, 1994; Baker & Jones, 1998). Coordinate bilinguals are said to operate all functions in both languages while subtractive bilinguals use one language for certain functions and the other language for other functions. Neither model seems wholly convincing since it is difficult to establish a test case in which an individual could operate equally in both languages or ambilingually, though Steiner (1968) claims to do so. But my first approach does not really conform to either coordinate or subtractive bilingualism since it is not about bilingualism, but rather about a special type of monolingualism. While it is true that that is how people appear to operate, that we all have a repertoire which is mixed and complex (whether linguistic or dialectal), nevertheless, it is of only indirect interest to set out to describe one individual in all his/her linguistic features: indeed to do so seems to be less scientific than artistic/ literary. Thus a stylistic description of James Joyce's *Finnegan's Wake* would set out to provide an appreciation of the whole text but that would be integrative and stylistic rather than rule-extracting and analytic. There is another view of this approach, that 'everyone is a native speaker of his/her own speech' which is brought into prominence by the special case of the gifted emigré writer such as Kafka, Conrad, Beckett, Borges or Nabokov. If indeed 'the modernist movement can be seen as a strategy of permanent exile' (Steiner, 1968: 17) then what such emigré writers convey to us is the great strength (possibly giving them that extra gift of genius) of their mixed code, their own unique speech/language. And if this is true in the writer's special case it is equally true, though not of course so obvious, for us all. Writing of Nabokov, Steiner (1968: 10) suggests that his writing is made up out of 'a private mixed idiom' and again 'the multilingual, cross linguistic situation is both the matter and form of Nabokov's work' (p. 7).

Underlying this view is the identification of language and thought. This appears to be the view that Steiner takes of literature and of language. It is not surprising therefore that in different ways he finds common ground with both Chomsky's (1986) arguments about universals and innate ideas and with Whorf's linguistic relativity (Whorf, 1942). While it does seem to be true that Nabokov and other such writers in exile are indeed concerned with their language loss and language gain and with preserving as best they can the medium that used to be native to them and which is no longer so prominent because less used around them in their daily lives, Steiner's comment contains elements of reductionism and of being patronising. Reductionism because it equates native speaker and code with the total use that the writer makes of his/her language(s); patronising because it implies that exiled second language writers have no control over the way that they write, that they cannot distance themselves from their medium, cannot do what Donaldson (1978) argues all normal children must do, and that is dissociate themselves from the immediate and think about it.

The Second Approach: First Acquired Language

The second approach states that we are all native speakers of the language we first acquired, that is our mother tongue. Now with the caveat which I considered in discussing the mother tongue (Chapter 1) and remembering that for many people it is not clear what the mother tongue is, then I can say that being a native speaker does mean having a first acquired language. All that does, in fact, is to reduce the definition back onto the question of what having a first acquired language means or, in other words, what knowledge of a language of which one is a competent user means. That is the competence question and so that is where the value of discussions of competence resides. Thus being a native speaker according to this definition means having linguistic (and perhaps also communicative) competence in a language (see Chapter 6).

The Third Approach: Unitary Competence

The third approach moves on from this competence-in-one-language definition to the idea of competence in-more-than-one-language. This is a very real and live issue since it affects the view many second (and foreign) language users have of their own control of a second or foreign language. But of equal importance is what view so-called bilinguals (especially those who acquire more than one language in early childhood) have of themselves. And the view we must take of them.

Now in part this is a question of what competence means. But it is also, as I noted earlier, a philosophical question of whether or not one can be a native speaker (have competence in) more than one language, to be not just bilingual but ambilingual. In one sense this must be rare if not impossible, that is in the sense that no-one can be equally at home in every aspect of life in more than one language: apart from anything else, functions and domains will differ. No-one, one might say, talks to his/her grandmother in two languages; or at the other extreme no-one goes to school in two second languages. Of course there are claimed exceptions to both these cases but it must always be possible to find one more function of language use which the bilingual feels at greater ease with in one or other language, for example counting, prayer, talking to animals, dealing with bureaucrats.

However it may be that competence in two or more languages does not require ambilingualism, which is after all a matter of fluency. Perhaps competence is at some kind of higher, more abstract level. We will come on to that when we discuss what is meant by competence.

The Fourth Approach: Semilingualism

The fourth approach proposes that while some individuals are fully lingual (that is competent), others are not and may be called semilingual. Note that semilingualism must assume the existence of competence because semilingualism has meaning only as the negation of lingualism or of the possession of linguistic competence. What semilingualism argues (Skutnabb-Kangas, 1981) is that in certain situations, either of a multilingual character or an impoverished one, which creates a climate of disadvantage, children may be brought up with no fully developed linguistic system and what they have will be either (a) a set (two or more) of partial systems or (b) one inadequate system.

It must be said that the first of these views (the set of partial systems) is the one more usually adumbrated, the second (the inadequate system) being suspect both on philosophical grounds (what does it mean to have an inadequate system only?) but also on psychological/developmental grounds since normal development in language as in other areas seems, whatever the input, to lead to a fully formed system. It seems to be the case that even impoverished language input, however non-standard, however non-fluent, will trigger off the child's language learning ability and provide enough evidence for a full competence to develop. The hearing child of deaf parents appears to gain from them a competence in signing and from neighbours and relatives an oral language competence which the parents cannot display (Swisher & McKee, 1989; Sutton-Spence & Woll, 1999).

This does not exclude all consideration of non-normal development and of faulty or inadequate use of the system, since use is not in itself in any way an indication of a speaker's competence. It is also the case that on libertarian, political, anti-racist grounds it would be difficult to maintain an argument about a speaker possessing only a partial system, an argument that may be used about disadvantaged groups, such as blacks, working class, foreign workers' children.

Two or More Systems?

The first view of semilingualism, however, is more meaningful: that is the view that the speaker has a set of two or more systems. Now if this means that second and foreign languages (that is all those that are not 'first') provide only a partial system then this view reduces in these terms to the second view of semilingualism, that is that there is one system (the L1) and then a set of inadequate proficiencies. This can be dismissed. But there is a more attractive and persuasive view and it applies particularly to situations of multilingualism (including bilingualism) from early childhood. Because what this posits is that such learners may compensate for what is lacking in one system by a corresponding replacement component in another system or in other systems.

Now this does seem to make sense in areas such as function or domain, for example in Celtic languages we may posit that the domain of home and of religion employs the local language (Welsh, Scots Gaelic, Breton) while the domains of the school, play, shopping and so on employ English or French. This is an old argument and seems to make sense: it is probably the case that this is in reality for most people who are 'bilingual' what bilingualism means in that there are some things they do in one language and others they do in other(s); to do everything in one language would be possible but impractical because it would require a series of switches involving not just the speaker but his/her whole network of acquaintances and a whole set of institutions; as well as learning how to do it. Increasingly, it seems, bilingual scholars recognise the need to take account of social context: 'from very early on, the bilingual child makes contextually sensitive linguistic choices that draw on a developing knowledge of two separate language systems' (de Houwer, 1994: 248).

A Patchwork Linguistic System?

Such language systems are whole not partial: 'bilingual children do not differ much from monolingual children in their approach to the language learning task' (de Houwer, 1994: 248). But what is meant by semilingualism as being a set of (two or more) partial systems is that some part of the linguistic system is handled in one language and some part in the other(s). Now there are areas of linguistic activity where this could be held to make sense, for example in terms of various linguistic levels: thus it would be possible in the Celtic situation we have just been looking at for the syntax to be Welsh and the phonology or the lexis to be English or for the morphology to be English and the syntax to be Welsh (it does seem that it is the syntax which is least permeable).

Such imbalances do, in fact, occur: both in situations of language loss, decline and death where gradually one system after another is eroded and taken over by the incoming code; also in situations of pidginisation and creolisation where new languages are being formed. If this is true then it does seem that those bilingual (or recently bilingual as in the case of creole) situations where languages are being currently lost or gained are those in which subsystems are shared.

Again it is not clear that this is what is meant by this version of semilingualism. What does seem to be meant is that within one language level, that is within syntax, there is a mixing so that, for example, the subject may be the province of English and the predicate of Welsh; or the tense is English and the modality Welsh; or the negation is English while the interrogation is Welsh. Well, once again there is a plausibility about such arguments in cases of language loss and undoubtedly there are cases in language acquisition where negation, for example, will be supplied, when using the second language (L2), by the first language (L1); but when using the L1 then L1 forms for both negation and interrogation will be used; but that is not the claim of this view of semilingualism which must be that the speaker controls (for example) negation only in English and interrogation only in Welsh.

In other words the speaker does not have full command of either Welsh or English but only of a mixed code which at the same time is somehow adequate. Now, as we have said, this may indeed be the case in situations of language loss particularly where the community is remote and has little or no access to education and other modernising developments. It may perhaps also be the case among the children in recent immigrant communities: though on logical grounds this seems unlikely since the children of an immigrant community will either acquire the language of the parents, who are presumably – according to the usual argument – competent in their L1 or they will acquire that partially and then the language of the school environment. How well they will be able to acquire the language of the school environment, especially in literacy skills which matter so much in education, is a moot point and is some times confused with their accession of competence.

Semilingualism then as a view of competence – although the discussion helps clarify our view of competence – seems to hold up only in situations of language loss. I shall need to return to the topic later when we discuss communicative competence (Chapter 6) because the same sort of issue arises in terms of internalising of the culture (or of more than one culture). But I leave it now and turn to the main topic of this chapter which is competence. We have skirted round it long enough.

A Dictionary Definition

The Longman *Dictionary of Applied Linguistics* (Richards *et al.*, 1985) defines competence as follows:

> in Generative Transformational Grammar [as] a person's internalized grammar of a language. This means a person's ability to create and understand sentences, including sentences they have never heard before. It also includes a person's knowledge of what are and what are

not sentences of a particular language. For example a speaker of English would recognize:
1. I want to go home
as an English sentence but would not accept a sentence such as
2. I want going home
even though all the words in it are English words. Competence often refers to the ideal speaker/hearer, that is an idealized but not a real person who would have a complete knowledge of the whole language. A distinction is made between competence and performance, which is the actual use of the language by individuals in speech and writing. (Richards *et al.*, 1985: 52)

As will be obvious the difficulty with this definition is that it assumes the existence of a language out there, outside people: 'for example a speaker of English would recognise:

1. want to go home

as an English sentence'. That can only mean that there is an English code to be recognised by a speaker and that this English has a set of rules which are learnt, accessed by speakers rather than provided by them. We can leave for the moment the question of just what this English (or any other language) is; that, after all, is a linguistic question and we will come to it in Chapter 3 when we look into the linguistic questions. This approach to competence is strongly structural, even more it is cognitive-developmental. It indicates that competence is seen metaphorically as some kind of motor programmed to acquire English on behalf of the child. The question of whether the learning of a second/foreign language makes use of the same competence in the same way will be returned to shortly. This motor or, better, piece of software has a built-in general programme (perhaps universal grammar) which permits the child to acquire whichever language s/he is exposed to, has input and opportunity for. What the input and the opportunity provide is a shaping of the software based on general grammatical lines (universal grammar) in such a way that all learners of the 'same' language will have the same or a similar shaping to their software.

The Longman definition refers to an internalised grammar, to ability and to knowledge. In addition, we are told of the *ideal* speaker/hearer, not a real person. The dictionary definition, in other words, enables us to handle the issue of competence so as to bracket both the real and the idealised world. A neat definition and one that certainly reflects the ambiguity with which competence is surrounded such that it is used to mean both what it is that speakers of the language do and in addition what no one speaker knows or obtains, that is what the ideal speaker knows or what all speakers know after redundancy is eliminated. These two views are not incompatible in that what every speaker has is partial but based on what is accessible to all but which no one individual alone possesses.

Competence Characteristics

Let me attempt to characterise competence as follows:

(1) Competence means performing without thinking (the notion of automaticity). The child can perform in limited ways, the ideal native speaker in all areas.
(2) Competence does not mean performing in valued ways, that is doing it well; just as what distinguishes two runners or two pianists is not competence (they both have that) but level of performance.
(3) Competence means knowing, being familiar with, all structural resources of a code, (though not with its rhetoric), and being able to make judgements about structural realisations.

So to take the quoted sentence

(1) I want going home

competence would label that sentence as ungrammatical. But here we meet problems over the idealised native speaker; we can accept that the idealised native speaker does not make errors, is not dependent on context and separates variety from non variety. Does this suggest that the ideal native speaker would know if 'I want going home' can be grammatical in some varieties? (cf I like going home). Since grammaticality is not language-based but variety-based or is more abstract than related to one variety and operates above any lexical realisation level, then the ideal native speaker is seen to be a goal only for an explanatory model, rather than an operable one on the grounds that even structurally related varieties of one language cannot have exactly the same grammar. Then the ideal native speaker becomes more and more simply a characterisation of the (universal) human linguistic ability, quite unrelated to particular languages. It is not therefore surprising that the goal/object of linguistics should have been defined as being not about language at all but about grammar (Smith & Wilson, 1979). In my view this is an unnecessarily narrow definition. Linguistics can be about all systematic language behaviour including grammar. The narrow definition is also ultimately self-defeating, since grammar only has meaning insofar as it relates to language use in human language. Without these data it becomes philosophy or psychology.

The Two Cognitive Systems Hypothesis

Felix argues strongly for a type of Universal Grammar hypothesis by which 'the principles of Universal Grammar are themselves subject to an innately specified developmental process'. This strong Universal Grammar (UG) view 'incorporates two parts: a set of parametric constraints on possible mental representations and a maturational schedule for the emergence of these constraints' (Felix, 1987: 114).

What this means is that it is the parameters (for example the settings for word order, feature deletion) that uniquely distinguish native speakers. Felix helpfully poses the right question: why is it that after puberty a second language learner cannot become a native speaker? And Felix means *cannot*. He accepts (though he does not discuss) the possibility of a pre-pubertal second language learner becoming a native speaker, but he would presumably not regard that as second language learning. In other words, second language learning is in complementary distribution to native speakerness in that the second must happen before puberty and the first only afterwards. No doubt Felix would also accept that a pre-pubertal learner cannot become a native speaker without adequate input (for example a situation where a foreign language is taught in the primary or elementary school).

But Felix's argument is more interesting still in that he proposes two different cognitive systems at work from the onset of puberty; he calls them the language-specific system and the problem-solving system and says that they 'begin to compete in the processing of language data' (Felix, 1987: 140). And since this, in his view, is what prevents the post-pubertal second language learner from becoming a native speaker, this competition has 'rather unfortunate consequences in the case of language learning' (p. 140). We discuss these systems later.

On the face of it this is a revival of the critical period hypothesis (Lennerberg, 1967; and Chapter 9). But Felix argues that this bilingual or nativist explanation is unsatisfactory in assuming that L1 and L2 acquisition for children and (in the case of L2) for adults are 'both governed by a common set of basic principles' (p. 142). Felix is sceptical of the importance given by teachers to external environmental factors in second language learning, although he makes no comment on the issue of unequal success for individuals: once environmental conditions are discounted as criterial, then either there is a differential ability at work (which would not, it seems, be acceptable to Felix although he might settle for equivalent competence and differential performance) or there is motivation. But motivation is an unsatisfactory answer to a non-question since it can only be an answer to itself, i.e. what motivates? ... motivation? (rather like the famous Levi-Strauss comment on incest: the answer to a question which has not been asked!). Felix takes a clear Chomskian line: 'the human mind is organised in the form of an infinite number of independent cognitive modules each having its own specific properties – a person's (tacit) grammatical knowledge represents one such module, while a different module contains what may be called 'conceptual knowledge' (p. 154).

The effect of this view is to provide support for Felix's proposal of the existence of two different cognitive systems: both are available for language learning – the first, the system of language-specific cognitive structures and the second the system of problem-solving cognitive structures. The first, the language-specific one, is available only until puberty. After that all second language learning has to use the problem-solving system. These two systems are in competition with one another. Athough both remain available after puberty for cognitive operations, it appears that adult second language learning typically makes use only of the problem-solving capacity/system. Felix considers the problem-solving system much less efficient than the language-specific system and his argument is largely a logical one that has to do with the hypothesis of a special language faculty.

Choosing Between the Two Systems?

But can the second language adult learner choose between the two systems? Felix thinks no, that while both are 'available', adults typically tend to approach language learning in a problem-solving manner (Felix, 1987: 161). Child language acquisition and second language acquisition (adult) therefore differ in this crucial respect that for child language acquisition only the language-specific system is available; for second language acquisition (adult) both are available. For the adult (unlike the child) the two systems compete, but although the problem-solving system is less efficient for language learning than the language-specific system, the adult typically chooses the problem-solving system for second language learning even though it is the wrong system to use for any language learning.

The adult is programmed into using this wrong system because adults approach all learning tasks through their problem-solving system. It is partly the wrong system because environmental factors, which do not in Felix's view affect the language-specific system, 'strongly affect the operation of the problem-solving system' (p. 165). And the fact that the adult may make use of the language-specific system in addition to the problem-solving system makes things worse, because the two systems are in competition with one another. Felix produces data to demonstrate the differences between the types of utterances produced by adults and children which he maintains 'reflect the operation of the problem-solving system' (p. 172).

Felix's scenario is relevant to our concern. He makes after all a convincing case for a psycholinguistic-learning distinction between a child's first-language and an adult's second-language learning and, in doing so, provides a rationale by which we can distinguish between the native speaker and the non-native speaker, as follows: that the native speaker learns one or more first language according to one system (the language-specific) and that the non-native speaker learns a second language by a combination of the language-specific and the problem-solving system which are in competition with one another. Thus we seem now to have an explanation for why a native speaker is a native speaker.

This explains why native speakers can be regarded as different from non-native speakers: native speakers move from a position of insecurity to one of security, while non-native speakers move in the reverse direction. Native speakers, however defined, start off seeking meaning: they learn the language offered them in order (in part) to gain the meaning they seek. As they progress, the gain in meaning gives them greater and greater security as they come, through the medium of language, to control their environment. Non-native speakers, in contrast, already have that control in their L1. Their learning of an L2 means that they must abandon the security of their L1 to become less and less sure in the L2 of what was so familiar in the L1.

Cook insists that L2 is different from L1 acquisition precisely because there is an L1 already in place: 'a major factor in the different courses of L1 and L2 acquisition must be the developing links between the two languages. In a sense any investigation of L2 learning or use that does not involve this relationship is not SLA research' (Cook, 2001: 499, 500).

Eventually, if non-native speakers make sufficient progress in the target language, they also gain security in the L2 as well as in their L1. Felix shows that differential acquisition results in a difference in grammatical sentences whereby non-native speakers provide evidence of 'numerous instances of utterances which do not exhibit any detectable syntactic patterns' (Felix, 1987: 172). And in the differences of expression exhibited and illustrated elsewhere in this account. What Felix does not, however, show is whether post-pubertal non-native speakers cannot, in principle, become native-speaker-like in the target language and therefore indistinguishable from native speakers on all parameters except of course the biological one.

Relevance to Applied Linguistics

The main applied linguistics interest in psycholinguistics is in Second Language Acquisition (SLA) research. The two central issues are: (1) that of the generality of the development process in terms of context and learner variables; and (2) that of the relationship across languages of SLA, which is essentially a further generalisation from the first question (Corder, 1981; Ellis, 1985).

The first question is discussed by Winitz (1981), who describes the 'cross-over effect' whereby adults' initial superiority in language learning is lost as the L2 is acquired. Winitz suggests that this may arise from the mismatch between linguistic and cognitive development in the adult, especially when the adult is presented with an oral language input equivalent to that of the L1 learner.

For both questions the native speaker acts as model and goal. The applied linguistics interest is in the approximation of SLA to native speaker models, the ordinary assumption (the so-called null hypothesis) being that all SLA is similar, that, as with child language acquisition, the particular model of input is unimportant. But to examine that question it is necessary to describe the available native speaker models, the basic question being whether all learners approximate to the same native speaker model, however inadequate their native speaker (or non-native speaker) input may be. For such a fundamental applied linguistic concern we have to agree what we mean by the native speaker.

Summary

In this chapter I have looked briefly at the native speaker from a psycholinguistic point of view. I have examined the question of what it means to say that everyone is a native speaker and argued that there are four ways of answering this question: the native speaker as a speaker of his/her own idiolect (which raised the interesting question of the creative writer in a second language), the native speaker as a speaker of his/her first acquired language, and the native speaker as a bilingual. The fourth answer, that of semilingualism, I have rejected but not before it has pointed us (as of course does the issue of bilingualism) to the need to take account of more than one system. That I suggested is a necessary implication both for language and for cognition. I considered the view put forward by Felix (1987) that what is essential for native speaker development is the dual cognitive system. That is a reminder of earlier critical age views. What it does for us in this discussion is to help explain, if that is what is needed, how native speakers are special. While native speakers move from insecurity (searching for meaning) to security, so non-native speakers move in the other direction, since they come to their target language full of the security given by their own native speakerness in their first language.

I turn now from psycholinguistic considerations to linguistic ones. If native speakers have, as has been suggested in this chapter, language-specific cognitive systems, what is language specific, that is what is linguistic about the native speaker? In Chapter 3 I deal with this linguistic question.

Chapter 3
Linguistic Aspects of the Native Speaker

Discussing the 'fundamental and surprisingly complex problem of defining what is meant by an error in the language clasroom context', Allwright (1988: 202) gives the following short text:

Teacher: I started at Essex on the fifth of October. When did you start? (nominates by gesture)
Student 4:   I start in Excess since the eleventh of January.
Teacher: When did you arrive? You arrived on the eleventh of January, did you? You must have started the next day, did you?

Allwright (p. 209) comments that the complexity for the analyst of deciding just what was going wrong 'meant a parallel amount of complexity for the classroom teacher'. The trick for the teacher is not just to understand what the learner is trying to say but also to provide some way of remediation. That, as Allwright says, is an overwhelming task for the classroom teacher who has to operate – unlike the analyst – in the real time and public setting of the class-room.

The Grammarian's Task

Linguistics has as its aim the description of competence and this refers both to the idealised model of competence and to what it is that individual native speakers know. Note that while the second task stimulates and provides data for the first, it must be the case that for purely linguistic purposes the aim of the linguist is to describe the idealised model which underlies the internalised grammar of a person, his/her ability and his/her knowledge of the grammar of the language s/he is acquiring or has already acquired. But this is not straightforward and there remain severe problems, such as whether it makes sense to speak of *has acquired* (as a product) or is language always in the process of being learnt? We seem to need both senses.

Native speakers are still always *acquiring* in an absolute sense but *have acquired* in comparison with non-native speakers. It is clear then that linguistics is concerned with uncovering, revealing, describing, explaining the knowledge of the idealised native speaker. Note the precision of this definition: it restricts the knowledge of concern in terms of content to that of language (or rather to linguistic behaviour) and in terms of kind of knowledge to that of an idealisation, that is removed from any one person. And this is the nub of the problem for us in our consideration of the native speaker in linguistic terms. For what does it mean to be a human native speaker – linguistically – if linguistics is about ideal speaker/ hearers? In other words what relationship does the real living native speaker have to the idealisation? When we say:

I am a native speaker, or

s/he is a native speaker, or

you'll have to ask a native speaker, or

don't ask me, I'm not a native speaker.

what is it we are appealing to? What is it that human native speakers know if linguistics considers the concept to be an idealisation and if competence is, as we saw in the Longman dictionary entry (in Chapter 2), the possession of the ideal speaker/hearer? The examples used in a discussion of what the ideal native speaker/hearer knows are created from (1) the grammarian's own knowledge of his/her own speech or that of an informant; and (2) what the grammarian thinks s/he knows of representative, usually educated, native speaker use. This must, of course, vary in time and in space since all samples of native-speakers are selected both chronologically and geographically (not to speak of socially). 'Ideal' is, therefore, to some extent a creation of what is real, non-ideal, data-based plus contexts of acquisition. We refer to this later as 'systems of individual speakers'.

Three Types of Grammar

The core question in this chapter then is what sort of knowledge does the native speaker have? We can offer such qualifications as partial, potential, fallible. But much more important is the opposition between (a) evidence (getting at the abstraction of competence) and (b) the ambiguity of what it is that the individual knows and what it is that an individual shares in terms of knowledge with other individuals. In other words (as far as my (b) is concerned) it would be absurd to deny that a person is a native speaker of his/her own speech, that is s/he is not just trying to speak like him/herself. Or to put it another way we are not trying to be idealised versions of ourselves. Certainly what we think we are doing is becoming fully proficient (native) speakers of the language we are acquiring. And this is where the ambiguity, and it is a deep systematic ambiguity, resides. For there are indeed two senses of what is meant by approaching the native speaker linguistically. In the first sense, what is sometimes traditionally called the descriptive linguistic sense, the aim of linguistics is to describe an individual's linguistic system: thus this (this grammar) is my grammar, of Alan Davies, what I will call Grammar 1. Free of mistakes, of course, or, as is usually said, free of performance errors. This is my system, this is the best account of the grammar I am making use of when I speak and so on, me, after editing as it were, but not the data of my speech not a transcript of everything I have said or written but the underlying rules on which I draw in performing these data.

Now what is true of me is not necessarily true of anyone else. You and I may be both native speakers of language X but your grammar and mine at the descriptive level will not be identical: note this is not because we are now talking about differences between performance errors, not at all. Those will have been removed from both of us. What we are talking about is the fact that we both appeal to different sets of rules, that our grammars are different. How different is a matter of just how far apart our speech is while still being intelligible. At the extremes (the English of England and the English of Scots) the grammars will need to be quite different; at a nearer position, say my speech and that of my father, daughter or other close relative, the differences will be minimal but they will still be there.

In the second sense – and here is the other side of the ambiguity to construct a linguistic grammar which accommodates both my daughter and me, my father and me, me as an English-speaking Welshman and you as an English person and so on, requires more than a descriptive grammar: putting two or more descriptive grammars together means providing an explanation of some kind, showing what it is they/we have in common, indicating what it is that, at a deeper level than description, at a level of abstraction, enables one individual to share with another some set of rules which can be regarded as being 'the same'. Of course, they will not be exactly the same, they can only be similar; we shall call this Grammar 2.

So far we have considered two types of grammar (or competence) which we will call: Grammar 1, which is what an individual has in terms of his/her own language; and Grammar 2, which is what one individual shares with another because they share the same language and are, to a large extent, mutually intelligible when they use it. As will be obvious by now there must also be a Grammar 3, the grammar of the human faculty of language, which is what all speakers share whether or not they share the same language. Grammar 3 underlies all language use; it is competence at its most abstract level, what has also been called universal grammar.

Problems of Abstraction

Indeed, this is exactly the argument for the revolution made by transformational grammar in the 1950s (Chomsky, 1957), in that it broke away from the 'old' descriptivist tradition of linguistics which had been about languages (but as we now know was, in fact, about the systems of individual speakers) and took as its proper pursuit the explanation for the human faculty of language. That is how it is that language can be learnt, by analogy with other forms of human learning and development. Whether or not this is what linguistics should be about is a moot point. Certainly it is very persuasive since it can be argued that this is a higher order, more abstract, more theoretical study than the description of individual languages or of individual speakers. Furthermore it must (if it has any truth) underlie individual languages and individual speakers and is therefore logically prior to any such description. There are, however, problems about investigating at such an abstract level – abstract since no-one actually speaks a universal grammar. I will use the analogy of the study of literature (any art form would be equally apposite). Let us suppose that instead of investigating, researching into individual writers of individual literatures it was decided (and indeed we see such tendencies in the post-structuralist movements), to investigate literature – in general – that is what is universal about literature which (presumably) enables separate literatures to be written, individual writers to write. The problem that would arise would be just what it is that is to be investigated, what data could be examined. In effect, what would happen would be, a constant to-and-fro movement between the universal hypothesis and sample data from one or more literature. Such an investigation would attempt to operate at a highly abstract level using genre and structure in literature but would become, for much of the time, an updated comparative literature study. Language, in fact, lends itself more readily to such an abstract study since it is curiously like a type of logical account. But what happens is that the study of universal grammar becomes either (as with literature) comparative language study or it becomes comparative linguistics, that is to say an updated version of contrastive linguistics, 19th century philology brought up to date with more sophisticated methods of doing the grammar; or cognitive science which operates at the level of universal human abstraction, arguing sensibly enough that what is true for one human being is potentially true for all others (Harris, 1988).

Thus modern linguistics in its pursuit of Grammar 3 becomes either philology or psychology (in its present manifestations as psycholinguistics, cognitive science, artificial intelligence and so on). The difficulty with this type of investigation as an account of language is that (as with behaviourism in an earlier paradigm) it tends to remake human cognition on the model of what is possible for a machine. (Of course we recognise that there is a two-way process here and that machines become or attempt to become more true to what humans can do and do do.)

Grammar 2

For the moment then let me leave Grammar 1 and Grammar 3 as somehow both being the real stuff (though in dispute) of linguistics, Grammar 1, the more traditional view or descriptivist approach (the grammar of the informant, of one person's speech), Grammar 3, the more contemporary, the 'structuralist' (in its more recent sense) explanatory and universal and cognitive (universal grammar, the human language faculty).

I still have to account for Grammar 2 from a linguistic point of view. Let me rehearse the differences between Grammar 2 and both Grammar 1 and Grammar 3. Grammar 1 concerns the system of one speaker and this may or may not be the system of a monolingual; as should be clear by now this does not matter and indeed there are arguments such as those by Gumperz (1964) which state that single combined systems can be derived from individual users in multilingual contact situations.

That really takes us too far ahead of ourselves. Grammar 3 concerns the human faculty of language – not one person's language use, ability or knowledge, not the system of a language or of one language but universal abstract systems, what makes language possible. Such a quest, that for universal grammar, is indeed akin to the search for scientific generality (which no doubt is why cognitive science has latched on to this type of investigation). Grammar 2 is not about individuals and not about universals though obviously it relates both ways); what it is about is separate and distinct languages, the grammar of French, the grammar of Japanese, English and so on. What it is also about is the native speaker: it is here that our question comes home to us in its linguistic role; since it is irrelevant to ask of Grammar 1 and Grammar 3 whether or not they are concerned with the native speaker because of course they both are, but unimportantly so, since it is trivial (but true) to say in Grammar 1 that X is a native speaker of his/her own speech; and of Grammar 3 that X possesses the human faculty of speech, is a 'native speaker' of universal grammar. In both cases such definitions are quite circular.

The problem with the Grammar 2 pursuit, as we have already seen, is that individual speakers of English and of all other languages disagree with one another as to what the grammar is (see Chapter 9). But that must be the case if Grammar 1 makes any sense at all: unless it is believed that the pursuit of Grammar 1 allows us to generalise to all other users of the language with which X (that is any one person) identifies. The issue then is the boundary one, an issue I will return to when I consider the socio-linguistics of the native speaker in Chapter 4. Where does one language end and another begin?

The answer to this, in my view, is largely sociolinguistic; and has to do with concepts such as those of language standardisation. But there is a continuum between the individual and the universal – so much is straight-forward in any theory of particulars or commonsense view of the categories society imposes on the world. Along this continuum it may be possible to determine major differences between one linguistic code and another – and we are here considering only linguistic distinctions between languages which are manifestly different languages but still related, such as, for example, French and German.

There are two ways of approaching this: the first states that such distinctions are arbitrary or they are determined by extra-linguistic considerations – in both cases we would have to say that if this is true then Grammar 2 has only a sociolinguistic reality. The second approach suggests a linguistic status for Grammar 2: this is that there are indeed major linguistic distinctions, cut-offs, along the linguistic continuum, so-called dialect boundaries, and these have to do with issues of descriptive efficiency, that is that it is more efficient to analyse this area here of the continuum on its own and separately from that area over there. As is obvious at extremes it makes sense to analyse, for example, English separately from Chinese; but problems do arise when we ask the question of just what it is linguistically that distinguishes say one dialect of Chinese from others, or what distinguishes British from American English, and so on. There are reasons to speculate that we can also claim intelligibility as another reason for making such distinctions, but as I shall argue later (in Chapter 7) it is really more satisfactory to regard intelligibility as a sociolinguistic factor.

The Linguistics of Grammar 2

From a linguistic point of view then where does this leave the native speaker with Grammar 2? I have already dismissed claims that the native speaker concept has any meaning at all in regard to Grammar 1 and Grammar 3. No doubt there is a linguistic argument in relation to Grammar 2 which states that there is a level of abstraction above the individual's speech which does account for that individual as well as for other individuals who are in membership with him/her in some sort of community (note that I cannot avoid making an immediate societal leap). In this regard being a native speaker would mean being close linguistically (not of course identical) to other speakers.

And that is of course exactly the case in reality. To return to my relatives, although we do not have the same set of rules, my father and I, or my daughter and I, do share enough rules in common for us to behave as if we did speak the same language. Which in an important sense means that we do. And although we are here once again appealing to a variety of non-linguistic but social or sociolinguistic considerations, nevertheless our description, once we have decided what it is we are describing, will be linguistic. Thus the common language of any speech community, be it of a family, town, tribe, village, region, island, country and so on, these are all possible objects of grammatical description and when they are completed what they provide is, in our terms, a statement about Grammar 2.

To be a native speaker linguistically, then, means operating a Grammar 2, an operation which allows for access to and intelligibility with other operators of the 'same' Grammar 2. In his construct of langue Saussure similarly links the social to the linguistic, thereby providing an explanation for the existence of Grammar 2. Grammar 2 linguistics thus seems predicated on some kind of sociolinguistic interpretation of social life: while of course Grammar 1 and even more Grammar 3 are predicated on a psycholinguistic view.

At least for our present purposes there is some reality about being a native speaker; but it does mean that the linguistic agreement, the acceptance and automatising of linguistic rules, the same rules come only *after* membership has already been decided on other than linguistic grounds. For example, my being a member of a family determines that I share a Grammar 2 with other members of that family, rather than my membership being decided on by the Grammar 2 I control (see Chapter 9).

Research Evidence of Linguistic Differences

Second language acquisition studies have, over the last 20 years, given a good deal of attention to the linguistic differences between the native speaker and the non-native speaker. (In such investigations it is usual for the researcher to accept self-ascription by individuals of native speaker status). What comes through very powerfully in this body of research is the consistent differences found by researchers in terms of the various measures (both of linguistic features and of communicative strategies.) That is to say that while principled ways of distinguishing native and non-native speakers may be difficult to reach there is no doubt that in practice, according to this body of research, they are different (Ellis, 1985). Some of the common differences found in this research are noted later (and see Chapter 10) but a word of caution is first necessary. We should not be easily persuaded that, because these differences are found consistently (as they are), there is a fundamental distinction between native and non-native speakers: indeed the argument of the book is that this distinction is fugitive and subtle.

In a typical study Porter reports that

> native speaker input was significantly different from learner input on four variables: rating, quality, total words and monitor. *Ratings* by ESL teachers showed native speaker input to be twice as good as learner input. In *quality*, native speaker input was about one-third as 'faulty' as learner input ... The native speakers did not use the kind of ungrammatical language sometimes found in foreigner talk; rather, their errors were those of performance, such as subject–verb agreement and pronoun reference. Native speakers had significantly more total words than learners ... Native speakers *monitored* their own and their interlocutor's speech more closely than did the learners, this pattern being parallel for self-correction and for other-correction' (Porter, 1986: 207–10; emphasis in original.)

We must remember just who are sampled in these researches. They tend to be, on the one hand, well-educated native speakers, usually speakers of the standard code, certainly literate and therefore familiar with the written, if not with the spoken standard. The non-natives, on the other hand, tend – inevitably and quite properly – to be learners, whether intermediate or advanced, still active learners. There is good reason for this because this second language acquisition (SLA) research is not about native and non-native speakers but about learning and if indeed very advanced learners appeared as part of a sample for one of these experiments and they were thought to be too native-like they might very well be excluded from the experiment.

In other words what this research shows is that second language learners are probably different from native speakers: that is a view which we have no argument with; indeed it is one with which we agree. But it does not, I submit, mean that a native speaker is uniquely and permanently different from a non-native speaker. Furthermore, as Long (1981, 1985) points out, much of the research on which this argument is based lacks data from one side of the equation: many of the studies, he says, have failed to obtain baseline data, that is evidence of native speaker performance, against which to compare the performance of non-native speakers. There is plenty of evidence of what non-native speakers do, but that it is different from the way native speakers behave is, to an extent, surmise. We are not concerned here with grammatical errors: the fact that second language learners make grammatical errors is obvious and not worth rehearsing. But in the important area of foreigner talk we can observe what appears to be a systematic difference between native and second language learners in terms of language control. Foreigner talk (the analogue of motherese or caretaker language for first language learners) is said to be the register used by native speakers when they address non-native speakers. What is important here from our point of view is not just the realised differences and the articulation of language control (that is that native speakers can do this) but also the clear awareness among native speakers that they have this capacity, strong evidence indeed for our argument that the main criterion for definition of a native speaker is self-identification. Ellis (1985) mentions three explanations that have been put forward of how native speakers are able to adjust their speech: these are:

(1) regression,
(2) matching and
(3) negotiation.

Ellis prefers the third of the explanations (but see Klein, 1986), that of negotiation, largely because such an explanation is basically descriptive and makes no assumptions about what the psycholinguistic processes are (Ellis, 1985: 138).

However, all three explanations do, in fact, appeal to simplification and in doing so, link up helpfully with what is known about other simplified codes such as motherese, interlanguage and pidgins. Then it seems to make sense to suggest that simplification through reduction, whether of form or of function, is a central linguistic ability and one available to all native speakers in regard to their first language (Meisel, 1980). Second language learners cannot, so easily, simplify their target language because as Corder (1981) pointed out, you cannot simplify what you do not have.

Foreigner talk has both formal and functional characteristics, labelled by Long (1981) input and interactional features respectively. Note that three levels of foreigner talk are distinguished; first the functional (or inter-actional) reduction; second, the functional plus the reduction of the formal input but limited to standard forms; and third both of these plus the use of non-standard formal input. Ellis (1985: 135–6) provides useful tables of these features, which include the following ones.

Foreigner Talk Examples

Interactional modifications

More 'here and now' topics
More confirmation checks
More clarification requests
More other repetitions
Shorter responses

More topic initiating moves
More comprehension checks
More self repetitions
More expansions

Input modifications

Standard	Non-Standard
Pronunciation	
Slowing down speech	Addition of vowel to final consonant
Separate word/syllable articulation	Fewer reduced vowels
More careful pronunciation	Exaggerated intonation
Heavier stress	
Increased volume on key words	
Lexis	
Restricted vocabulary size	Special lexicon of quantifiers, intensifiers and modal particles
Difficult items replaced with more frequently occurring items	Use of foreign or foreign sounding words (e.g. 'savvy')
Fewer pro- forms	
Repetition of words	
Use of analytic paraphrases	
Use of gesture	
Grammar	
Fewer contractions	Omission of copula, 'it', 'do', verb inflections
Overall shorter Length	Use of interlanguage forms (e.g. 'no' + verb)
Grammatical relations made explicit	

Coordination preferred to
  subordination
Less preverb modification
Topics moved to the beginnings
  of utterances
Fewer WH questions and more
  yes/no questions
More uninverted questions
More 'or-choice' questions
More tag questions
More present temporal markings

Relevance to Applied Linguistics

Our applied linguistics concern here is that of the teaching model for second language teaching, what is sometimes called pedagogic grammar (Rutherford, 1987). The problem is critically one for text-book writers, spoken language materials and examination/test constructors. The choice on the face of it is very clear: it is for Grammar 2. Pedagogic grammar is of relevance, therefore, because it is intended to provide the adult learner with a rapid learning experience. That this is necessary is shown by the demands that adults place on themselves to learn a second language quickly because they are unwilling to go through all the childhood learning again (see the Winitz, 1981, reference in Chapter 2). And yet they may reckon that the best environment to learn in is to replicate the child-like environment. Burling's humorous account (Burling, 1981) shows the absurdity of such a self-imposition and, at the same time, places a query against the extreme forms of communicative language teaching (see Chapter 6).

Grammar 1 is too idiosyncratic and Grammar 3 too abstract. In the event Grammar 2 is hard to pin down in exact detail. However, the applied linguistic moral of this chapter is, I suggest, that we should be relaxed about securing the right model. Grammar 2 is flexible and, in my view, exchangeable among dialects. In other words, Chapter 3 encourages confidence about our own awareness of the standard and of learners' ability to move between standards. In that sense, the view presented in Chapter 3 is intended to liberate us from a sense of grammatical imprisonment.

Summary

In this chapter I attempted to characterise the linguistic knowledge or competence of the native speaker, adding that to the discussion in Chapter 2 of the native speaker's systems of cognitive structures. I proposed three types of Grammar: Grammar 1, the grammar of the individual's idiolect; Grammar 2, the grammar that we share with other native speakers with whom we identify and Grammar 3, the human faculty of language. I noted that while Grammar 1 and Grammar 3 have traditionally been the object of linguistic investigation, it is in Grammar 2 that we need to seek for an understanding of the native speaker. This leads on to our later discussions (beginning in Chapter 4) of sociolinguistics and, in particular, of standard languages for it is there that we hope to find the most useful helpful definition of the native speaker. And so it is to the sociolinguistic aspects of the native speaker that I turn in Chapter 4.

Chapter 4
Sociolinguistic Aspects of the Native Speaker

Our discussion of Grammars 1, 2 and 3 (Chapter 3) suggests that we should look to Grammar 2 for a definition of the native speaker. This then is the background to our discussion in this chapter.

I begin with another cross-cultural interview example, which illustrates the problem for an interviewee who does not interpret questions in the light of the overall purpose of the job interview (Williams, 1985: 173). The interviewer, I, is a native speaker of Australian English; the interviewee, M, a young man from Bali, who is being interviewed for a position as sales assistant in a record shop in Australia.

I: erm ... this place you now have in Freemantle – this is a permanent address? You're staying there permanently, are you?
M: Yes.
I: And you are over in Australia to stay, or would you like to travel later on? ... or
M: I think I would like to travel.
I: You would like to travel. Er, where would you like to go?
M: Europe.
I: Europe ... mm ... Any idea when ... when you would like to go?
M: Er ... depend when I get the job, you know.
I: Good, O.K.
M: After I'm ... getting ... after I get a job, I think, then earn some money, and then ...
I: So how long would you like to work for us for? If we gave you a job, how long do you think you'd be working for us before you wanted to travel?
M: Mm. Until enough money to ... until enough money to go to travel.
I: Right. O.K. So that's really why you want the job is to get some money for travelling.
M: Yeah, for travelling. I love travelling.

Williams comments:

> the process of miscommunication is ... hidden. M assumes the intention of the interviewer's questions is to put him at ease and he answers accordingly. He seems unaware that her seemingly innocent questions are probing his commitment to the job and the music shop firm. Since he doesn't share the same background knowledge as the interviewer about the job interviews, he is unaware that the candidate must recognise all questions in the encounter as potentially gauging job suitability. M fails to interpret the interviewer's questions in this light and answers inappropriately. (Williams, 1985: 174)

M's sociolinguistic (pragmatic) failure here loses him the chance of the job. The relevance of this example to the discussion in this chapter is that sharing linguistic rules does not guarantee understanding – the failure is sociolinguistic. This is my topic for Chapter 4.

As we have seen, Grammar 2 is about that shared set of rules which seems to bring together members of the same language group; it lies therefore between Grammar 1 (the system of one individual) and Grammar 3 (the abstract set of rules for language, the human faculty which is, so it is assumed, the same for everyone). Grammar 2 then is the grammar of English, the grammar of Japanese, the grammar of Welsh, of Swahili and so on. It is a well-tried axiom that linguistics is about language while sociolinguistics is about *a* language (or languages): what this implies is that it falls to sociolinguistics to define just what determines the distinction between one language and another. Languages can be distinguished from other languages, on the one hand, and from dialects, on the other: let us take these in turn.

Defining Languages

Languages are generally defined (a) linguistically, (b) sociolinguistically in terms of comprehension (or intelligibility) and (c) politically, in terms of attitude, identity and power (Haugen 1966).

Linguistically, languages can be defined and distinguished one from another in terms of their historical development or in terms of language typologies. Such definitions relate to the shared set of systems they control – and while this in part overlaps with my third category because it is a concern of attitudes, it is also a matter of shared history. Thus American English and British English can be said to be one language not two because they have such a large common history; and the same might

be said for the German of the two former Germanies and the German
of Austria; again the same type of sameness might be claimed for the
Scandinavian languages. But shared history does not in itself mean that
the contemporary languages spoken in America, Britain and so on share
very much. It is the same sort of argument as that about blood relations
where a shared ancestor does not necessarily mean much remains in
common. French and Italian, Maltese and Arabic, the Bantu languages, and
so on: these all exemplify shared histories and yet it seems to make little
sense to claim that they are in each case the same language.

Let me turn to my second category. The sociolinguistic argument is in
part an argument about actual understanding, shared understanding or
intelligibility. History alone, the fact that two languages have the same
origin in one parent language (like the Romance languages), will not do if
too long a time has elapsed since the split (as in the case of Finnish and
Hungarian) or if speakers no longer wish to understand or believe they
understand one another (as was the case perhaps with Dutch and
Afrikaans). What matters even more strongly is whether or not speakers
understand one another now, which on the face of it is a simple enough
question. As I will show, it is not simple. Politically, languages are defined
institutionally,that is to say they symbolise the claims of nationalism and
are therefore, on the one hand, like flags, airlines and membership of the
United Nations and on the other hand, like the preferred ethnicity which is
regarded as the norm of the nation even though it may in fact be so only
for a minority of the population. I could suggest Bahasa Malay for
Malaysia or Kiswahili for Tanzania or Chinese for China or English for the
USA and so on. Hence too the problems that arise when there are two or
more languages in conflict as representatives of the nation, for example
French and English in Canada or Flemish/Dutch and French in Belgium or
the regional languages as well as English in India. In observing areas where
there is conflict it is also salutary to observe countries such as Switzerland
which until recently seemed to avoid such interlingual conflict.

What languages also do politically is to allow individuals (and groups)
to identify with other individuals and groups, in some cases out of a desire
to share a selected group's prestige, in others solely out of a desire to
belong because of what is felt as a shared ethnicity. Note that this second
reason may, in fact, be a derivative of the first in that a wish to identify is
normally predicated on a desire to share perceived prestige, albeit this
prestige may be hidden or negative (Welsh and Irish are possible
examples). The obvious explanation for this role of language is that languages allow for identification, that is to say that speakers of the same
language will identify with one another in the same way that members of

any other ethnicity such as race, colour, religion or gender will identify with other members of the same ethnicity for no other reason than a sense of belonging. In the case of language it might be more sensible to say that the sense of identity comes from a source other than a perceived ethnicity, thus there may be one very salient non-linguistic category of ethnicity, such as race or religion, which subsumes all others.

In such cases, it can be the symbolic rather than the communicative value of a language that provides a sense of identity, especially in the diasporic communities of such groups as Jews and Poles. Such an approach indicates the importance in all questions of identity or attitude. Members' beliefs about their identity (real or wished for) will cause them to assert that identity and act it out in their lives. Their behaviour is reflected in members' views towards such language factors as the speech community, the standard language and stereotypes of language use.

The Speech Community

The speech community is most helpfully seen as a primitive sociolinguistic category which escapes precise definition but nevertheless has a useful heuristic value. A speech community is that portion of human society in which language behaviour has some important shared community meaning – note that here I have deliberately stated *language* not *a language* because the typical speech community is multilingual.

What seems to define membership of a speech community is that members share common attitudes towards appropriate language use (Ryan *et al.*, 1982) and agree on which language it is right to use for which purpose (for norms of language use see Labov (1972) and for correctness see Thomas (1991), Davies (1991) and McMorris (2001)). Hence they share the same views not just about what it is appropriate to say (which language or which register in which situation, what counts as a joke, when swearing and other forms of opprobrious language are and are not appropriate – and what counts as a swear word or a curse) but also about which features are formally correct. Such views often reduce themselves to shibboleths, no doubt (whether in English to use *due to* or *owing to*, whether to say *It's me* or *It's I*) but what they reflect is a common (a speech community) view towards the language which is thus being defined in these very stereotypical ways as defining and indicating and belonging to and as identifying with the group of significant others.

Thus in a speech community there is common agreement as to what is the standard language: rather as in a common culture there is agreement as to what is high culture as well as what is correct or proper behaviour or comportment ('table manners'). Such agreement need have nothing to do with individual (or even subgroup) use. It is perfectly possible for a group never itself to use the standard language (or as in the West Indies for only a small minority to use it) while at the same time accepting completely the status of the standard language in question, even going so far as to stigmatise itself in its own language use as being inferior. It seems that spoken language use in Birmingham (England) provides a good example of such stigmatising (Giles & Powesland, 1975).

In extreme cases such social attitudes, such attitudinal affect, can lean over into the question of intelligibility and, as we have already suggested, influence whether or not individuals (and even groups) understand one another. Wolff (1959) cites cases of unidirectional intelligibility among groups in West Africa. There, according to Wolff, where the codes of the client group and the patron group are mutually intelligible as judged by an outsider, only the client group will admit to sharing a common code with their patrons; in other cases there may be a type of false intelligibility which has arisen because the client group has this time actually learnt the patron group's code. The two codes have no linguistic connection and the client group has adopted the patron's code as their own since they aspire to be part of the patron community.

Here there is a denial of one ethnicity (and language) in favour of another more prestigious one. Claims in such cases of intelligibility are correct since the client groups has, in these cases, actually learnt as a superposed code the patron's code which is for them a second language. In the other instance of one-way intelligibility there is in fact also a real intelligibility but one that is not admitted by both parties. The reason is that the client group will claim that their code is mutually intelligible with the patron's code. The patron group, however, will deny that this is the case and insist that the client group is somehow alien and does not share with them any common language. How the dynamics of such a situation work is hard to say because in reality both groups must understand one another and therefore what the patron group is saying is that although the client group do in fact understand them they do not understand the client group talking among themselves because when they do so they are using a different code from the one they use with the patron group. Such a view is hugely attitudinal and has no objective behavioural validity in terms of an outside evaluator's strict linguistic judgements. However, it does seem to be the case that intelligibility is as much a matter of attitude as it is of linguistic nearness.

One area of sociolinguistics which is on the edge of studies of political identity but is really more the concern of linguistics itself is that of

linguistic variables, the area of research that has been called secular linguistics, which concerns primarily the issue of language change over time
(Labov, 1972; Trudgill, 1983). This research indicates how speech communities define themselves since members are acutely aware of the
existence and the meaning of such features in terms of social stratification:
features such as the use at the end of English participles and gerunds of the
/ing/ form (for example walking, running, talking) and of the glottal stop
intervocalically. All members of a speech community systematically use (or
admit the use of) stigmatised forms according to context but in different
amounts and contexts (Labov, 1972).

Members of a speech community know implicitly what the conventional stigmatised forms mean socially in which contexts. Linguistic
features are not stigmatised in themselves but depend on context: the
glottal stop is a good example. The fact is that all speakers of English use
the glottal stop but the feature is stigmatised only in those contexts of
linguistic use which are in heavy use by lower social classes in society.
This is perhaps another way of saying that what is stigmatised in any
society is the use of the language by the poor and the socially inferior.
Or we can also say that what such a judgement illustrates is that the social
and the linguistic are closely linked and that secular linguistics is also very
much bound up with the sociology of language.

I have referred to the speech community and the standard language and
linguistic variables in the context of the speech community. I also need to
consider the question of the relation of the language of the native speaker
to the speech community. The point I have been making is that the speech
community is primarily built on the attitudes of its members. And that is
of keen relevance to the views that first language (Ll) speakers take of their
language. So I now propose to look at the distinction between a language
and a dialect. These are distinctions that have no meaning in terms of two
of the three Grammars we discussed in Chapter 3 either for the individual
(the speaker of Grammar 1) or for the abstract level of universal grammar
(Grammar 3). Dialect only has meaning in terms of Grammar 2.

Distinguishing Dialect from Language

What we find in distinguishing dialect from language is exactly what
we find in distinguishing one language from another language. The
distinction is partly a linguistic one and partly a sociolinguistic, political
one. In *linguistic* terms a dialect is intelligible with another dialect while a
language is not intelligible with another language; or to put this another

way languages do not share a recent history of similar origins while dialects do. They share some kind of common origin as well as a current identity of system, morphological and syntactic, such that a speaker of one dialect will find another at least partly intelligible.

The need for a sociolinguistic distinction arises from the fact that the linguistic one does not hold up on its own – it is exactly the same dilemma as we found earlier in distinguishing on linguistic grounds alone between languages, indeed it is precisely the same problem because there are languages which are mutually intelligible (for example Hindi–Urdu, Norwegian–Danish) and which could therefore be called dialects of one another but are in practice called languages for political and national reasons. On sociolinguistic grounds therefore dialects are dialects of the same language because their speakers claim them to be so, and they are distinguished from languages in terms of power. 'A language is a dialect with an army and a navy' (Briand in Haugen, 1966) it has been said; and again 'a dialect is a language that did not succeed'.

Language Variety: The Case of Gender

One of the basic sociolinguistic concepts is that of variety. Language varies across time, diachronically and across space: thus there are different language codes, dialects, family use, social class variation, work and professional use, speech and writing differences, differences according to formality and informality, age and gender differences. As I argued earlier, such differences are more those of language use rather than of language system and it may be therefore that we can ignore them for our purposes on the grounds that in our pursuit of the native speaker it is system rather than use with which we are concerned.

Nevertheless it will be useful to consider briefly one of the contemporary issues in variety, if only to examine to what extent variety in general is relevant to our consideration of the native speaker: and this issue is that of gender-related language (and see Chapter 8). Gender, it has been pointed out (Spender, 1980; Cameron, 1985), is a variable which may affect the language system and certainly does affect language use. Let me take these arguments in turn.

Systematic differentiation does seem to be the case in certain languages (for example in Thai) where both men and women address members of the same sex and members of the opposite sex in systematically different ways. Of course it must be the case that each is aware that the other sex speaks differently. This is not the point any more than it would be the point to say that a first language speaker of language X learns language Y as a foreign language and then knows what its systems are.

The point for us surely is whether the man or the woman in such cases 'knows' not only what s/he uses but also what members of the same sex use and the answer would appear to be that they do know since what they are claiming all the time is not just 'this is how I speak' but 'this is how men or how women speak'. And that claim must be respected: that they know and the other sex does not. Of course there is inevitably an air of secrecy about it, a touch of linguistic relativity such that it is necessarily unfalsifiable. If a woman says 'that is what women say' to a man then he has no *locus standi* in the discussion simply on the grounds that he is not a woman.

At least in variation of this kind we can rest on the (fairly) firm ground that we know what categories we are dealing with (men and women) and that those are determined before we examine their categorical language. That at least avoids the circularity of much variety description which rests not on an external criterion but on the language itself. No doubt there are cases where even the basic categorial distinction breaks down and we may find that sex change or sex reversal has taken place but, by and large, we do accept that there is a category of sex and that other distinctions (such as distinct language systems) will be correlative. But that is where the problem arises and where we need to look at the other aspect – that of variation according to language use.

Here what is often suggested as being gender specific is, on the one hand, the polite (women) and the lurid (men) and, on the other hand, the self (women) and the impersonal (men). Aspects such as frequent use of tag questions and references to the self, frequent use of first person; use of colour terms and of terms of comfort and endearment (women) are contrasted with swearing, abstraction and references to fact (men).

Much of this is sheer speculation and reflects stereotypes and social attitudes rather than reality but what is interesting from our point of view is the feminist argument on this. Because what some feminists say is that all such differences have to do with the imposition of power by men, the majority, on women, the minority, where the majority is not defined in numerical terms, and that it is all either stereotype or learned, that is socialised behaviour, which has no basis in anything systematic (except in the sense that in due course learned behaviour does become automatic). What they claim is that there is nothing in the language that makes for such systematic differences and that therefore what we have referred to as systematic difference is in fact just another (and perhaps more accepted) example of the imposition of power and that it is all really a matter of language use. There is no reason, they would perhaps say, why men and women should talk differently and they only do so – if they do – because men impose such differences to keep women in their place (Cameron, 1998).

I recognise that in the context of discussing the native speaker such an attack does not in any way question the construct of 'a language'. Indeed it probably strengthens it, in the sense that what feminists are claiming is that men and women do not have different systems and should not have different uses because they do (necessarily for the argument) all speak the same language. I will observe in passing that there are clear distinctions that simply cannot be ignored, for example class inclusion through pronominal use, for example *he* referring to everyone or even as the unmarked term. Such uses, it may be argued, should be deliberately changed so that the marked non-inclusive gender difference disappears.

As I have indicated this criticism does not in itself affect a stance in terms of the native speaker controlling a system which is shared by other speakers of 'the same' language. Rather it reflects an attempt to change our perceptions of categories and what importance they have politically in the social world; and from this angle the argument is not really about language at all. Nevertheless it does have implications for the concept native speaker in that it exemplifies the partiality of the term if, as with other subgroups, men and women are to be regarded necessarily as native speakers of different languages. Which, to follow one strong feminist argument, must be mutually unintelligible. Such a position, in my view, has to be untenable both in terms of commonsense and of the earlier argument concerning Grammar 2 (Chapter 3); it links also with our later consideration of Standard Languages in the next section.

Standard Languages

I now move on to a consideration of the role of standard languages in relation to the native speaker. In remote communities, so it is sometimes anecdotally claimed, there is a high degree of uniformity both culturally and linguistically; indeed it may well be that not only are the members of such a community monolingual, they are also monodialectal. In such communities, it is further argued, there is no bilingualism or bidialectalism, there is no variation according to functional use (Fasold, 1984). Such a view seems to fly in the face of all experience but I do agree that this is because of the particular view I take of culture and social life, a view which says that behaviour adjusts itself to different demands and situations and that this adjustment is systematic and that the behaviour includes linguistic behaviour.

Now if this view is not accepted, I am led to conclude either that all use is idiosyncratic, which would at the end of the day make understanding impossible; or to believe that, if there are differences between, for example, legal language and advertising language, these are random and lawyers and advertisers can use one another's style. Such a view does not seem to me tenable. I submit, therefore, that we must accept that variable language use is systematic in some sense.

Even in remote communities there is variation in terms of age and sex and if there is marrying in and out perhaps other languages will be brought in. If the community is literate there will be variation according to speech and writing, but as will become clear shortly, we assume for this argument that the community is not literate. Such variation does not compare with the variety that exists in a big city or across a country. The remote community can manage, be coherent within itself, communicate fully in interaction by using the language of daily life which is everyone's language while of course honouring what built-in variation there is. In the city, in the country at large, where above all there is administration and education often in multicultural and multilinguistic situations, then it becomes necessary to impose one language as the official language. This may be a local language, even our remote community's language (although this is very unlikely – but see Clayton (2000) and Davies (2001b) – the code normally chosen already belongs to a majority group) but the language chosen or designated as the official language will then undergo, on a permanent basis, the process of standardising which will functionally make it fit to serve the whole community, internally and externally, in writing and in public spoken language use.

Such a process is essential for a large complex community which requires the acceptance by everyone of one code as the official means of communication, particularly in education, official business, the professions and the media, both in writing and in public spoken use. The value of the standard language then is that it makes for efficiency, it provides for intelligibility and it avoids uncertainty – what to use in which context and how to spell or say it. As such it cuts down on local distinctions, thereby not advantaging (or disadvantaging) one community (remote or not) over another; it does what all positive political development is really about – it makes for greater equality among its members.

Now as far as English is concerned there are two warnings I must immediately offer. The first concerns the belief that, unlike French (and other Romance languages), English is not standardised because there is no academy on the model of the French Academy. (One was very nearly started in the reign of Charles II but it became the more useful scientific Royal Society instead.) This argument is also used in a slightly different form to point to the difficulty of separating British English and American English. The truth is that a language does not need an academy for it to be standardized. The very fact of official, administrative use, the fact of publishing in bulk, of exposure in the media, both newspapers and broadcasting, of a centralised education system, all of these influence a language towards standardisation – the simplest example of which perhaps is how to spell words in common use.

It is necessary for the types of modern state activities mentioned here for there to be an agreed dictionary because otherwise time would be constantly wasted while everyone wondered how to spell words; and then how to understand what s/he is reading since other people's spelling would be different. This just does not happen in developed states even in the absence of an academy. It does not happen because of the social fact of the institutions I have mentioned, institutions which, unlike the academy, have roles other than language roles to play but for which language is vital. Perhaps that is a good reason why when there is an academy, as in France, which has this central responsibility for the language, the academy nevertheless cannot in practice control that use; it cannot, for example, prevent the spread of franglais, of anglicisms in modern French.

Whether or not an academy can really prevent language change is doubtful and reminiscent of King Canute's wise failure to turn the tide. This may illustrate the lack of real importance in the standardisation process of the academy (except perhaps in emerging nations which lack the institutional layering of developed societies) and the greater importance of education, the media, the public services and broadcasting and now, of course, of computing and as far as English is concerned, of the international use of the language. Which presumably means that the effect of the increasingly wider use of English internationally will not lead to a break up of the language into non-intelligible varieties, as happened to Latin (Burchfield, 1985). On the contrary, the opposite is likely, with English becoming more rather than less uniform because in its international guise that is what is needed. We return to this question later.

The second warning about English and standardising is that not everyone is equally disadvantaged. There is a social class differential which advantages the middle and upper classses, who comprise most of the élite in society and whose control of the standard (through their long association with education, the media, the public service and so on) both gives them a special claim on it and a facility in it. At the same time this may perhaps cause them to make it increasingly the language they use all the time. In the sort of remote community we have mentioned earlier there is likely to be little access to the standard and children who may be selected for education away from home in a city school will find themselves disadvantaged, doubly so, first because their life experience is less 'modern', which does seem to be of relevance to success in school, and second, because their facility with the standard language, which will typically be the language used in the school, will be minimal or non-existent. And so they will start with a disadvantage which only the ablest will be able to overcome (Davies, 2001a).

Symbolic and Institutional Roles for Language

It is for this reason that, so it appears, in the Third World there is an increasing demand by middle-class, professional parents for their children to have access to English or French earlier and earlier so as to provide them with the means to get a headstart with the education which, in such societies, is still the chief means of élite selection. Those who are already members of the élite wish their children to join them there and English (or in former francophone territories French) is seen as both the symbol of that access and also the means to ensure that it is available. For the same reason English then becomes one, perhaps the only one, of the chief selection devices for entry into selected or prestige schools.

It may seem bizarre that in such situations, often ex-colonial, a foreign (or perhaps a second) language, itself the ex-colonial language, should occupy such an important place but it is not a new phenomenon. We may compare the role of Latin in the Roman world or Mandarin in the Chinese empire. It is in part a kind of symbolic magic and in part an acknowledgement of reality. The magic is exemplified by the use of the 'neck verse', the Latin verse from the Psalms offered in the Middle Ages to those seeking the benefit of clergy by reading which they might save their neck. The neck verse is defined in the *Shorter Oxford Dictionary* as: 'neck Verse 1450. A Latin verse printed in black-letter (usually the beginning of Psalm 51) formerly set before one claiming benefit of clergy by reading which he might save his neck. Now only Historical.' The acknowledgement of reality accepts that in order to make a success of education it is crucial that the child should be as fluent and as proficient as possible in the language which is to be used as the medium.

An established standard language is likely to become adopted as the first language of the élite. I do not mean here that any language is ever fully standardised: standardisation is a process which, as I have noted, is ongoing and never completed, if only because what is now the standard must change as time goes on. Certain stratified societies can arrest change to the standard by the acceptance of diglossia. In a diglossic situation there are typically two functionally distinct (High and Low) codes which, as in the case of Arabic, can endure in a stable state over a long period (Ferguson, 1959). Indeed from the point of view of social cohesion it could be argued that there is merit in such a state of diglossia in that the community has within its grasp both the security of certainty (which we have used to define a standard language) and at the same time the opportunity to change (which we have remarked all languages must do). If for some non-linguistic reason, perhaps because of colonialism (as in Haiti) or perhaps because of religion (as in Egypt) diglossia arises then inertia may well make change (that is to lose diglossia) difficult.

In societies where the major institutions do allow for change then language like other social behaviours will also change.

The Standard Language as L1

We return to the adoption of the standard language by the élite as their own first language. There are two important effects of this. The first is that the existence of the standard language outside people, e.g. in books, educational materials, dictionaries and materials (tapes, video and so on) for teaching the language to foreigners, has an effect on those who speak it, as well as on those who are learning it and that effect is that, in some way, both speakers and learners will become, the term is apt, more standardised, more like one another. I can even refer to this effect as speaking like the book and it surely is the case that those people who use the standard language all the time are more open to the norms of published materials than those for whom the only authority is the oral tradition and the language use of their family and neighbours.

The second effect follows on from this: it is that this induced homogeneity may well have a real effect on the language systems that are being used, making them more like one another: and it is in this sense from the sociolinguistic point of view that I can most appropriately speak of a native speaker as someone who regards the standard language as his/her mother tongue (Aitken, 1973).

It is also in this sense that it becomes more possible, easier, to speak of common speakers of the standard language as both being native speakers of it and of being as it were equivalent native speakers: indeed Jespersen

(1922) used the term common language to refer to exactly this type of sharing. Of course there will still be differences; two such speakers of the standard language will still be distinct and recognisably so, e.g. on the telephone and in writing. Furthermore, they will almost certainly disagree in certain areas of grammar, as Ross (1979) has shown (see Chapter 9).

But it may well be the case that native speaker is a more useful term in situations where the standard language has an important role to play than in the speech encounters in remote and isolated communities. This is not intended to disparage in any way at all the reality of the knowledge that a remote villager has of his/her first language, and we shall come back to this. The point being made is that in the standard language situation it may be that access to the native speaker is more frequently sought because it is the standard and because therefore it is in demand (in education and other areas) while in the remote community it really is only the linguist who wants such access. It may also be the case, indeed it probably is the case, that in standard language situations the language is more explicit, as we have already seen. It is as though in such situations (partly on the grounds of power, partly on the grounds of speaker transfer to the standard as the first language) the act of describing, of standardising, in effect is also the act of defining native speakers: you are a native speaker if you speak the standard language (or on the paradoxical ground we mentioned earlier if you accept it as yours even when you do not speak it or do so inadequately). The fact of explicitness makes a reality of what was before a concept: the process of standardising is an operational definition of the native speaker.

High mobility situations

In situations of social stability (or stagnation) being a native speaker does not, as we have suggested, arise; it is taken for granted and does not have to be claimed. It becomes an issue in situations of mobility where individuals move from one community to another. There are three such situations we should consider, all of which have a bearing on our definition of the native speaker.

Before I consider these three mobility situations it will be as well to remember the apparent circularity of any attempt to define the native speaker. In spite of the difficulty of pinning down the definition to a simple condition such as 'born to two native speaking parents, both preferably monolingual, and raised by them in a native speaking community', it does seem increasingly as though that is the canonical case, the baseline against which all other definitions measure themselves. However, a simple definition is, I have suggested, too simple. No doubt it does play a part in our conceptualising of what we mean by the native speaker; and gets very close to a stereotype of the ideal native speaker. That being so, our quest for a definition of the native speaker is not in vain: it is not as though we are obstinately refusing to pick up the simple definition. There is no such simple definition in reality.

The immigrant ethnic community

The first high-mobility situation is that of the immigrant ethnic community which (in the simplest case) consists of, for example, a non-English-speaking family going to live in Britain, Australia, Canada or any other metropolitan English-speaking country. Now is that family made up of native speakers of English? (Let me use the destination UK as the representative case.) Commonsense suggests that for the migrant adults themselves it cannot be the case, since we have defined them as being non-English speaking. But once in the metropolitan country they will send their children to school. Now there may be a difference linguistically between the child born in the immigrant country and the child born in the UK in the sense that we would probably not use native speaker (of English) to refer to the child born out of the UK to such a family (it would of course depend on the age at time of settlement in the UK). The limiting question is whether we would speak of the child born in the UK to a non-English-speaking family as a native speaker of English.

This is, as is obvious, a hugely political question; but it is one quite germane to our discussion. And if we have no answer to it, then this may well indicate our lack of clarity as to what we mean by the native speaker or rather perhaps that we mean different things by it depending on which way we are looking at it, where we are approaching it from.

The issue in such cases is one of input: does such a child have adequate input to gain the necessary linguistic competence to become, as it were, indistinguishable from the child whose parents are themselves mother-tongue speakers of English, of which variety seems to be irrelevant? My argument tends at this point to become circular because I still do not have a criterion for native speaker. It cannot surely be defined in terms of who your parents were, clearly other caretakers will have just as much linguistic influence in terms of input. But it may have everything to do with timing of input, timing probably more than kind of input, indeed necessarily so since claims on native speakerness and indeed recognition of other claimants seem to have little to do with the kind of input in terms of dialect and so on. All I can say here is that such learners, who are likely to be bilingual in some guise (or semilingual: see Chapters 2 and 5), appear to develop a full grammatical system in the second language and in that sense to become indistinguishable from those who have had only English input since birth.

What may be lacking to such speakers are the resources of the language for childhood itself, the kinds of things that are said to children and the kinds of things that little children say to one another. This may be an exaggeration in the sense that what is being suggested here is not linguistic at all, rather it is one means of becoming linguistically active. Again when the English second language child grows up and then wishes to rear his/her own children in their former second language it is unlikely that they will then not have access to that English motherese creativity for their own children, that simplifying function, from which they themselves benefited in their original first language.

However, there may still be something lacking and that is the language use of children, the games, stories, songs and so on which mean both childhood and language-in-childhood for children and adults. In such cases it is difficult for English second-language children to recapture, except at second hand through books, an experience they did not themselves have because they experienced it in another language. This is more properly an issue of communicative competence than of linguistic competence (see Chapter 6). It seems undeniable that this language use is lacking and what is of interest to us is whether it matters or not in terms of our definition of native speaker. (Of course it matters individually if the child and growing adult miss not having had it.) As I have already suggested, it seems unlikely that it prevents the development of the full English linguistic system, which means that the child growing up in an immigrant community will, if born in the UK, acquire the second language (English in this case) and become linguistically a native speaker. The child brought to live in the UK will only achieve the same result if brought early enough and here current thinking is in favour of the critical age view (Patkowski, 1980; Felix, 1987; and see Chapter 2). But there are other voices too, as we report later in Chapter 8.

New Englishes

The second high-mobility situation is the one which it is suggested the New Englishes raise, situations such as Singapore, West and East Africa, India, Pakistan, situations where, it is said, people speak Singapore English, West African English, East African English, Indian, Pakistani English and so on. The question I want to address is in what sense we can speak of a speaker of Singaporean or Indian English as being a native speaker of English (Tay, 1982; and see Chapter 1). As will be clear there are really two distinct questions here: the first is the native speaker question, similar to (but not the same as) the one we have just been discussing, the other is which English such a speaker is a native speaker of (see Chapter 8).

The native-speaker question appears to be different this time because I am not dealing here with a situation in which English is being used as a first language in the environment. No doubt in Singapore as in India there will be first-language speakers of English, Singaporeans, Indians and so on who have opted for English as their first language. But for the most part English users will be bilingual second-language users. The question then becomes whether there is sufficient exposure for the child in English for him/her to develop a linguistic competence. Note that this time it is not just that the input is lacking in the home (as in the immigrant community in the UK), it is also lacking or partial in the surrounding situation. When the child goes to school then no doubt there will be full exposure in an English medium (and of course it is precisely in such situations that parents of the élite group choose an English school, nursery or whatever, as early as possible for their child). Does that provide adequate exposure?

The answer must be in two parts: the first is that as with my immigrant community child example there will be the lack of communicative competence in terms of the language of childhood; the second is that there will be the absence of a wider and essentially intimate language use unless in such cases the child plays with other children in English, shops in English, talks to old people in English and so on. Of course there will be plenty of exposure in official and public use, but paradoxically the intimate and non-public uses of language ((what Bernstein [1971–5] referred to as the 'restricted codes') Bernstein, 1971–5) will be missing. This again would seem to be a matter of communicative competence rather than one of systematic linguistic competence.

As to the other question, that of which English such speakers are speakers of, the answer is again in two parts, the first linguistic, the second sociolinguistic. In terms of the first, the linguistic issue, the question is really whether (a) there is an identifiable Singaporean English which can be described in a systematically different way from any metropolitan English which, essentially, means British Irish, American, Canadian, Australian, New Zealand, South African. Now no doubt this is the case in terms of phonology (Mugglestone, 1995), but we are normally concerned with more than phonology, salient though it is, when we wish to distinguish one language or one major dialectal variety from another. There are systematic differences in grammar (Platt, 1977; Platt & Weber, 1980) and lexis but it does indeed seem to be the case that there is no (or little) intelligibility problem and that the difference between, say, Singaporean and British English is no greater than the difference between British and American English. Linguistically, therefore, it looks as though I do not need to regard Singaporean English as a separate variety of English. Nor indeed American English (examples of Singaporean English are quoted in Chapters 2 and 8).

And this is where I want to look at the second part of my answer, the sociolinguistic one. This is the issue of identity and of attitudes towards community. The logic of my linguistic argument seems to lead to the conclusion that speakers of Singaporean English may properly consider themselves as members of the community who speak standard (British or other metropolitan) English. But it is debatable if this is what Singaporean English speakers would wish to claim for themselves. They may very well prefer to claim that their first language or their dominant language is Singaporean English of which therefore they would claim to be native speakers. For me to say to them that they can regard themselves as native speakers of (British) English is intensely patronising since I am already deliberately excluding from such an admission those aspects of communicative competence I have referred to.

In any case I am leaving open the question of whether the exposure to (British) English is adequate. On linguistic (but not communicative) grounds they may claim to be speakers of British English; if they prefer on attitudinal and identity grounds they may claim to be speakers of Singaporean English, which is equally true, *mutatis mutandis*, for Americans or Scots!

Should I then consider describing such Singapore English speakers as being linguistically speakers of British English and communicatively of Singaporean English, a mixture? I am forced back on the distinction betweeen the interests of linguistics and those of sociolinguistics, linguistics being about universal grammar and therefore not about languages at all, and sociolinguistics being about group use and therefore indeed about group language behaviour. Now on linguistic grounds Singaporean English does not exist, but nor of course does British English! This also means that the concept of acts of identity (Le Page & Tabouret-Keller, 1985) confuses the concerns of linguistics with those of sociolinguistics. What does exist is the individual speaker.

If a speaker defines him/herself as a native speaker of Singaporean English then this is a sociolinguistic decision; on linguistic grounds there will indeed be some, perhaps many features that speakers of Singaporean

English share with one another (for example, they share some parts of the same grammar) but the idea that there is a separate Singaporean grammar distinct from the grammars of other Englishes and at the same time homogeneous across all speakers of Singaporean English is, in reality, a myth; it is an artefact of the idealisation that is at the heart of all linguistic analysis. Of course there is the additional intervention of the standardisation process, such that when Singaporean English is described, itself as we have just observed the product of an idealisation routine, the very fact of its existence will cause speakers of Singaporean English to identify with it, to claim that they are native speakers of it and also to become perhaps a little more accommodating towards it themselves. They will, in other words, move their own speech in some ways towards the new standard, the effect being that they approximate, however little, towards the other members of their Singaporean speech community, thereby pushing forward the standardisation process.

There remains the further question in such cases of the extent to which in Singapore and other second-language environments for English the internalising of rules is possible. Greenbaum (1985), for example, suggests that the base for internalisation is limited when there are few speakers who have more than a limited use of the language. Of course this then becomes an empirical question. I have argued that on sociolinguistic grounds such speakers may properly decide that they are native speakers if they wish to identify fully with the Singaporean-English-speaking speech community.

Leaving aside for the moment the semilingualism explanation, I would need to accept that all such speakers have a full set of internalised rules, although they may be at very different stages and may be unstable. If this is so their use of English is that of an interlanguage – and there are quite persuasive arguments which suggest that there is an interlanguage aspect to the new Englishes (Platt, 1977; Davies, 1989a). Of course exactly the same argument can be used of monolingual native speakers of English whose own intuitions will show grey areas between speaker and speaker and between individual and idealised standard. Instability, in other words, is the default mode (Ross, 1979).

International English

The third high-mobility situation in which I must consider the native speaker is that of so-called international English, today's *lingua franca* for world public affairs (see Chapter 8). There have of course been many *lingua francas*. What distinguishes international English is its use by so many in power all over the world. It seems to me that the most useful way of looking at International English is to see it as one more development in the standardisation process; that International English is a further development of the standard Englishes that we now have. To what extent this makes it different in any serious way from existing standard Englishes is difficult to understand. If it means that educated users of one or other existing L1 standard Englishes automatically become speakers of International English then the problem disappears. If, however, it implies that second-language users are also speakers of international English by virtue of being second-language users we are back into the same problem we were dealing with just now of Singaporean English and with exactly the same sort of solution.

Knowledge and Proficiency

If it is suggested that foreign-language users of English may also be speakers of International English then any relevance of this concept for the native speaker must collapse because it confuses level of proficiency (foreign-language user which I maintain means having a certain proficiency level in English) with an internalised knowledge or competence. Now it is possible that I can determine knowledge that is competence (but see Chapter 9), in terms of proficiency. Indeed this is what tests of language proficiency attempt to do and by equating knowledge and proficiency this search for a definition of the native speaker becomes very much easier since most proficiency testing uses the explicit published standard as model, a model which is in effect no-one's language, an idealised artefact (see Chapters 5 and 9 for a fuller discussion on the knowledge–proficiency connection.)

Such foreign non-native speakers may suffer from disadvantage – I have already considered this as an issue in relation to the immigrant community and to a lesser extent in terms of the new English communities. Is it also the case for other non-native speakers who include both second- and foreign-language speakers? The answer can only be that of course they are at a disadvantage until they have acquired enough of the language for their purpose, whatever that may be. But as foreign-language speakers they may well have no disadvantage at all when they use their foreign language in such domains as international agencies, interpreting and academic conferences. Problems only arise if they themselves wish to identify with the community which they regard as defined in terms of target native speakerness, British speech community or Singaporean speech or other community. In other words the problems have to do with acceptance not with knowledge, which may be partial; but of course if such speakers wish a kind of identity which they are denied then they are indeed at a disadvantage (see Chapter 8).

Passing as a Native Speaker

There is a sense in which learners may wish to 'pass' as native speakers, be indistinguishable and fail to do so because they do not have, usually, the appropriate phonology or whatever. But there is equally a sense in which non-native speakers do well not to try to be taken for native speakers (Braine, 1999), situations in which what is demanded of them, because they appear to be native speakers, is native speaker cultural knowledge and reactions (like my 'why bother!' example in Chapter 6 and in the same chapter the examples I give of the language of childhood which the children have not fully acquired but which their linguistic competence may pretend to). Further it is also the case that non-native speakers may, in practice, prefer to rest at some level of approximation, to choose fossilisation, because it suits them to be outside, not indistinguishable, because then the kind of expectation I have been suggesting is not made of them.

This may be the explanation for the foreign accent which many adult immigrants retain, the only sign perhaps of a non-native origin but it would be wrong, in my view, to regard this as necessarily a disadvantage for users since what it can also mean is a choice of identity and they have chosen not to belong to the native speaker community of the speech community they now reside in.

There is also the case of the temporary resident and of the student: the student may be resident for a time in the metropolitan community (overseas students in the UK, in the USA, in France and elsewhere) or they may also be studying in the medium of English, French and so on at home. In both types of experience they are very much at a disadvantage: but this is not because they are not native speakers, a status they perhaps would not seek, but rather because their proficiency in the language they are studying in or using is not high enough. Native speakers do have advantages as students over non-natives in terms of overall proficiency and in interactive skills. But it is doubtful if they have any advantage in terms of study skills by virtue of native speakerness. If they do then that must be attributed to educational or cultural factors. And in any case, native speakership does not in itself guarantee success in studying. If it did native speakers would never fail. But alas! they do.

There is an assumption that for studying to make any sense at the higher education level a minimum level of proficiency is required, an assumption based upon some (idealised) notion of what native speakers of the same education level are capable. But the studies of the relation between proficiency and subject content are contradictory (Davies, 1984a; Alderson & Urquhart, 1983) and it is therefore difficult to know the extent to which it is necessary to have that minimum level. Commonsense suggests that it is essential but there are ways of getting round what is straighforwardly necessary, for example by using the input of colleagues. However, in the subjects which rely on argument and exposition rather than on interaction and field or laboratory work, a minimum level of language proficiency does seem to be essential if studying is to make any sense at all.

Langue Again

I return now to the concept of langue (see Chapter 1). Langue, as Saussure maintained, is what members share, it is a metaphor for this sense of native speakerness which we have just been discussing. To put it another way, it represents shared competence, the competence common to the community not just to the individual. That means that while linguistic competence refers only to Grammar 1 and Grammar 3, langue relates to Grammar 2. It is because of langue that one native speaker can address another and make assumptions about his/her language understanding.

We have suggested that there is no principled way in which a boundary can be drawn between one 'language' and another (any more than between one culture and another). What that means is that langue *either* represents what is stated in descriptions about, for example, the standard language, itself as we have seen essentially the grammar of an individual, Grammar 1, expanded perhaps by the best guess to include possible others; *or* that it represents a metaphysical sharing. For as long as it remains undescribed (that is to say, not written down and fixed) then it is metaphysical; once written down it becomes in its linguistic status (though not perhaps its social) like the standard language.

But in spite of what I have said about the common assumptions that native speakers have, it must also be true that these assumptions will be affected by variability. In other words language, whether explicit in terms of a written grammar or implicit in terms of what it is that native speakers share, must represent a non-coherent set, with the boundary set arbitrarily. Langue then is, and I come back to this, a metaphorical attempt to paraphrase what it is that native speakers share; it does not in any way describe what it is they actually share or who those speakers are because there must always be more or less sharing and more or less agreement. One langue (in this sense) then leads into another langue and it is as difficult to separate langues as it is to separate languages. Being a native speaker remains ill defined if we are considering native speakerness in terms of our Grammar 2; even though, as we have seen, this is the sense in which it is most frequently used.

In one sense native speakerness is always partial, and I draw attention again to the British English–Singaporean English distinction, on the one hand, and the British English–Scottish English distinction, on the other. Scottish English (not Scots here) and British English share a common langue although they would not be identical in, for example, the use of modal verbs and in a number of communicative features of pragmatics.

To some extent what is regarded as British English is itself an artefact, an outcome of various standardising procedures and based on the English of England. To be fair, the same might be said of Scottish English, that it also is an artefact and corresponds therefore only at some idealised or abstract level to the way Scots speak. However, Scottish and *British* English belong together, with Scottish English either slightly overlapping or included as a series of options at certain points. Scottish English and *English* English, on the other hand, would need to be regarded as separate in the same way that British and American English are.

The same exactly is true of Singaporean English, if it is to be regarded as a language with its own native speakers. If not, then of course it simply becomes subsumed within British (or American) English. I do not raise again here the question of whether or not Singaporean English has native speakers; I have discussed this earlier in this chapter. The issue here is that the langues of native speakers form a continuum which has no obvious breaks; furthermore what is true for English is also true for other languages and indeed for all languages in that the continuum for English must continue into other continuums such as the one for Friesian, Dutch and German. Discrete langues, like discrete languages, exist only in idealisations and in standard language descriptions, rules and norms.

Langue is the sociolinguistic correlate of competence and, like it, is a metaphor for the human faculty, both to be a language user/maker and a language interactant as a social being. What grammars do for competence so descriptions of discourse and pragmatics do for langue but as with all maps, such generalisations are, at best, generalisations, especially when they try to distinguish what it is that one group knows and can do from another group. Overlap is endemic.

For this reason writing a linguistic competence grammar which uses the data *of the individual* in order to reveal what is universal is easier than attempting to produce a description, whether of grammar or of pragmatics *of a group* – unless such a quest is intended to be sociological, that is to use language data in order to determine what it is that makes a group a group. But that is not really what sociolinguistics is about or says it is about.

Relevance to Applied Linguistics

The discussion in this chapter of high-mobility situations underlines the developing multicultural state of many western societies and of the need for applied linguistics to present a coherent policy of maintenance, replacement and balance. Such situations in any one country change quickly. The USA has seen the rise and fall of the ethnic movement (Fishman *et al.*, 1985) and Australia, soon after implementing its own language policy through the former National Languages Institute of Australia, has now acknowledged that its phase of multiculturalism/ multilingualism is ending (Lo Bianco, 1987; Taft & Cahill, 1989). It appears to be the case that without a regular influx of new L1 speakers into the country, homogenisation is inevitable and the migrant children born in the immigrant country do not (wish to) maintain the language of their parents.

At the same time, cross-cultural communication is a permanent need for all societies and is particularly difficult in situations where the speakers think on linguistic grounds that they understand one another. It matters therefore that both the analysis and the attention to remediation be adequate to prevent the situation which an Indian English speaker has described as being 'on parallel tracks which don't meet' (Gumperz, 1982: 185).

Nevertheless, the fact of immigrant countries and therefore of language maintenance and language loss is universal. The applied linguistics requirement is to recognise the need for a systematic and fair plan which provides real opportunities for gaining language skills in the relevant language and is also sympathetic, but realistically and non-hypocritically so, to the sentimental attachment to the old first languages, as is seen for example in northern Canada with Inuit.

Summary

In this chapter I considered a number of fundamental sociolinguistic aspects of the native speaker. I discussed the importance in language definition of attitude and feelings of identity and noted that individuals can regard themselves (and others) as native speakers for symbolic rather than communicative purposes. The politicisation of native speakerness with particular reference to the language and gender question was considered and I estimated the necessary role and importance of standard languages, arguing that the process of standardisation is an operational definition of the native speaker. I then introduced the notion of high-mobility situations arguing that it is only in such situations that being a native speaker matters. Three such situations were described: the immigrant ethnic community, the New Englishes situation, the international English situation and I took further the question of the possibility of non-native speakers becoming native speakers, with the side issue of whether that is how they wish to be regarded.

This topic, that of the non-native speaker being regarded as a native speaker, is now taken up in Chapter 5, in two special senses, those of bilingualism and semilingualism. I maintain that bilingualism in the sense of being a native speaker of more than one language is indeed possible under certain conditions which I specify but that semilingualism (except where it is used, rather trivially, to mean differences in proficiency, fluency and so on) cannot be supported on logical grounds.

Chapter 5

Lingualism and the Knowledges of the Native Speaker

My conclusion about langue in the previous chapter is that it is the social correlate of linguistic competence but that it is quite unlike a study of group dynamics, although that is part of it. Langue must be about the internalised grammar of the individual along with the social use of that grammar, unlike linguistic competence which does not appear to show interest in any aspect of interaction. As I have already shown, there are therefore no bounds to the area of interest of langue either in terms of which groups of people nor in terms of which aspects of their behaviour.

I discuss the twin topics of bilingualism and semilingualism in this chapter. Both topics are illustrated in the following example of switching between Black English and Standard American English. What the text shows is how bilingualism (in this case bidialectalism) operates and at the same time how inappropriate it would be to label the Black English sentences as semilingual.

The text is an excerpt from a longer example in Gumperz (1982) where he is discussing a black protestant religious broadcast sermon. We quote part of the sermon, using italics to show the code switching.

(The preacher refers to a previous announcement):
6 I hope that you don't forget the announcement
  We expectun yu to be with us
8 Praise the Lord
9 we're expecting you to be with us
  [Lines 10 and 11 omitted]
12 *and ah ... don-fuget if yu enywhere in yu car right now you*
13 you can probably sense the glory of the Lord in this place
14 *jes jump in yu car an run right on down here to the Ephesian church*
15 Immediately after the broadcast we'll be having a musical service here ...

Gumperz (1982: 191) claims that the preacher is here 'contrastively using two ways of speaking [and] that this contrast is meaningful within the context created by the sermon' (Gumperz, 1982: 194). The italicised sentences are the Black English switches. Bilingualism (or bidialectalism) is shown here to be a fact. And semilingualism cannot be treated seriously. In the first place the speaker controls more than one system; in the second place the 'semilingual' Black English examples are indicators in their own right of a full dialect/ language.

Bilingualism and the Native Speaker

I have referred to the topics of bilingualism and semilingualism and want now to discuss them further. Bilingualism is of interest partly because it is such a widespread phenomenon; it is only in certain countries of the North, from which, ironically, many linguists in the past have originated, that there is any assumption that one has a choice about being bilingual or that indeed being a bilingual is not the normal state (Baker & Jones, 1998). Bilingualism is also of interest to our discussion of the native speaker because it removes the comfortable notion of monolingual competence as uniquely coherent and unified. This cannot be true of the bilingual and one of the fortunate spin-offs of considerations of bilinguality (Hamers & Blanc, 1989) is that it compels us to realise that there is no such state as monolingualism since even those who appear to control only one language do have in their repertoire other forms of variety, for example, dialectal or registral.

The extent to which the native speaker is taken for granted is shown in the use made of the term in Hamers and Blanc. For example they define a balanced bilingual as one who 'can be recognised as a native speaker in either one of his languages' (Hamers & Blanc, 1989: 132). It is true that they provide a definition (in their Glossary) of the native speaker, as follows: 'an individual for whom a particular language is a "native language"' [that is] 'the language or languages which have been acquired naturally during childhood' (pp. 269, 268). As I pointed out earlier, the native speaker is used as a primitive definition, like speech community, its meaning being taken for granted. As we also saw, this leaves real problems.

The type of bilingual I am concerned with is indeed the native-speaking bilingual; or rather I am interested in whether it make sense to speak of a native speaker of more than one language. Therefore I am not concerned for the moment with those who acquire a second language later in life, after first childhood, however well they do this; I am concerned here with, as the canonical case, the child who acquires the two languages to become a native speaker in both. Is this possible?

First, on philosophical grounds, is such a phenomenon possible? The answer has to be yes it is — if my definition of native speaker allows for it. If, however, I define native speaker as competence in one language only in some exclusive way, then of course it is impossible to be a bilingual native speaker. It may be the case that it is not possible for linguistic or other reasons to be such a bilingual but again that is not the point. Our question here is really how to define native speaker and it does not seem to be necessary to restrict our definition thus. So it is at least acceptable to consider the question.

On linguistic grounds (including sociolinguistic, psycholinguistic and practical grounds) can a child acquire two languages to equivalent competence? Here I am less sure. However, it does seem to be possible to internalise the grammar sufficiently to acquire a linguistic competence in two or more languages. I have accepted the possibility of a learner becoming a native speaker when reared outside an environment where the language is spoken and where the only input is that of the parents; and so it does seem acceptable to claim that a child can become a native speaker of two (or more) languages and, therefore, that the bilingual native speaker is possible in terms of linguistic competence. Genesee (2001: 163) agrees:

> Detailed analyses of the grammatical organization of bilingual child language indicates that it conforms with the target systems, taking into account development.

But what about the other aspects of native speakerness to which I have given attention, aspects of communicative competence? Indeed when I discussed the question of the English as a Second Language (ESL) speaker I suggested that communicative competence might be more important than linguistic competence. My sureness here is less immediate: the problem is one of use. For all of us there is a set of functions for which we need language, for example, talking to our families, writing letters, working, reading newspapers, watching television, studying, following instructions, attending religious services, listening to sports commentaries, engaging in politics, courtship — the list is obviously endless.

Now in many cases there is at least the possibility that bilinguals will be able to operate in parallel, that is in both languages in the same function. But there do seem to be limitations in specific tasks in which we are proficient in one language, for example listening to grandparents, paying compliments, complaining, playing hockey or just playing in the school playground and skipping or playing tig, reading a favourite newspaper.

And perhaps this last example is the crucial one since it illustrates that there are tasks which have such specificity that they can only be carried out in one language – reading a favourite newspaper is one and, for most people, talking to or listening to one's grandparents is another. There are in most people's lives activities that are quite specific to one language and would be unthinkable in another. This is one reason why in a very different context it is so difficult for language policy changes to be fully implemented, for, let us say, lecturers in Indian universities to switch completely from English to the regional language or in Tanzania for secondary school teachers to switch from English to Kiswahili. Their problem is that they have learned to do what they do, to carry out their professional life, in one language and it would involve a whole relearning for them to switch to another code.

For this reason if among the criteria of native speakerness I include important features of communicative competence such as being able to lecture and commune with family members, then I might have to deny the possibility of the existence of a bilingual native speaker. However, perhaps these demands are too high, either because I must accept that in some societies (such as isolated communities) the number of functions demanded of the first language is limited, much more so than in our modern urban centres; or because what I am talking about is the *use* of the code rather than the code itself.

That is to say that the child who always talks to her grandmother in language X and never in language Y is in a position to switch if the grandmother insisted. Practice in one language (as is clear with foreign students) in a particular sphere eases the switch to another language in the same sphere. If, however, there has been no use of the first language and all practice is in the second language (as with learning to be a medical doctor in English when there is no medical training available in one's first language) this is much more difficult.

At the same time it is not impossible. The medical doctor accustomed to practising his/her medicine in language X could switch the practice of medicine to language Y if there were pressing enough reasons. It could be done. My conclusion has to be that bilingual native speakers are possible in terms of linguistic competence but not in terms of communicative competence although it does seem to remain a possibility that the communicative competence practice that has not been experienced could be made up on in the appropriate circumstances. But as a note of caution in this area – how often have we all said to others (or they to us): 'I know how to do this in language X but I just have no idea at all in language Y'. At the same time it is only proper to admit that in such admissions language Y does tend to be a second language which was not acquired as a child.

Grosjean (1982: preface) offers a cautionary view:

Contrary to general belief, bilinguals are rarely equally fluent in their languages; some speak one language better than another, others use one of their languages in specific situations and others can still only read and write one of the languages they speak.

Grosjean points out that bilingualism for the child has both negative and positive attributes. Among the negative are: restricted vocabulary, limited grammatical structures, unusual word order, errors in morphology, hesitations, stuttering. Among the positive are: more diversified structure of intelligence, flexibility of thought, cognitive flexibility, creativity, divergent thought. It does appear that while the negatives are largely linguistic, the positives are largely cognitive. In our view this suggests that the positives heavily outweigh the negative because there will be maturational time when the linguistic deficiencies can be repaired.

Grosjean also quotes differences between the bilingual and monolingual child in terms of task performance. In naming tasks, decoding tasks and reading aloud tasks monolinguals do better than bilinguals who, in their turn, do better than trilinguals. Once again I want to maintain that these are features of practice rather than of ability and that in time the bilingual can catch up. Furthermore it is important to ask, as Long (1981) does for input comparisons, to what extent the base-line data are adequate, that is who were the monolingual native speakers who were assessed for task performance.

However, let me give Jespersen the last word on bilingualism, even though his considered view is pessimistic (and very much contrary to his own personal experience):

It is of course an advantage for a child to be familiar with two languages: but without doubt the advantage may be and generally is purchased too dear. First of all the child in question hardly learns either of the two languages as perfectly as he would have done if he had limited himself to one. It may seem, on the surface, as if he talked just like a native, but he does not really command the fine points of the language. Secondly, the power required to master two languages instead of one certainly diminishes the child's power of learning other things, which might and ought to be learnt. (Jespersen, 1922: 220)

It is clear from this quotation that Jespersen's definition of the native speaker must be someone who was monolingual as a child. Well, we must take seriously the views of so great a linguist, but we do not, of course, have to agree with them.

Semilingualism and the Native Speaker

So far I have accepted at least the possibility of bilingual native speakers. I turn now to semilingualism (see also Chapter 2). What about semilingual native speakers? The issue of semilingualism is, in fact, very close to that of bilingualism since in both cases the concern is with the amount of system that can be acquired by the child. I have argued that the child can acquire bilingual linguistic competence. Can s/he acquire semilingual competence? My answer must be in two parts: in the first the answer is perhaps yes when the subject is a bilingual child who acquires part of the system of one language and part of another. Having said that however, it really does not make very much sense because semilingualism is no more about inadequacy of input (on the grounds of input coming from more than one code) than is bilingualism itself.

The only area in which such semilingualism might be contemplated is that of language loss (Lambert & Freed, 1982; van Els et al., 1984) where there is severe impoverishment in the home language (called by those native speakers of Welsh who are uncertain of their command of their own variety 'Welsh pot jam'). What seems to happen in the case of Welsh is language decay in the linguistic system (Dressler & Wodak-Ledolter, 1977), accentuated by the lack of use of Welsh, as domains are appropriated by the second language, in this case English. An alternative arrangement occurs when there is inadequate input of the second language (where there is teaching in the second language by teachers who themselves have very low proficiency). But in both such cases the quality of 'semilingualism' applies only to one of the two languages functionally available to the user. Children may be impaired in such situations in terms of a lack of practice in particular domains but it still remains problematic to what extent their linguistic competence can be held back.

The other type of semilingualism to which I have previously referred is the kind where there is only a monolingual input which is somehow, for whatever reason, severely restricted. Once again it does seem strange to think of the child whose own learning does not enable him/her to use that limited input and to build on his/her own universal grammar in order to develop a full adult competence. Because even if the input from the family is restricted there still remain other children.

The stereotype of semilingualism remains that of the immigrant community child who is in the process, through community change, of language loss and who does not get far in the second language because of inadequate stimulus in school. Even then we would have to hesitate about that *semi-*. That child may remain illiterate, and in a sense, uneducated. But there is no evidence at all that anyone's native speakerness depends on educability or on being schooled (Scribner & Cole, 1981). The very fact of immersion exposure in the school to the second language should be adequate for such a child to gain the full adult competence in the second language (Swain & Lapkin, 1982). Martin-Jones and Romaine (1986) totally reject the concept of semilingualism as being without meaning.

Age and the Native Speaker

The problems of semilingualism and of bilingualism both raise the question of age with becoming a native speaker. The question is whether it is possible to become a native speaker after a certain age (Harley, 1986). Now in terms of child first-language acquisition it does seem to be the case that acquisition is age related. Towards the age of three there is a major grammatical advance, with the appearance of sentences containing more than one clause (Crystal, 1987). Other systems vary in onset and development period and the acqusition process is long and drawn out. 'Recent studies have shown that the acquisition of several types of construction is still taking place as children approach 10 or 11' (Crystal, 1987: 243).

In the case of second-language acquisition the question is whether a child who starts acquiring it within the normal age range can then change before puberty and become either a bilingual native speaker in both the existing code and the new one or switch to being a native speaker only in the new code. This question, already discussed in Chapters 2 and 3, reduces to whether childhood acquisition is necessary for the native speaker. Ellis (1985: 106) remarks that the results of investigations into the age question

> may appear confusing and contradictory, but a fairly clear pattern emerges if route, rate and success are treated as separate, if due account is taken of the differential effects of age on pronunciation, vocabulary and grammar, and if starting age is not confounded with the number of years' exposure to the L2. (Ellis, 1985: 106)

He points to the important distinction between fluency and accuracy and claims that the research evidence indicates that while length of exposure influences fluency, starting age affects accuracy. In spite of this quite dramatic conclusion it still remains unclear whether in terms of starting age there is one critical period. Indeed, as Seliger (1978) suggests, there might be several critical periods. At the same time the weight of opinion (if not of evidence) seems to be in favour of a major differential between children and adults. Neufeld (1978), for example, has argued in favour of 'primary' and 'secondary' levels of language. What distinguishes children is that they are more likely to succeed with the secondary levels, for example complex grammatical structures and different language styles.

To return to the question we set ourselves: is childhood acquisition necessary for the native speaker? The answer appears to be that there are probably some features of native speakerness which can be acquired only in childhood.

I turn now to the question of defining the native speaker in the light of what it is the native speaker knows and what it is the native speaker can do; in other words what are people's expectations of the native speaker?

Defining the Native Speaker?

It is now time to start bringing together the various qualities of the native speaker which have been mentioned earlier, but before attempting to present an overall picture, I want to look again, first, at linguistic competence and then at communicative competence.

So far I have claimed that the native speaker above all has a linguistic competence in the language of which s/he is a native speaker; and indeed that is a totally circular definition. Perhaps I can amend it a little by suggesting what that competence means. It means that the native speaker can operate as a grammatical being, that s/he can generate sentences that s/he has not heard before and understand ones that s/he has not heard before: naturally this is a syntactic not a content definition. Similarly for communicative competence, the native speaker has built-in antennae, his/her own monitor, for distinguishing between acceptable and unacceptable utterances; i.e. s/he is, in short, able to put the grammar into action and know when that is being done by others. Of course such crude definitions leave much to the imagination. Does it mean all the sentences that are or might be heard? Does it mean all situations and occasions when the language is being heard? And in any case what counts as the language: which language? It is time to try to define the native speaker thus far and see what else to add to the catalogue, enabling us either to arrive at a definition or to accept that the native speaker remains like the unicorn, inspirational but always a mirage as we get near.

A Game Analogy

In order to disentangle the clutter of qualities and stereotypes associated with the concept of the native speaker let me approach a definition by way of a game analogy.

Game analogies are common in linguistic discussions (e.g. de Saussure, 1916; Wittgenstein, 1953), one of the more famous being the chess example. So when, perhaps on a journey, a new acquaintance claims to be able to play chess, what exactly does s/he mean? Let me examine the claim in terms of four kinds of knowledge:

Knowledge 1:   knowing the rules, the sequences, the moves each piece is allowed and is not allowed to make, the purpose of the game, why the game is being played and what indicates winning.

Knowledge 2:   knowing or being able to recognise the shape of each of the pieces even if the set is a new, previously unseen one.

Knowledge 3:   acknowledging and sharing the courtesies of the game, such as how long to wait between moves, whether or not to talk, move about, how seriously to take it, what to do if a piece gets lost, whether or not to penalise one another if a move is retracted. And so on.

Knowledge 4:   how to play with skill. In chess, as in all games, many of those who play don't play very well, hence the prevarications: 'Yes I play but not very well' or 'I don't really play' or 'I know how to play'.

Knowledge 2 may be less clear since the pieces may be quite new to the claimant. However, since s/he knows what sorts of pieces to expect (two bishops, eight pawns and so on), even if the pieces in this new set are distinguished only by colour s/he will very quickly identify them for what they represent and will also be able to negotiate with the inviting player who may have begun with a different piece identification. That does not matter as long as they agree as to which object stands for which piece in the game.

So much for the rules: without the knowledges indicated here, playing a game of chess would not be possible. If the two players have different ideas about which moves may be made, in which order or which piece stands for what, then there can only be chaos or randomness or, of course, total and instant victory for one side.

Describing the Four Kinds of Knowledge

Knowledge 1, in spite of what has just been said, is a form of convention. Rules may, in fact, be formalised conventions, whether they are the operations of a computer or a motor or the rules of a nation state or the rules of a game, but once fixed they cease to be conventions (or thought of as conventions) and become law-like. Rules may originate in conventions but they must then be elevated above conventions in order for the game to proceed at all.

Knowledge 2 may appear to be more convention-like than rule-like but as we shall see later it is safer to regard it as rule-like. Of course, like Knowledge 1, it takes its origin in convention, in tacit agreement as to what shape indicates which piece: this is the Queen, this the King, Bishop and so on. But although at the outset which counts as which is immaterial, as time goes on the player forgets that it was only a convention and for him/her the connection between the object and the chess piece becomes unquestionable. Of course the new player may find this uncomfortable (and if s/he does not know chess incomprehensible) but will readily accept the distribution of object to piece because this is what s/he expects. Knowledge 2, like Knowledge 1, draws on a set of routines and their combinations in skilled and planning ways, leaving the neophyte lost and puzzled because s/he does not understand what is happening, nor why it is.

Knowledge 3 is more obviously conventional and overlaps with very local arrangements which can be negotiated separately for each chess encounter. No doubt in some cases the types of convention listed here (for example how long to wait between moves, talking, moving about, whether or not to allow a retraction of a move) are more rule-like and may indeed be governed by a rule book just like Knowledge 1 and 2. But other aspects of Knowledge 3, for example how seriously to take it, whether to bet on a game, how generously to interpret the 'rules' and whether to behave sympathetically to one's opponent, these features of behaviour must be left to individuals. Indeed the problem with Knowledge 3 is that it tends to spread over into very personal and quite individual characterstics like how often to smile during a game, whether to eat, smoke, drink. These move beyond even the negotiated interpersonal and local, becoming wholly idiosyncratic.

Knowledge 4 is of a different order. It is possible to say, in answer to the question we first asked, 'Yes, I play chess'. But that does not imply well or badly. Modesty normally requires a simple answer without qualification: or rather the unmarked form would be 'I play, but not very well', whereas 'Yes I play' could mean I play very well indeed. Modesty here is conventional except in the Stephen Potter gamesmanship ploys which deliberately downplay beyond the reach of modesty, for example 'Do you play chess?' – 'Hardly at all', meaning 'Yes I'm a Grandmaster!'.

But Knowledge 4 is really about level of skill and the point we must make is that this is a quite separate attribute from Knowledges 1–3: Knowledges 1–3 are required for chess players. Knowledge 4 is not required in the same way. Knowledge 4 is, of course, necessary to some modest degree. To take a different sort of game, to have only Knowledge 1–3 for tennis is of no value if you are invited to join a friend on the tennis court for a game since you will not find it possible to translate your knowledges into some kind of performance, however low level. Knowing the rules of tennis (or of chess) is no guarantee (indeed no assurance of any kind) of being able to play the game for real.

The game analogy helps in two ways. First, it indicates the distinction between performance and competence. Performance (in chess, tennis, games – and language) means putting into action Knowledge 1–3, that is playing the game, producing, using the language. There are, of course, different levels of performance and I will return to these. Second, it indicates that what the performance shows (for the moment, again, leaving aside its level of skill) is the extent of the informing Knowledges 1–3, whether the player or user knows the rules (Knowledge 1), is familiar with their representation (Knowledge 2) and observes the interactional courtesies (Knowledge 3).

What Knowledge 4 indicates brings me to the heart of the 'how well do you play?' question. First of all let me dispense with the explicit fallacy. Just as Knowledges 1–3 may be present without Knowledge 4, so that the player or user knows in theory but cannot play in practice, so Knowledge 4 may be present alone, the player can play or use but is not able to explain this understanding in terms of Knowledges 1–3. In both cases we probably need to suspend disbelief and assume, given subjective normality, that the unpractised player who has Knowledges 1–3 can, through practice, articulate Knowledges 1–3; and similarly the player or user who has Knowledge 4 can acquire Knowledges 1–3.

However, this need not be the case both ways. Knowledges 1–3 are possible for armchair players who never acquire or articulate Knowledge 4.

In the reverse case we know that Knowledge 4 is possible with no explicit Knowledges 1–3. Of course we assume that Knowledges 1–3 must implicitly underlie Knowledge 4, that is that no-one can play chess or tennis or any other game, without some knowledge of the rules, the moves, the conventions and the courtesies. Even more interesting in terms of Knowledge 4 is the threshold question. Should I assume that Knowledge 4 necessarily requires knowing how to play *skilfully*? No doubt we do make major distinctions among players, we provide hierarchies and championships and honours, we choose teams and we (probably) distinguish even when choosing opponents ourselves. And yet although this is common and indicates an important aspect of game knowledge it is not, I suggest, necessary. We can all be chess players, however badly we play (although there is one caveat which is that we do need to have some small acquaintance with Knowledges 1–3). Knowledge 4 is paradoxically less necessary. Some modicum is necessary but no more than a limited amount. Perhaps in addition to the possession of Knowledges 1-3 there also needs to be some motivation to develop Knowledge 4.

The point of the analogy should now be obvious. Knowledges 1–3 have to do with competence, Knowledge 4 with a combination of performance and proficiency; and what the performance of Knowledge 4 demonstrates in illustrating levels of proficiency is precisely the extent to which Knowledges 1–3 have been internalised.

Knowledges and Language

Let me now move back from the game analogy to language, indicating the parallels of Knowledges 1–4 and relating, in each case, the different kinds of knowledge available to the fugitive native speaker. (We should also note the parallels to the continuing debate on the relation between implicit and explicit knowledge (Ellis, in press).

I must say, first of all, that, as with all analogies, the parallels between games and language do not easily hold up. Nevertheless, I will make whatever connections are possible and, when necessary, point to the discrepancies.

Metalinguistic knowledge

Knowledge 1 is metalinguistic knowledge, knowledge about the language (Alderson *et al.*, 1997; Elder *et al.*, 1999). Native speakers may or may not have this explicit knowledge though it is customary to say that they have internalised it in some sense. What it means is the ability to talk about the language, to know and describe in however elementary a way, the parts of the sentence, to have some awareness, which can inform discussion, of accent, style, register, linkages in discourse and so on. But Knowledge 1 in language refers more importantly to a manipulative ability with these structures, to be able to put together sounds, intonation, stressing, rhythm, sentences, discourses, registers, styles, perhaps within a very limited range (especially at above sentence levels). Note that we are teetering here on the very edge of rule-governed behaviour (and are already moving into the arena of Knowledge 2 and Knowledge 3).

Knowledge 1 involves having the construction ability to assemble the parts of common sentence types or texts and to recognise them receptively as meaning bearing whether or not they are understood. What matters crucially then is a recognition of language use as being an exemplification or realisation of the structural resource which they do have control over. Of course this is a strong argument in support of the centrality of grammar: it assumes that all language use is a particular, local or contextual adaptation of the grammar. As I will show, the power of the local or contextual is not so easily dismissed. But for the moment, to use another analogy, it is generally accepted that skills are transferable in activities such as reading (whatever script is used, given constancy of code), driving a car, whatever intricacies and developments the car may have, farming, medicine and so on. In all such cases there are constants, the important core remains and what changes is how to use that core. Similarly with language: the grammar of any one 'language' remains quite (if not fully) impermeable to change but what uses it is put to vary, with time and demand.

Discriminating knowledge

Knowledge 2, which I will call discriminating knowledge, enables the native speaker to recognise what counts or what does not count as being part of the language. There are perhaps three aspects to this, none of them foolproof for reasons discussed earlier in connection with the L1–L2–FL (Foreign Language) relation, that is that any one native speaker is vastly limited in what s/he knows of his/her own language, but it does include a recognition ability of the rote kind of idiom, metaphor and so on.

However, given those constraints, I propose these three attributes to Knowledge 2. First, the native speaker knows what is his/her language and what is not (it is English, say, not French). Second, the native speaker knows that a sentence/text/sound could be his/her language but it does not sound quite right. It belongs elsewhere but is not somehow familiar; in other words it must belong to some other dialect. Even if in my idiolect 'term starts again on Monday already' is not possible, I recognise that it is possible in some idiolects of English.

Third, the native speaker knows that a new word or expression, one that s/he has not heard before or even one that s/he chooses to invent 'belongs' to the language. It conforms to the rules and is acceptable not only to him/her but to others. This does not mean it will be used extensively or even at all after the first occasion. That is not the point. What is at issue is that it is usable in the way that a non-native borrowing is not. In other words the native speaker has the capacity and the authority for generative creativity in the language. For example, the Lewis Carroll inventions in the Alice books or a coinage such as de-car (compare with de-train, de-plane) would be immediately recognisable as acceptable even if thought to be peculiar or ugly.

Language creativity

Indeed creativity of this linguistic sort is of major criterial importance to the native speaker and seems to act as a defining criterion for who is (and is not) a native speaker. It seems to be the case that often non-native speakers will invent terms, whether words, expressions or sentences, which native speakers choose to categorise as errors: and yet by the same token similar inventions or creations by the native speaker are not regarded as being errors. Instead they are creative potential additions to the language. It then does indeed become criterial to my attempt to define the native speaker to determine whether this is a significant point in the progression 'non-native speaker to native speaker' (that is in the development of the acquisition by the non-native speaker) i.e. the point at which his/her errors are no longer regarded as errors but as native-like creations.

Of course there is circularity here in that if the non-native speaker is a writer as capable as Joseph Conrad then his inventions, however bizarre, are regarded as creative even though in a lesser or unknown writer they would be considered to be errors. In similar vein the Nigerian novelist Amos Tutuola's writing is indeed full of errors but his work received so much praise in the literary world that his novels are often regarded as hugely creative (see Chapter 8). The question I pose is whether they are genuinely creative, that is deliberately so in the way that James Joyce is; creative through luck (but then that may imply implicit intuitive knowledge); or whether they are full of errors, which in his case (but not that of uncelebrated learners) are glossed over. Indeed the whole relation between creativity and error is of central interest to our theme and we will come back to it in Chapter 8.

Communicational knowledge

Knowledge 3, which I will call communicational knowledge, concerns the handling of the rules, in a relation of courtesy to others. In the case of the game analogy I have suggested it means responding (accommodating to) one's partner or opponent, on the sensible premise that games usually need two or more players. But it is not just courtesy to others that matters, it is also courtesy to – a seriousness about – the game itself. Otherwise it becomes trivial and meaningless: the vacuousness of cheating oneself is well known.

In terms of language this means knowing how to seek appropriateness and how to recognise it, how to match background knowledge and context in such a way that messages are understood and understandable. There is, as I will show later, overlap here with Knowledge 4 since doing Knowledge 3 well does indicate a valued level of skill, reaches above what is normal, given knowledge. But that is not intended here. What is being suggested is that there is a type of knowledge of using and handling language which indicates a recognition or relationship and thereby seeks to provide in speaking and writing the rhetorical clues that help understanding. To clarify what is meant, let me return to the game analogy.

Here, in tennis for example, the true tennis player (not, note, the 'good' player) takes the game seriously, is adequately equipped, has enough time for the game, does not cheat or act overbearingly or take advantages, gives the opponent (if there is no umpire) the benefit of the doubt when a line call is uncertain and yet tries his/her hardest to win, that is does not waste his/her opponent's time or act patronisingly.

The language analogy means, above all, taking the interaction seriously, seeking to make and achieve communication whether in speech or in writing, not to utter (again in speech or writing) a list of unconnected sentences. This means that foremost among the linguistic devices to achieve communication must be the building of coherent discourse through a combination of interlocking information structures and cohesive devices. If Knowledge 1 refers to sentence construction, Knowledge 3 concerns discourse structure; it also covers pragmatics, the interface between language and context as well as the matching of linguistic units into appropriate language use. Once again I am not here making any claims for how well or badly this is actually done. For the moment that is not the point. Furthermore I am not at all claiming that the native speaker gets it right every time. Far from it. What is, however, being claimed is that this area of knowledge – Knowledge 3 – is relevant to our concept of the native speaker even if what I am building up is an idealised picture. This is a topic which I address more fully in Chapter 6 where I discuss communicative competence.

Skills knowledge

Knowledge 4, which I will name skills knowledge, is about the level of skill the player (in a game) and the speaker or user in language bring to the event. I shall use the common distinctions whereby Knowledges 1–3 are knowledge/what (or that) and Knowledge 4 is knowledge/how. Or again I can characterise Knowledges 1–3 as knowledge and Knowledge 4 as control. But in effect as I have indicated both knowledge and control are present in Knowledge 1–3 and probably in Knowledge 4 as well.

For even in Knowledge 4, in relation to games, there is a distinction among players, first of all in terms of knowledge. Let us take two tennis players, both equivalent in terms of Knowledge 1, 2 and 3. Player 1 (P1) plays better than Player 2 (P2) not only because, let us say, s/he hits more accurately (that is has greater control) but also because s/he transfers his/her knowledge – Knowledges 1–3 – more effectively, thereby enabling him/herself to hit harder. P2 may be accurate on occasion but is unable to make the connection between Knowledges 1–3 and Knowledge 4. Of course there is the much simpler case of Players 3 (P3) and 4 (P4) in which what distinguishes, say, P3 from P4 is only control even though again they are equivalent in terms of Knowledges 1–3. But the point I wish to make here is that the distinction between knowledge and control is fragile and quite tenuous even though every knowledge implies a control.

To return to the original discussion on the four types of knowledge, we can say that only Knowledge 1 is a pure knowledge and the rest are control. But even (pure) knowledge itself contains a bifurcation between a knowledge and a discrimination of that knowledge. In other words the fundamental distinction at all levels of knowledge is knowledge what/that and knowledge how: both are types of knowledge and, furthermore, in the context of a skill (a game, language) it is virtually impossible to keep them apart except perhaps in the extreme Knowledge 1 sense of an external commentary on the rules.

Proficiency (that is control) therefore appears at all levels, though it is of course most available at Knowledge 4. But even there I want to be careful because what really distinguishes Knowledge 4 from Knowledge 1–3 is that Knowledge 4 represents performance as against the competence of Knowledge 1–3. At the same time, and for the reason just mentioned that proficiency is more clearly perceived in Knowledge 4, it is in Knowledge 4 that we find distinctions among native speakers in proficiency. How then can this be? How can native speakers differ in terms of proficiency from one another? This is an intriguing and, at the same time, quite basic question. Let me approach it from the opposite angle.

Language Proficiency

Is it the case that non-native speakers differ in terms of proficiency? This question seems hardly worth asking since the answer must be that of course they do, unless there is a catch in it. But there is no catch. Non-native speakers, even those with similar language learning experience and other matched variables, show differential language proficiencies. Note that the issue here is not one of range of language experience (though that might well be a legitimate assessment parameter). It refers to the grammar and the semantics, the comprehension and the production of texts. Now if we can accept without a demur the fact of non-native speaker differentiation why would there be any problem about the native speaker?

Let me consider the issue of native speaker proficiency by a question and answer procedure:

(1) Do native speakers differ in control of style?
(2) Do native speakers differ in control of oratory?
(3) Do native speakers differ in control of register?
(4) Do native speakers differ in control of range of vocabulary?
(5) Do native speakers differ in control of range of accent?
(6) Do native speakers differ in control of sentence structure?

In my view the answer to questions 1, 2, 3 and 4 must without any doubt be affirmative: some native speakers write better, speak with greater power and so on than others. Question 5 is more difficult: and while it may be (perhaps it is) the case that native speakers do differ in terms of accent range somehow this is not regarded as important. It would seem to relate to an ability to mimic (to perform as an imitator) rather than to demonstrate language control. In the areas of style, oratory, register and vocabulary level (Questions 1–4), non-native speakers differ just as native speakers do; this is less obviously the case for range of accent (Question 5). The sticking point is control of sentence structure (Question 6). For here it is crystal clear that non-native speakers differ among one another in terms of their control over sentence structure. This is, after all, the precise variable which crucially distinguishes native speakers and non-native speakers But what happens to this argument if it can be shown that native speakers also disagree among themselves about certain sentences (see Chapter 9)?

Now if I include in this discussion dialectal variety, then it must be the case that native speakers differ since not all native speakers share the same dialect, leaving aside for the present the issue of whether it makes sense to speak of different dialects as having native speakers in common. Similarly, and in a sense making the same point but for a different area, educated native speakers may differ from uneducated ones in terms of the structures they recognise, use and accept (for example: she has/she have). In all such investigations there is a need to distinguish carefully between the production/comprehension data and between the performance/ competence claims; undoubtedly, in social and in geographical dialects there are serious problems of eliciting just what structures speakers have in common (Quirk, 1990).

My question here, however, is, given an equivalence of background, do two native speakers (both, say, using the standard code) differ in terms of their proficiency in sentence structure? I have already agreed that they can indeed differ in terms of other language proficiencies.

The answer can only be provided in terms of the actual question that is asked. Let me go back to the previous non-native speaker question: *is it the case that non-native speakers differ in terms of proficiency?*

Two non-native learners with equal educational background may very well differ in terms of their control over grammatical structures. If they do not appear to differ when tested, then that may be because of the salience of educational background in the test. Or it may have to do with a non-valid test or with random test effects. Absolute equivalence of proficiency is unlikely precisely because of differential abilities which tests are constructed to reflect.

The same applies to these two native speakers. If they test out equally then again that may be because of chance or because of what we have built into our definition of native speaker. No doubt there is a certain agreement among native speakers on the structures of 'their' language (the 'core') but there comes a point as, for example, Ross (1979) has shown where this agreement disappears (see Chapter 9). In other words, in terms of the earlier discussion in Chapter 2, it seems to be the case that what happens in the development of native speakerness also takes place in non-native-speaker development, that is that universal grammar parameters are reset for the target language.

Relevance to Applied Linguistics

Two important applied linguistics issues arise out of the discussion in this chapter. The first, raised by both the bilingualism and semilingualism debates, is that of disadvantage. From an applied linguistics point of view it is interesting that each has been represented as the cause and the explanation for linguistic (and therefore cognitive) deficiency, leading to disadvantage educationally. In neither case is this true. In the case of bilingualism the evidence for disadvantage comes from inadequate sampling in the studies undertaken. Cummins (1984) refers to this as 'the myth of bilingual handicap'. In the case of semilingualism the weakness was not experimental but intellectual in that the term semilingualism was being used to cover/explain inadequate education. That is why it is very reminiscent of earlier debates on restricted and elaborated codes (Bernstein, 1971–5; Rosen 1972; Atkinson 1985) in which the false assumption was made of the restricted codes being somehow innate. It also relates to the important topic of simplification which has both pedagogic (Davies, 1984c) and linguistic ramifications in, for example, pidginization (Romaine, 1988).

What the discussion of both the restricted codes and semilingualism indicated was the need to provide proper educational access in, for example, literacy and not to rush from educational problems to popular and easy explanations. What applied linguistics offers is a debunking of such beliefs/fallacies and a willingness to explore the truly empirical areas of proficiency which the other major discussion (on Knowledges) in this chapter opens up. In the next decade it is likely that one of the major tasks of applied linguistics will be the investigation of adequate proficiencies, and that requires an operational definition of minimal native-speaker ability. (The issue of proficiency is taken up again in Chapter 9 but the optimism I expressed 10 years ago that we would gain insight into adequate proficiencies in this period has proved vain.)

Summary

In this chapter I considered the non-native speaker's relation to the native speaker from the points of view of bilingualism and semilingualism. I maintained that it is possible to be a native speaker of more than one language as a 'bilingual' under certain conditions, for example adequate exposure to each language before the critical age. I also maintained that on logical grounds it is not possible to sustain the notion of semilingualism, although in practical terms it must be the case that some speakers are less fluent and proficient than others. But the use of semilingualism to mean some form of cognitive deficiency I dismissed as untenable.

In this chapter I also used a game analogy to introduce four types of knowledge which I labelled: metalinguistic, discriminating, communicational and skills. The suggestion was made that Knowledges 1, 2 and 3 refer to competence and Knowledge 4 to performance; and from another point of view that Knowledge 1 is 'pure' while Knowledges 2, 3 and 4 relate to control or proficiency. I commented on the apparent fundamental bifurcation at all levels (even within Knowledge 1 itself) between a knowledge and a discrimination of that knowledge, that is between knowledge and control. Proficiency, I argued, is most evident in Knowledge 4, and it is for that reason that native speakers as well as non-native speakers can be distinguished in terms of proficiency.

Whether or not I should wish to distinguish among non-native speakers in terms of linguistic competence is, I argued, largely a philosophical issue. More relevant, and of more applied interest at this point in the discussion, is the special claim of the native speaker to communicative competence, and it is to this topic that I turn in the next chapter, Chapter 6.

Chapter 6
Communicative Competence
Aspects of the Native Speaker

Rintell and Mitchell (1989: 248–72) quote the following oral request
from a foreign student:

> Miss Mary, I am really sorry to say that, but the assignment, I couldn't
> hand it to you on time, didn't, because there are some problems in
> my family. I didn't have much time to think about the assignment.
> So, would you please to give me one more time, and I think I will hand
> it to you as soon as possible, as soon as I finish it, and I promise this is
> the first time I will do it and it is also the last time I ask for your favor.

Rintell and Mitchell comment:

> the non-native speaker may feel particularly insecure in a face-to-face
> situation. Another concern appears to be the need for clarity. Thus the
> learner uses a phrase, then begins anew or uses a second phrase, albeit
> redundant, to clarify his or her point ... On the other hand, a native
> speaker's facility with the language allows him or her to respond
> spontaneously, whether orally or in writing, without the need to
> search for the most appropriate, or the most correct, word or phrase.
> (Rintell & Mitchell, 1989: 266–7)

I want to suggest that the facility which Rintell and Mitchell refer to here
stands for communicative competence. Can the native speaker be defined
as privileged in terms of this ability? (See also Davies (1989b) and Hymes
(1989) for a discussion of this question.)

Rationale for Communicative Competence

In terms of language use it is clear that the native speaker knows; which is
another way of saying that s/he possesses communicative competence. The
rationale for communicative competence (Hymes, 1970; Campbell & Wales,

1970) was the redressing of what Hymes regarded as the inadequacy of linguistic competence. And what he was concerned with was precisely what it is that the native speaker knows other than linguistic competence. This latter, he felt, was a narrow concept and one that did too little justice to what we expect of the native speaker, especially the educated native speaker. But what do we expect of the native speaker in addition to the linguistic competence which, as suggested in Chapters 2 and 5, seems to mean the internalisation of linguistic rules, the rules of grammar (Kramsch, 1998)?

Let me say what I expect of the native speaker. I expect the native speaker to have internalised rules of use, the appropriate use of language, to know when to use what and how to speak to others. I expect control of strategies and of pragmatics, an automatic feeling for the connotations of words, for folk etymologies, for what is appropriate to various domains, for the import of a range of speech acts, in general for appropriate membership behaviour in him/herself and of implicit – and very rapid – detection of others as being or not being members.

As will be clear what I am really talking about here is culture as much as language, since what we expect of the native speaker in terms of appropriate behaviour is that s/he should have immediate access to the culture of which s/he is a member; part of the cultural behaviour to which s/he claims access is, of course, appropriate language use. In this sense it would seem that being a native speaker is as much (and indeed perhaps more) about knowing the conventions, the ways in which language and culture meet, as it is about how to form grammatical sentences. It may be difficult for us to examine the one without being secure about the other. Nevertheless, it may well be that while native speakers do not agree about the grammar ('all grammars leak'), they share more agreement about the culture; and that is why, as I was suggesting earlier, it is quite difficult to claim native speaker status without early exposure to the language (and the culture and their interface) of childhood.

Here is an example: a British-born academic who has worked for 25 years in Australia tells me that even after all those years in Australia his problem of communication with friends and colleagues has nothing to do with the linguistic system; his problem is entirely one of culture in that he gets the swearing wrong, his use of irony and allusion are not quite right and so on. It is precisely, if we accept his story, that he lacks communicative competence in the culture.

This discussion of communicative competence reaches over into the approaches of ethnomethodologists who take the view that the object of a social science should be to reveal what it is that members of a group know and how they operate that knowledge (Garfinkel, 1967; Heritage, 1984; Atkinson & Heritage, 1984). Such knowledge is, as it were, common-sense knowledge and it must indeed be the case that much of the time we act not out of full understanding of what others mean but out of our best guess as to what they mean. In other words, there is a good deal of tacit understanding, of taking on trust, a trust that can only operate if we reckon that others are also likely to behave in the same way. At its extreme this is the assumption about a common humanity; but ethnomethodology goes much further and makes assumptions about a common 'common sense' among members and a common cultural understanding which relies as much on getting by, on 'ad hocking', as on rules or even conventions.

Membership

It does seem clear that membership is a useful model for the native speaker: membership of 'the same' cultural group means an assumption of behaviours from other members as well as a knowledge of how to behave oneself in the normal range of situations of daily life. 'The normal range of situations of daily life': this orientation suggests a ritualised view of behaviour and indeed it is an appropriate one since for much of one's interactive daily life, whether cultural or linguistic, it is probably the case that behaviour is ritualised, participating in activities such as meals, shopping, working, dressing, washing, religious performance, artistic activity, sexual interaction, childrearing and so on. And among these behaviours are those, also hugely ritualised, which I will treat as part cultural or as solely linguistic: talk, rehearsing information, chat, gossip, as well as the to and fro of communication at and in work, even daily reading and writing in literate societies are hugely ritualised. It is not surprising, therefore, that I take seriously the ethnomethodological approach to shared cultural understandings.

Being a member is what counts; thereafter others expect of us and we of ourselves 'proper' behaviour, cultural and linguistic; and although our behaviour does act as a criterion for acceptance into membership it is probably the case that membership comes first (Barth, 1969) and that we can be accepted as members even if our behaviour is quite marginal to the norms of the group. Obvious examples would include those with pathological impairment as well as the handicapped; that is to say we do not automatically exclude the deaf from native-speaker membership because they cannot speak or because they use sign language. Similarly, we do not exclude those who cannot work, dress themselves and so on. In other

words we make the obvious distinction between knowledge and performance and we do not demand performance as a test of membership.
Indications of knowledge are enough.

Linguistic Relativity

The membership claim is seen in a different guise in the continuing
argument over the relation of language, culture and thought. In this
argument there is a sense of the uniqueness of the native speaker who has
both the responsibility for and the rights to the culture and the language:
the best known and most publicised expression of this view is found in the
Sapir–Whorf hypothesis (Sapir, 1931; Whorf, 1942) which, in its extreme
form, says that there is an identity between language and thought such
that thinking is determined by the language of the thinker. For the
purposes of the argument thought and culture are amalgamated. Sapir
(1931: 578) put the view thus:

> The relation between language and experience is often misunder-
> stood. Language is not merely a more or less systematic inventory of
> the various items of experience which seem relevant to the individual,
> as is so often naively assumed, but is also a self-contained, creative
> symbolic organization, which not only refers to experience largely
> acquired without its help but actually defines experience for us by
> reason of its formal completeness and because of our unconscious
> projection of its implicit expectations into the field of experience.

Whorf, himself a pupil of Sapir's, reported that the views of time and
direction taken by the Hopi (American) Indians were determined by the
Hopi language; similarly, he argued, the views of time and distance
accepted in Western European culture (which for his purpose included
North American Anglophone and which he combined under the generic
heading of Standard Average European) was traceable to the languages of
Western Europe. It is not my business here to detail the problems of the
Sapir–Whorf hypothesis; the usually accepted view is that in its extreme
or strong form the hypothesis is untenable but that in its weak form it
must be accepted, in that there must be some relation between language
and thought/culture (Gumperz & Levinson, 1996).

But for my purposes here what is of interest is the way in which
any hypothesis of this kind relates to the native speaker since if it is true,
and I have just argued that in some weak form it must be, then native
speakers may be distinguished in terms of thought (culture) as well as of

language. This relates to the assumptions that we make of one another, assumptions we take, as I have just suggested, in connection with an ethnomethodological approach, about our shared understandings with community members.

It is not at all easy to distinguish these features of the weak Whorf hypothesis from what is said to belong to the concept of communicative competence. In general, communicative competence discussions tend to relate to questions of appropriateness while those of the linguistic relativity argument more often concern issues related to the ways in which we categorise the world, for example in colour terminology or the lexical naming that we employ. We expect fellow native speakers to make the same assumptions as we do and for events and ideas to have similar implications to them as to us so that, for example, a well-known festival (such as Christmas) will arouse not only similar and immediate accord about what to do, how to celebrate and so on but also agreement on what it is appropriate to say and perform in terms of language. An example such as this indicates that linguistic relativity is closely related to ideas of communicative competence and also to assumptions about shared world knowledge.

Culture peels away like the layers of an onion: it is indeed possible to be a member of more than one group, to be, for example, both Scottish and British, to be an Edinburgh man/woman as well as Scottish and British and so on. This means that if you are Scottish and British but not an Edinburgh person even though living in Edinburgh, you may find yourself lost in some of the intricacies of Edinburgh social life. This is even more complicated if you are British (but not Scottish, say English) and during an encounter in a corner shop in Scotland find yourself misunderstood and yourself misunderstanding: you share the overall culture but not the subculture; you do not know what to say, how to ask for things, what greetings to begin with and how to bring the encounter to a close (Davies, 1988; McDonald, 1989). It is the immediate, the essentially ritualised script, the restricted code, that you cannot handle, just as if you were British and visiting the USA and were unaware of the significance of a local holiday, such as Thanksgiving. In the corner shop, as a sharer of the over-arching culture, in this case, the British, you would very soon observe what the ritual was and although you might find the phonetic accommodation beyond you, you would certainly make use of the correct routines for buying and for starting and finishing such an encounter. What is more the misunderstanding we have suggested would arise because of what is a local issue, the correct way to handle that encounter. But if there were some other more general cultural allusions, something about politics, television, the newspapers, the mail, drinking hours, school holidays, hospital care, where the bus-stop is, how your wife, husband, mother, father, children are, the price of petrol, and so on then, whether you were from Edinburgh or not, whether Scottish or not, comprehension would be possible between you and the shop-keeper on such matters, on how to talk about them and on the common assumptions behind them.

Even when there is this problem of different subcultures there is general agreement on what counts as a question form and even if the form were not one that you would yourself use, yet it would be possible to pick up clues in the context as to what is intended, what the unusual (to you) form is functioning as. This is unlikely to be the case if the customer is not a native speaker of (in our case) British English. What it is legitimate to talk about and how to do it would be less easy unless of course the customer (to follow the shop example) has become very fully a member of your speech community, has changed his/her first language and is trying to participate or 'pass' as a native speaker. But I repeat my earlier warning that even in such extreme cases there is always the problem for such learners that they have large experiential gaps (such as childhood in the language) which nothing they can do − except vicariously − will fill for them.

Davies (1984d) considers the Catch 22 certification problem of the English second-language learner attending a secondary school in the UK who is required to gain a certificate of English for L1 students. This L1 examination turns out to make literary and cultural assumptions which cannot be met by the second-language learner (McDonald, 1989).

Bilingual Communicative Competence

Earlier in this book (Chapter 1) it was suggested that it may be harder for the non-native speaker to achieve native-speaker levels of communicative competence than of linguistic competence. It was argued that the reason for this is that the non-native speaker misses out on the nexus of experience (Davies, 1984d) which contributes essential structure and information to the native speaker and which is assimilated only in childhood. In making this distinction I pointed out that I was excluding the bilingual child with full bilingualism (so-called ambilingualism) who must necessarily acquire both linguistic competence and communicative competence equally well in the two (or more) languages. Here, however, my concern is with the adult second/foreign language learner who comes to the target language after acquisition of an L1. What is it then about the components and the layering of communicative competence that makes it, unlike linguistic competence if

our argument stands, apparently inaccessible to the second/foreign language learner? I suggested earlier that if it is the case that true bilingualism
is unattainable, it is precisely for this reason, that is, that communicative
competence is attainable in only one code. As I will show, it may be
necessary to revise this view.

In its simplest terms communicative competence is concerned with
appropriacy of language use, that is to say with using (writing, speaking
and so on) the right sentence in the right context. The claim is not as
hugely exaggerated as may appear: it is not (like my Skill Knowledge,
Knowledge 4) concerned with the best appropriate utterance. What it has
to do with is articulating the right sort of utterance on the right occasion,
knowing and being able to offer some sort of suitable language use.
Observe, first, that the proposed utterance may be an error because your
analysis of the situation may be wrong; and, second, that you may fail to
think of a suitable utterance. However, there is here an important escape
for the native speaker (and this may be quite crucial in our native speaker
definition) and it is this: that the native speaker is very very good at
circumlocution, at finding ways round, at paraphrasing and explaining in
alternative ways: non-native speakers generally are not so good at this.

Defining Communicative Competence

When Hymes (1970) at much the same time as Campbell and Wales
(1970) proposed the term communicative competence it was as a
deliberate counter to the narrowness of Chomsky's (1965) linguistic
competence. In effect, as is now clear, it was unnecessary, even irrelevant,
except in symbolic terms. What Chomsky had done was to indicate what
for him linguistics should be about. His argument was not without merit
since it was coherent, his concern (Smith & Wilson, 1979) being with
grammar and grammar as a human faculty (our Grammar 3 in Chapter 3).
Hymes was not at all concerned with grammar and therefore in respect to
that particular argument his alternative formulation proposal fulfilled a
useful function because in spite of his own genuine wish for linguistic
competence not to be applied to areas such as language learning and
teaching, Chomsky's theory was very widely made use of in applied fields.
Hymes was therefore responding more as an applied than as a theoretical
linguist, even though he claimed (1989) that his contribution was intended
to be theoretical. And in his paper, addressed felicitously to a conference
on disadvantage among L1 speakers, Hymes attempted to return our
concern to language, to indicate that whatever it is that recent linguistics

may have seen as a goal (Harris, 1988) language is very much wider, more varied and enters at many levels into the lives we lead and the problems we face.

We now distinguish the facts of communicative competence from the learning of communicative competence. In this way we will both distinguish between the native speaker and the non-native speaker, and, at the same time, gain some understanding of what it is that the native speaker controls as his/her repertoire.

The Facts of Communicative Competence

There are four types of facts of communicative competence; these correspond to the criteria Hymes laid down, though it should be noted that the distinctions he made were new only in so far as the names he accorded to them. I will use the following terms: historical, practical, effective and contextual.

Historical

This refers to a sentence which may be well formed grammatically but fails to make any sense or connection in the present. Thus, for example, letters however formal beginning: 'Most noble . . .' and ending 'I have the honour to be . . . faithful/devoted servant' would be thought quaint and somewhat forced or even hypocritical. Certainly the writer would be regarded as behaving inappropriately, as not knowing the language even though at one time (the 17th or 18th century) s/he would have been expected to write in this way. The example chosen here is by no means arcane or recherché or very out of date: I could choose an Anglo Saxon example or even something from Middle English, for example, to call someone, however worthy, today 'a gentle perfect man' would seem excessive. Changes of word meaning provide very obvious common examples of the changes of the originally intended speech act. Take for example Wordsworth's:

A poet could not but be gay
In such a jocund company

which is now difficult to say without a homosexual meaning. Words like *sad* and *nice* now have almost opposite meanings to those they had formerly. Because language varies, rule output cannot keep tabs on that change: the fact of abstraction in language is what permits change: but that change is in itself also arbitrary and so the rules alone are no guide as to what output over time is appropriate.

Practical

The rules of grammar are unthinking. In that sense they do provide a perfect analogue for a machine, for example a computer which when programmed will produce sentence after sentence usable and not usable. Thus it would be possible and quite grammatical for a sentence to be produced which constantly repeats, either through recursion (for example: 'This is the boy who saw the girl who saw a cat who saw the mouse who ...'); repetition (for example: 'Mary is a very pretty, pretty, pretty, pretty, pretty, pretty ...'; or the repetition may not be of the exact lexical item but of a repeated category, for example: 'Mary is a small, pretty, happy, fat, big, beautiful, young, intelligent, smart, lazy, sweet, rich ...'). Grammars are, as it were, mindless and need both restriction and intelligence to constrain what it is that they produce. To this extent they are not like machines since machines necessarily output meaningful content, that is they are programmed for an intelligent output.

Grammars are themselves programmes. Hymes's point, which as Harris (1988) pointed out, is an old one, is that grammars do not act alone, they are necessarily only part of the linguistic apparatus, providing the syntactic mechanism for the linguistic message. Grammar needs semantics, pragmatics and so on, just as the body needs the mind and the emotions to tell it what to do.

Useful

Not all sentences are useful or rather, some sentences are more useful than others. Thus if I say 'Inflammable!', which has a very clear grammatical pedigree of meaning 'Fire risk' there is a sense in which (as Whorf showed) the *in* prefix may be ignored and lead to hazardous outcomes. His solution (which is redundant in a strictly morpho-grammatical sense), was to add 'Non-' (Non Inflammable) to indicate precisely those conditions in which a container was safe and to leave the 'Inflammable' (or just the 'Flammable') when it was unsafe.

Language manuals (for example, Fowler, 1926; Webster, 1961; Peters, 1995) are full of recommendations on how to avoid the non-useful; and in a certain sense what they are recommending in terms of norms and correctness of use are precisely the most useful expressions. To cite an old example (and one in which these four canons of communicative competence are in conflict with one another) let me take *disinterested*. Now

Fowler and other normative writers say that the problem with disinterested is that it cuts down on choice in that it has taken over from *uninterested*, the negative meaning of interested, leaving as a result a gap for 'an absence of interest'. This is true in a narrow sense; but from the point of view of both language change and of usefulness the fact that the meaning of *disinterested* has shifted for many users must mean that 'an absence of interest' no longer needs its own lexeme or that it is already being provided elsewhere. This is a very pragmatic view: the user must judge whether or not *disinterested* still carries the meaning potential s/he needs.

The same analysis can be offered of the correctness arguments which arise when the language user runs ahead of the language and in so doing finds other/newer ways of saying; or just recognises that only some of the available resources need exploiting. Pronouns and relatives in English are of particular significance here (*It's I/It's me; the man who(m) we met last night; who(m)*). An even better contemporary example is the deliberate instrumentalist acting on the language by feminists (see Chapter 4) in an attempt to bring about political change through the language. It is not clear whether it is change in language use that is being advocated or change in language structure. Here again the communicative argument would be that present (that is traditional) use is not useful in that it does not accord with the views and relationships and sense of identity of most people (in this case women) and that therefore the grammar needs to be acted upon (in the extreme position) or extended (in the weaker position) in order to make the language more useful.

Contextual

This is the most interesting and perhaps most obvious of the communicative facts since in this case there would be general agreement that grammatical output can only be message bearing, that is meaningful, if it is context sensitive. The three other facts can even be seen as aspects of the need to relate language to its context; the context makes the largest contribution to appropriateness. Like everyone else, I normally tailor my tongue to the situation I find myself in and when I do not do so then I am said to be behaving inappropriately, though I may well be behaving in an exemplary grammatical fashion.

Examples

I want now to relate three of my own experiences. First, the 'Why bother?' example. I recall a foreign visitor, an academic phonetician, whose spoken English made him indistinguishable from a native speaker. I was expecting him and invited him into my office, asked him to sit down, remarked on the weather, took his coat and then said: 'I'll just shut the door'. He replied: 'Why bother?' My reaction was to shut the door, thinking as I did so that in my room I decided whether the door was to be open or shut and that my visitor was being aggressive and rude. In fact, as I realised later when I thought it over, he was trying to be polite and meant perhaps; 'Don't bother on my account!' 'Why bother?' though perfectly idiomatic was, however, quite wrong and I had reacted to his use of the idiom as if he had been a native speaker. Which suggests again that it is possible to perform too well in a foreign language and that a foreign accent may be a good badge to display – 'Don't expect me to share all your cultural assumptions!'

Second, the letter of condolence: about ten years ago a cousin of mine died under tragic circumstances. She was in her thirties, the mother of four children. She and her family were living abroad at the time. One evening they came out of a cinema and as they walked over to their car they saw that thieves were breaking into it: they ran towards the car, one of the men raised a gun, fired and my cousin was killed. She was a lot younger than me but we had been reasonably close and I found myself writing, trying to write, a letter of condolence to her parents, my uncle and aunt. I wanted to say something personal and to refer to the grotesque horror of the death. But I could not find the right words to do it in and after many trials I fell back on the highly ritualised form that we use when we write letters of condolence, the personal removed, the experience of death somehow muted.

My third example is children's jokes. My children were for a period – I can't remember exactly when but I think probably in the primary school, aged about 7 or 8 – very fond of jokes which they insisted on telling me, jokes no doubt they had been told. I was glad enough to listen but I never found the jokes funny. It was as if the children didn't know how to put the jokes across, exactly as in the famous numbered prison joke story. This story describes a new prisoner who discovers that at prison concerts no jokes are told in full because in such restricted communities every one knows all the same jokes. Instead each joke is numbered and it has become common practice for the number of a joke to be called out at an appropriate time. The new prisoner attempts to take part in the concert one evening by calling out some numbers. Nobody laughs and when he asks why, he is told that he hasn't learnt how to put the jokes across! Like the new prisoner my children knew the content of the jokes but not the telling of them.

In all such cases the grammar output is neutral: what is at issue is the context into which it is received where the real decision of its acceptance or not is made.

Demands on the Native Speaker

Before I consider context let me look at just what it is that these communicative facts appear to demand of the native speaker. In the first place the native speaker must be able to distinguish what is in contemporary use from what is not. In the second place, s/he must be aware of what is practical, that is speakable/writable and therefore communicable (what this underlines, of course, is the insistence on language as an interactive experience, since if it were only an individual affair, then this practical constraint would not have so strong a hold). In the third place, s/he must have a built-in critical awareness of usefulness. If it is agreed, as was suggested earlier, that usefulness can be linked to a rejection (a critical rejection) of norms of correctness, so that the native speaker is essentially 'aware' of both what is expected and of how far his/her freedom extends (that is whether or not to 'break' the norm), then there may be some sort of conflict here with the axiom that the native speaker is a native speaker precisely because s/he knows and observes the norm.

On the whole this does seem to make sense but I think there is an important qualification worth making and that is that an acceptance of those norms may/does indeed mark membership of the speech community to which the native speaker belongs and in which many codes may be in use. When we make a request we follow the convention of being polite just as we expect others to do to us. My request for help with directions in a strange city would normally begin perhaps: 'Can you please direct me to . . .'; but in a situation in which my interlocutor (for example taxi driver) has no English then I readily shunt into a reduced and less polite form ('Please show me X') or even a non-grammatical non-standard form, exactly as in the foreigner talk mode discussed earlier, for example, 'Where X?' (see Chapter 5). For within any such speech community the native speaker is in a position to make choices, choices precisely denied to those wishing to participate as members of the same speech community but who are non-native speakers and who therefore lack range, flexibility and confidence.

Now the problem with such a definition is that it is circular since we are (in part at least) defining the native speaker in terms of a relaxed attitude towards the norm. And it is certainly true that, in most cases, the native speaker will not act in this relaxed way. What remains central, however, is that the native speaker does know the norms (and then may or may not choose to observe them). Such knowledge is reminiscent of a similar order, equally demarcating, of cultural knowledge in a European context, for example in terms of when and where (for a man) to wear a tie and jacket, for a woman trousers or skirt; or in eating, cooking, dining, sleeping arrangements, what goes with what, what is indicative of a particular membership. Cultural membership is (like native speakerness) determined by such knowledge: equally those who feel sufficiently at ease can afford to flout some or other of the conventions.

It is probably the case that language is far more resilient as an exchange system than any of the other systems which are cruder and simpler. In language, therefore, flouting is easier (as long as it does not totally and immediately antagonise the interlocutor) than in these other more restricted modes. A group-related example is provided by Holmes (1988) who makes the interesting suggestion that since women apologise more than men (at least in English) and that they apologise most to other women, there may well be a mismatch between that fact and the strategies we offer to second-language learners in the area of apologising. Her argument is that since most language teachers are women they are more likely (as women) to teach, either explicitly or as models, their male students to apologise excessively. This is an intriguing issue about stereo-types and in this case the extent to which the major human distinction can be crossed on a linguistic bridge (see, for example, Taylor, 1976).

Or in another guise, the distinctions between speaking and writing, which mean that what counts as effective and acceptable prose would be thought inappropriate in speech. Another issue which has been discussed in language-maintenance programmes in recent years has been that of which language is suitable for which purpose, particularly for education. This issue has created controversy since, as Wells (1987) points out, what the mother tongue is means different things to different people:

That 'mother tongue' means different things to different people is also reflected in the teaching of South Asian languages in Britain. Urdu, for example, has been widely taught in mosques and community schools around Britain (Molteno, 1984) ostensibly 'as a mother tongue' to the children of parents mainly of Pakistani origin, who may speak Punjabi or Pahari/Mirpuri at home. However, the argument that Urdu and Punjabi and Pahari/Mirpuri are different languages and that most of these children are not native speakers of Urdu has provoked debate about whether Urdu is properly described as the mother tongue of most of those learning it. This has contributed to the decision by the Scottish branch of the National Council for Mother Tongue Teaching to drop the 'Mother Tongue' from its title and replace it with 'Community Language' (Wells, 1987: 5).

Or again the difference in acceptability of written English in different English language situations, for example this sentence from an article written in India: 'This polarity was experienced by Matthew Arnold in England in the 19th century itself' (quoted by Y. Kachru, TESOL 1988).

And this sentence from a West Indian newspaper: 'Mr X made the observation after the chairman pointed out that over 250 applicants at the interview only a small percentage of them could read and write a simple paragraph from the *Daily News*' (quoted in a Kenyan University examination paper, 1987).

I conclude therefore that the communicative facts demand of a native speaker that s/he can:

(1)   decide what is now in use;
(2)   be aware of what is speakable and writable about; and
(3)   have a relaxed attitude towards his/her own norms

Context

To return to context: what distinguishes the native speaker from the non-native speaker (given, as is necessary, matching on all obvious parameters) is that the native speaker normally has more awareness of the context. I can therefore distinguish three (at least) uses of context. *First, helping to understand the meaning of a word*; for example, mole in a government office and mole in a country churchyard. Here the awareness of the recent use of the word 'mole' to refer to spying in its various manifestations would suggest that in the first example we are dealing with a spy or spy-catcher while in the second we are dealing with the more traditional use. What context seems to mean in instances of this kind is keeping up to date in change of (above all else) vocabulary use. But note that no-one can hope to keep up with all such changes especially in the more specialised fields. Consider for example:

> The solution to Fermat that he constructs involves an incredibly large prime exponent (larger than $10^{\wedge}20$), but it is constructive. The main idea seems to be a kind of Heegner point construction, combined with a really ingenious descent for passing from the modular curves to the Fermat curve. The really difficult part of the argument seems to be to show that the field of definition of the solution (which, a priori, is some ring class field of an imaginary quadratic field) actually descends to Q. (Singh, 1997: 293, 4)

Second, helping to understand how words can be used quite differently in different contexts. For example the early loss of a human embryo by the mother is commonly called miscarriage when it happens 'naturally' so that women will refer to the miscarriage(s) they may have experienced. The term abortion in the common speech is restricted to the termination of pregnancy by deliberate means and is therefore subject to religious and/or legal sanctions in various countries. However, among the medical profession the term miscarriage is not used officially. Instead all terminations, natural or not, are referred to as abortions. We may speculate that this is because the medical profession (with its understandable caution about determining cause and with its central concern with diagnosis) is reluctant to claim that any terminations are natural. But this is pure speculation and all that concerns us here is the differential use of the term abortion.

Another example (and an interestingly different one from our previous examples because this time it involves geographical and/or social variation) is tea. For me tea (the meal not the drink) is a sweet refreshment including the drink tea and cakes/biscuits/light sandwiches taken at 4 or 4.30 pm in the afternoon and, it has to be said,increasingly rare now that most people are still at work at that time. However, the custom may still persist at weekends. And so when I was invited early on in my residence in Scotland to tea I arrived at about 4.30 pm expecting the kind of refreshment just indicated. But first I was early; tea in the Scottish sense starts at about 6 pm. Second, it was not light but a good knife and fork meal. Tea, that Scottish tea, is what is sometimes in England called high tea, what I call supper and some still call dinner.

Native speakers operate their own distinct version of these terms with ease; what we have not yet resolved is whether it is, in fact, part of native speakerness to extend sensitively, sympathetically that understanding so as to recognise that what I call the world, my categories, are not God-given. This requires the understanding to which we have referred of the different world views of different languages and cultures. In a curious way it is more of a problem within one dialect continuum like English since the need to operate different perceptions, at least to recognise them as different, is probably more likely to impinge. For most people the fact that Japanese, say, and English may categorise the world in different ways is less immediate and daily an issue.

Third, helping to understand what it is that is being written or talked about. Context here is related to the world outside the text, while the contexts I have so far considered have been more within the text. But in this aspect of my discussion of context the concern is with such important but largely nebulous features as world knowledge and individual experience. From this point of view (and it is not a wholly trivial one) context is different for every reader, every listener. And indeed this is precisely the argument of deconstructionism – that all texts have different meanings to different readers/listeners. My own view is Johnsonian, that common sense shows that there is some consensus about the overall meaning of a text. True, there will always be individual interpretations, but readers, within limits, do share meanings.

It is perhaps more convenient to turn the argument on its head and ask what sort of audience the writer or speaker has in mind. Is s/he in fact wishing to deliver a series of individual meanings in the one text? Rather as if s/he had written many letters or made many speeches/phone calls. This seems unlikely. It is far more likely that the writer/speaker wishes to get across some set of ideas, that is to share with others his/her experiences (conceptual, emotional, whatever) and while accepting that individual readers/listeners will access them individually, hope that the 'main' message will be understood (though not necessarily agreed to) by everyone. So that when readers/listeners debate the question about the text – 'What did s/he mean?' – they assume that there is a meaning to be detected and that given good will and adequate shared world knowledge with one another and with the writer they will achieve it. This is particularly true of scientific and other kinds of discursive writing. But for my purpose what it shows is that context is very difficult to delimit – that being a native speaker means operating the language rules one has automatised within a restricting world. But then this is what language is for – to relate the self to the world of the self.

And that leaves me with the question of how and if the self can relate to other worlds. This is an issue crucial for our understanding of the native speaker and I will come back to it (see Chapter 7). But now I return to the main topic and stay for the present with the facts of communicative competence. Let me recall these facts by considering a weak and a strong approach.

Weak and Strong Approach

The weak approach would be that communicative competence is being able to use the rules in appropriate ways within the normal context of use. Let us take an example: A is a taxi driver, B an economist, C a medical scientist. They will both share and not share a normal context of use. Therefore although they will inevitably differ in their communicative competence it remains possible for one to acquire the other's communicative competence through practice and apprenticeship. That is, what is needed is practice in the existing rules and skills rather than in totally new ones and to learn new ones by gradually acquiring competence in related skills. Thus it is probably easier to acquire skill in squash by generalising from, say, tennis rather than from chess.

On this account then the native speaker has an adequate facility in using the language in ordinary circumstances and is rather like the car driver who has learnt to drive and is able to manipulate the car in most normal traffic conditions. Two things are important here. First that we do not expect the car driver to be automatically capable of performing at a grand prix (nor, for that matter, of driving a bus or truck). Second, that what we say we are expecting of the normal driver is exactly that, since we also expect it of other drivers: in other words, there is a way in which competence in driving exists both in a knowledge of the rules of driving and of being able to do it. That is what we expect of one another.

Similarly for language use. We assume that being a native speaker means being able to cope with the language demands of normal daily intercourse, chatting, shopping, talking about children, addressing children and adults with different degrees of formality and so on. We do not expect more: when I add education to the native speaker then of course expectations rise and as well as literacy we now assume a greater range of styles and of fluency.

So much for the weak approach. The strong approach to communicative competence takes a more demanding line. This time it is assumed that the native speaker has available to him/her the whole of his/her life (like the drowning swimmer) as well as all knowledge relevant to the cultural background to the language (Fillmore, 1979). As soon as this is spelt out in this way it is manifestly absurd. Nobody can possess all that information and if we did then everybody would be the same. Or to put the argument in a different way: the fact of individuality means that we cannot all share exactly the same world view because to do so would be to deny our separate individuality.

Therefore the strong view either becomes a view of the native speaker (in terms of communicative competence) as once again reducing to the view I previously discussed of everyone being a native speaker of his/her own code, a view which, while true, is reductionist and basically trivial; or it becomes a more elaborate version of the weak view in that it notes that in operating communicative competence all of us in our native speaker roles take into account the experience we bring and have; but we also qualify that experience, if we are indeed wishing to exercise communicative competence, by our recognition that others are not quite like us. In other words the strong approach reduces to the weak one.

Communicative Competence: Learning

Now as for learning communicative competence I take it for granted that the native speaker learns through use. (I observe that for some analysts there is no useful distinction between communicative competence and linguistic competence, communicative competence being learnt in the process of learning linguistic competence.) The whole of native speaker development, therefore, goes towards the acquisition of communicative competence although it seems sensible to admit that, even more than linguistic competence, full communicative competence is unattainable. At the same time, and again in a strikingly similar way to linguistic competence, it has to be the case that the ability to communicate, in general, derives from the restricted input that is received.

What is remarkable about linguistic competence is that control over a potentially infinite set of sentences is achieved from a very restricted input, known as the 'poverty of the stimulus': to put it another way we all are able to use (or generate) sentences which we have never heard before. The very acquisition of structure triggers off a control over alternative structures, as in other areas of human development. Learning is transferable; that is walking up mountains and swimming in salt water do not depend absolutely on learning to walk up mountains and learning to swim in salt water but rather on learning to walk and learning to swim. If learning were not transferable (or generative) then human development would never have taken place, since I would only be able to repeat exactly what I had learnt. Generative (or transferable) learning is basic to human development.

Learning to be communicatively competent means the acquisition of a set of interactional skills for language in use: these skills include relating and accommodating to others, observing pragmatic protocol, being sensitive to context so as to access suitable linguistic units, performing in dialogue in appropriate ways and being able to relate the ongoing text (written or spoken) to the user's own understanding of the world. What this must mean is that there is less strain in interacting verbally with familiars than with strangers and to make the point even more strongly, it may also be the case that there is considerably more unfilled silence among familiars than between strangers (Tannen & Saville-Troike, 1985).

Native Speakers' Communicative Competence

The native speaker learns and operates these various skills largely without thinking. That, it will be remembered, was in part our definition of a native speaker. If the child-first-language learner can acquire a generative capacity for linguistic competence from the limited stock of sentences s/he hears, it must even more be the case that s/he can acquire ways of putting these sentences into use through direct observation of parents, other adults and peers. Communicative competence belongs to my Knowledge 3, which has, as do Knowledge 1 and Knowledge 2 (see Chapter 5), a proficiency dimension, that is, that native speakers differ among one another in terms of their communicative competence. That is why we all make distinctions and judgements among those who have communicative ability, using such value adjectives in their description as fluent, sympathetic, empathetic, understanding, brusque, fulsome, rude, courteous and so on. I take it that for native speakers it is criteria such as these that matter and it is these that we may wish to display as levels of native-speaker proficiency.

Non-native Speakers' Communicative Competence

But in terms of non-native-speakers' communicative competence the picture changes. Here the learner is normally exposed to a limited set of encounters and has little or no exposure to the cultural beliefs and knowledge which the target language bears. Of course much the same can be said for the learner's acquisition of linguistic competence – little exposure, limited range and often poor input. But in a sense the linguistic component contains fewer types to which the sentence tokens relate. In communicative competence there is far more information to carry and since for the most part the learner cannot live out the cultural routines, as native speakers can, learning them through doing, the only success s/he has is through knowledge, learning like a book. While this has often also been the case for the acquisition of linguistic competence, there are ways in which the interplay of sentences provides the practice in language that is lacking for the cultural routines.

Two Views

Two views of communicative competence need to be distinguished, views which emerge helpfully as we compare the facts and the learning of communicative competence. These two views are:

- *In terms of the facts the weak view must prevail.* That is, if communicative competence is in any sense generalisable across members of a group, that is across native speakers, then communicative competence reduces to appropriacy of language use in so-called normal settings.
- In terms of the learning of communicative competence the individual native speaker does acquire not only these facts but also everything else that contributes to making him/her an individual; but that in the course of this personal development what the native speaker does (must do) is to distinguish between what s/he is/has as a person and what s/he shares with others. This is true both for linguistic competence and for communicative competence but it does appear to be more difficult to make this distinction for communicative competence because of the greater resources that serve to inform communicative competence.

I am therefore led to conclude that both for the non-native speaker (learner) and for the analyst, it is necessary to define the nature of that shared communicative competence; this requires that we establish this definition at a sufficiently abstract level so as to avoid all individual confinement. What this means is that communicative competence ceases to be the impossible requirement for the second-language learner it has appeared to be. It becomes instead the articulation of linguistic competence in situation; that is the practice of interaction and the recognition of appropriacy. All else is individual experience.

Relevance to Applied Linguistics

The applied linguistics interest in this chapter is very clear. The concept of communicative competence has greatly stimulated language teaching studies in the last 25 years during which communicative language teaching (CLT) became the leading methodological model. Textbooks and tests were inspired by the excitement and the spin-off was considerable, ranging from English for specific purposes (Swales, 1984; Douglas, 2000) to the unit credit system (van Ek & Trim, 1984). Doubt has in recent years been expressed about the validity and practicality of CLT. What underlies all CLT models is now seen to be some version of the native speaker and with hindsight after our discussion in Chapter 6 we can surmise that the fault with most CLT is that its implicit model (of the native speaker) was too powerful. Such a native speaker, as Fillmore (1979) wryly comments, would have to be divine. The CLT idea, in other words, was based on an unanalysed version of communicative competence (Morrow, 1979). CLT was a methodology imposed on a teacher-driven enterprise. It arose in part out of the needs of UK-based EFL schools to provide materials for access for their students into the English-speaking life around them. Such materials were always UK-based. When transferred to non-English-speaking countries (and non-native-speaking teachers of English) they fell flat. They did so because they could not provide the range of situations in which proficiency could flourish. This is the heart of communicative competence, the linking of proficiency to situations. This is where the native speaker has a head-start, because s/he has more situation experience. Of course the non-native speaker can catch up but s/he needs the experiences of situations to do so.

Summary

In this chapter I related communicative competence to ethnomethodological notions of membership, thereby invalidating any support for linguistic relativity. I listed the parameters of communicative competence arguing for a distinction between the facts and the learning of communicative competence. The facts are that in terms of communicative competence the native speaker must: decide what is now in use, be aware of what is speakable and writable about; and have a relaxed attitude towards his/her own norms. The learning view of communicative competence implies that it must be generalisable and not simply an inventory of experiential encounters and facts.

I concluded that communicative competence represents the articulation of linguistic competence in situation; that is the practice of interaction and the recognition of appropriacy. All else, in my view, is individual experience and, as such, not attributable to a model of communicative competence.

The issue of communicative competence showed the importance of the involvement of culture in language and of the acquisition of culture as an analogue to the learning of language. In the next chapter, Chapter 7, I develop this theme and relate the important topic of norms and correctness to our earlier discussion of the standard language, extending the designation of standard beyond the set of official languages, proposing that an implicit (standard) language exists even where there is no codification.

Chapter 7
Intelligibility and the Speech Community

> For fifteen years – since arriving in this country, that is to say –
> I have suffered acutely listening to Australian voices. But all that will
> be changed. First thing in the morning, as I awake from sleep, I now
> clasp my hands together over my breast, and say to myself fifty times:
> 'Every day in every way I find there is nothing wrong with the
> Australian voice or speech.' I repeat this exercise as I drop to sleep
> at night, and firmly believe it will succeed with me as it has with
> Dr Mitchell.' – a correspondent in the *A.B.C. Weekly* 10 October
> 1942 (Mitchell & Delbridge, 1965: 68)

The irony, the humour, and the extreme stigmatising attitude in the
quotation from 1942 should serve to remind us of the strength of attitude
(usually negative attitude) among native speakers over what they regard
as theirs. The question at issue for this chapter is to what extent attitude
alone can affect intelligibility.

The Native Speaker and Other Natives

I have considered the type of knowledge and control expected of
the native speaker and in Chapter 9 indicate the judgements we expect
of the native speaker which distinguish native speakers and non-native
speakers. In this chapter I consider examples of native speakers in order to
illustrate some of the difficulties of reaching a definition and I also compare the status and construct of the native speaker in the field of language
to that of similar constructs in other ethnic fields.

Crewe's (1977b) discussion of the English of Singapore makes the very
valid point that while there are:

> certain features of Singapore English which most Englishmen and
> Americans feel intuitively are non-native – for example, the syllable-
> timed rhythm, the universal tag question *isn't it?*, certain intonation

contours – the difficulty is that the existence of native dialects possessing these or similar features would invalidate the point *ipso facto* ... it is virtually impossible to establish a criterion of non-nativeness with regard to any feature in any dialect which is not invalidated by the existence of a similar feature in a dialect within the acknowledged native speaker area. (Crewe, 1977b: 100)

To remind ourselves of the earlier discussion on knowledge and control, let us consider the comment which Harris makes on Saussure:

Theoretically, for de Saussure, a difference of a single phoneme or a single sign suffices to distinguish two separate sign systems. And he does not shrink from the conclusion that what are commonly called 'languages' (English, French, Latin etcetera) are not in his sense synchronic sign systems but conglomerates of historically related dialects and sub-dialects. It is at the dialectal and sub-dialectal level that the linguist will hope to identify the real 'idiosynchronic' systems which speakers actually use at any given time. (Harris, 1988: 92)

This is the argument I put forward earlier about the different understandings of the term grammar: that universal grammar, my Grammar 3, has become increasingly the object of linguistic study, very much at an idealised level, that the individual's idiolectal grammar, my Grammar 1, is an autobiographical account of each individual, necessarily different in each case, and that the common language grammar, our Grammar 2, refers to what Harris here calls 'languages ... conglomerates of historically related dialects and sub-dialects'.

According to my view of Grammar 3 everyone must be a native speaker of the same language, albeit at a very abstract level. In order to clarify my interest in there being native speakers of different languages there is no point in pursuing the notion of language in a plural sense; I will not proceed further with any consideration of Grammar 3. I am equally not concerned, for our present purposes, with making distinctions among every individual in terms of their very real differences such that in terms of our Grammar 1 every individual is a single native speaker of his/her own language (or, better, idiolect). This is not the point at present issue; but it will be useful to consider, briefly, why this should not be the point I am now concerned with. It is worth remembering that while my eventual interest is in Grammar 2 rather than in Grammars 1 or 3, I do not at all deny the reality of Grammars 1 and 3. I could, for example, take a quite general linguistic process such as phonology and claim (probably truly) that all languages contain a phonological system, allow meaning to be conveyed through a sound system: all languages provide devices to indicate the relationship between meanings and sounds.

So much for Grammar 3: then I can move directly to Grammar 1 and show that speaker A has one sound system (his/her own phonological system, not his/her own phonetic realisations, though that too), speaker B has another, speaker C a third and so on. Indeed, precisely as Harris (1988: 92) points out, 'a difference of a single phoneme or a single sign suffices to distinguish two sign systems', that is to say a single difference in one system creates two systems. That being so where does it leave Grammar 2? Or to put it more formally, what linguistic system can be attributed to those entities which are called languages, dialects, accents or varieties, which occupy the middle ground between what all humans share (Grammar 3) and what each human has alone (Grammar 1)? What is it that is systematically the case for groups of Grammar 1 or for subgroups of Grammar 3? Because, as Harris notes, this is exactly the position of 'what are commonly called languages (English, French, Latin et cetera)' or, to make the point even more dramatic, this is the position of the languages of the world. What is it that they share intralinguistically which they do not share with other 'languages' interlinguistically?

In passing it is worth noting that this problem is exactly the same problem for dialects and accents, indeed for all language categories which purport to be group related. And as I will show, it is a problem not at all unique to language but is shared by other group characteristics, culture especially but also religion, race, colour and tradition. In other words the issue is the very general one of defining ethnicity treating language as a type of ethnicity – and it raises the interesting and vexed question of the boundary marker (Barth, 1969) and that of group definition (Tajfel, 1981). I will come back to this later in the chapter.

Explanations of 'The Same' Grammar 2

To return to Grammar 2, is it a matter of quantity? Do we decide that person A has the same 'language' as person B because the only difference in their code is a single phoneme, whereas person C differs from both and therefore speaks a different language because s/he differs not only in that single phoneme but also in another phoneme? Is it a matter of least resistance, the lowest common denominator, as it were, of grouping together those whose codes are most like? But what is 'most like'? Person C may well differ from person A on two phonemes and from person B on two phonemes but they may not be the same two phonemes. The argument, the method of categorising, cannot simply be a matter of quantity. A straightforward example of the quantity problem would be that the English spoken in England and the English spoken in Scotland combine, with other Englishes, to make what is commonly referred to as 'a language' (British English) and yet in terms of phonology the systems of English and Scottish English are quite different. On what grounds then are they regarded as a single language?

The quantity solution can be rebutted at all levels, not just at the phonological one: at the lexical (British English, American English), the morphological (Scandinavian languages), the syntactic (Italian dialects) and even the discoursal (classical and colloquial Arabic). Examples can be found at every level: what are commonly called separate languages may or may not differ in the number of system units. The amount of system-sharing does not appear to matter. At the extreme this cannot be true.

To take an extreme case I would readily agree that while, say, Japanese and, say, English can be said to share (in some sense) Grammar 3 and also that an individual speaker of 'Japanese' and an individual speaker of 'English' each has his/her own Grammar 1, I would be hard put to argue for any sharing at the Grammar 2 level. It may be that a long period of contact, close contact, might cause some kind of mixing to take place, it might lead to a pidgin and subsequently a creole and then a new language. But in no sense could we say, synchronically, that Japanese and English are, together, to be regarded as a common language.

Nevertheless, in his work in Central India, and his insistent evidence in Khalapur, Gumperz (1964) showed that two historically distinct codes, one Indoeuropean and other Dravidian, have developed in part to become one language. Be that as it may, there is perhaps a more compelling argument in the Gumperz case; that is to characterise the phenomenon he describes as some kind of mixing which could lead to a new language. The point still holds that two very distinct languages may work together harmoniously because their speakers need them both. But can they be regarded as a form of Grammar 2? Gumperz would no doubt say yes, in that it might be possible to write a grammar of the new mixed common language. Indeed if there is in any sense a mechanism which allows the two codes to operate systematically together, then in some sense we can say that all Grammar 2s have the potentiality for merging with all other Grammar 2s.

There are explanations other than quantity for the combining we have spoken of – the overcoming of the fixed separation of every Grammar 1 as different and therefore its own 'language'. There are at least three such explanations: tradition, intelligibility and power.

The tradition explanation

The tradition explanation claims that two codes are the same code because of the past they share. At the extreme this would deny language change and at its most absurd claim that, say, Hindi and English were together one language, but a less extreme claim might be that the Scandinavian languages, English, Dutch, German, and Frisian are all so closely related that one Grammar 2 (a common language grammar) could be constructed for them all. Even this claim might seem exaggerated but when it is limited to, let us say, two Scandinavian languages (Danish and Norwegian) or Dutch and German, then we see both the nature of such a claim and also the problems it creates, problems that do not disappear completely when we limit the codes to one (English) and still have to take account of internal code varieties, including dialects and registers.

The intelligibility explanation

A more promising explanation for combining one native speaker with another is the appeal to intelligibility. This argument has two supports, the first general, the second linguistic. The general support is that while no two entities are ever the same, there does exist a relationship of similarity which enables us to make connections and relate objects and things. This is the argument from categories in that I can relate two tokens as belonging to the same type: a rose (Rose A) is in sufficient particulars close enough, similar enough to a second rose (Rose B) for me to consider them, see them, both as roses. So too with people; members of a family for example who may share very little in common, still have enough characteristic features for a relationship of similarity to be noted.

And so it is with language, although in this case, because a language has so many features, we require evidence of similarity to be more available than in simpler structures. But we are, nevertheless, predisposed to seek similarity wherever it offers itself and, when conditions are favourable, we are willing to agree that Scottish, Caribbean and Southern English are all English. When, however, we are negatively inclined, usually because of feelings of isolationism and of negative identity, then we can deny that another group's code is, in any sense, intelligible to us.

Intelligibility is also supported by the linguistic fact of redundancy. For it is the case that our messages are hugely oversubscribed in the attention they are given and the repetition they receive. In normal messages redundancy allows for a good deal of slack in the system. For example, morphological indicators are often redundant because of order, or number markers are redundant because of lexical indicators. In the sentence:

Those three girls were chosen

plural number is indicated in each of the first four words where, for the sake of efficiency, once would be enough. Native-speaking strangers can cope with each other's speech in normal circumstances partly because of such redundancy.

What this means is that there must be some kind of core in common which will allow native speaker 1 and native speaker 2 to agree that their idiolects are sufficiently similar to be regarded as one lect. I shall argue that this type of agreement, a decision of this kind, is heavily dependent on attitude and although there must (in the case of the intelligibility argument) be a modicum of linguistic (which means historical) sharing yet beyond that what seems to matter is that native speaker 1 and native speaker 2 wish to belong to one lect.

The power explanation

And this is where power as a force in its own right becomes important. In situations where one group is politically dominant over another group intelligibility can be claimed and indeed believed. Therefore, when we test for mutual comprehension between groups the power relation appears dominant. Much the same applies to the relation master/patron–servant/client in which it is typically the servant who learns the master's code (Wolff, 1959; see also Chapter 4). Now are the master's code and the servant's code mutually intelligible? The irony is that in some kind of programmatic way their codes are intelligible – strictly in this one-way direction.

Does this mean that speakers are intelligible to one another only because they choose to be so, that it is attitudes alone that matter; and that A and B understand one another, are mutually intelligible if (and only if) they choose to be so? I will answer this in two ways. First of all the negative is certainly true, that is that A and B will not understand one another if they do not wish to do so; at the worst they will not even listen, they will avoid; and at the best they will deliberately misunderstand and impute negative attitudes, and through any interchange allow negative stereotypes to influence what is being heard. For example a Scot might assume that a Southern England English speaker (especially an upper-class English speaker) is putting on airs, being arrogant, superior and so on; and it is that general view that will dominate the interaction. (Equally of course, in similar vein the Englishman will hear the Scot as dour, rude, mean and so on.) In another very familiar way close relatives react to one another's speech in semi-ritualised ways especially when the relationship is unfriendly; thus, the son-in-law will hear what his mother-in-law says to him as always saying the same negative thing; the parent always hears her teenage child making impossible demands. In such situations of negative attitudes messages are never exchanged, only feelings.

So much for the negative situation where we can say that intelligibility does not exist where people do not want it to. What of the reverse case, where people have positive attitudes to one another, is that positive feeling sufficient for them to achieve mutual intelligibility? The answer is really no, except in very trivial ways. A (an English speaker) and B (a Japanese speaker), each monolingual, cannot, however well intentioned, exchange much more than the phatic expressions of goodwill and courtesy which are, in fact, as much paralinguistic as they are linguistic. At the same time, there may be features of some kind of universal pragmatic code which can help to convey certain types of content, for example agreement, approbation, and their opposites, non-linguistically.

I will summarise the discussion on the role of power and of intelligibility in bringing about common languages by suggesting that these two factors are more usefully understood as describing what is going on rather than explaining it. An explanation must be sought elsewhere.

Is language a game?

Let me appeal again to the game analogy asking whether native speakers do combine within a Grammar 2 by virtue of tacit acceptance of playing the same game. The problem with the game analogy for language is that a game is necessarily competitive: the purpose of games is to win, that is the meaning and the only meaning of a game.

Strategy, tactics, cleverness of play, these all contribute to the formal repertoire of the player but the intended end is always the same — to win. Not so with language. Language is cooperative not competitive: neither side is out to win. Instead the purpose of language is communication, that is the exchange of messages and, unlike the unique aim of the game, the messages of language are frequently multivariate. However, games do, of course, require cooperation even though they are about competition and therefore about winning: without cooperation the game cannot be played. This need for cooperation in order to win is particularly evident in special cases of language behaviour such as argument and debate (and the place of winning and of losing in such events).

Does the game analogy explain native speakers' willingness to accept one another's idiolects as similar enough to their own for them to be regarded as 'native' by both parties? While it is true that players in a game accept, while they are engaged in play, the rules, these rules are not their rules, that is they do not relate to a play which the player, has in some sense, internalised. The rules exist only for the sake of the game and are therefore not at all like the rules of Grammar 1. But they do help explain how Grammar 2 acts as a tacit understanding among native speakers because that understanding is not unlike the acceptance that speakers give to the Standard Language. I will come back to that in greater detail.

The case of the native-speaker individual does not differ from language to language. It is one example of the more general case of the group or boundary question. As I have claimed there is no principled way of distinguishing the language of the individual (Grammar 1) from human language, that is universal grammar (Grammar 3). In the same fashion and for essentially the same reason, since the issue is not linguistic but social, there are no principled grounds for discrete determination of people into one or other ethnicity, whether ascribed (for example, race or colour) or attained (for example, religion, language, nationality or culture). The boundary fixed between groups is always indeterminate, artificial and imposed and always crossable. This is not to say of course that boundaries have no reality. Once placed (like bridges, roads, etc.) they cause those they divide, even when self-imposed, to act, behave and believe as if they are different.

The culture analogy

The closest analogy to language is probably culture. Like language, culture is acquired from birth and is probably just as impermeable, so that it becomes difficult in later life completely to switch cultures. Also like language, it is possible to carry multi-membership, both across, that is intra-cultural (so that a person may be both X and Y), and within, that is intercultural (so that being, say, American can also mean being American and Hispanic or American and Black).

A native speaker of a culture (whom we shall refer to as a native cultist or NC) is, exactly as with the native speaker, an individual culture bearer and although the NC is patterned in similar ways (in, for example, cooking or dress) to other members of the tribe, nation or region there will always be individual variation which will not just be random but systematic. Let us say that woman A and woman B both wear a sarong but the design and the method of wearing it differ. Why do I say they belong ('combine' as in our native-speaker discussion) with one another rather than with some other woman C who wears a dress not a sarong but designs it and wears it like A's sarong. What are the criteria, the determining factors that bind A to B and not to C? As with language, culture is complex and there are many categories, many layers that members use to recognise one another and to identify with one another.

And what matters even more for the link with language is that the indeterminacy of culture is evidenced in the ease with which, behaviourally if not declaratively, individuals can belong to different groups and sub-groups which can themselves be part of larger groups. The native cultist then can choose to belong to an indefinite set of groups with whom s/he wishes to identify from time to time and to whom s/he wishes to accommodate.

Grammar as (only) identity

Communities – and languages – are formed then by way of this grouping and regrouping in which the individual identifies with an infinite number of language users with whom s/he chooses to identify; this is the position taken up by extreme positivists. For example, le Page and Tabouret-Keller (1985) provide four definitions of 'a language':

(1)   a supposed property of an individual;
(2)   the actual behaviour of a people – the only kind of language to which we truly have access;
(3)   the linguist's description, using data from Sense 2 performance;
(4)   the layman's appeal to the systems assumed to be inherent in the linguistic behaviour of a community.

For Le Page and Tabouret-Keller (1985) only No. 2 is truly the language ('the only kind of language to which we truly have access'). What this accepts, or rather assumes, is that there is no Grammar 2 at all: it is a fiction invented at each moment as relationships are made and remade. But there are at least two faults with this view. The first is that it is not true that one can accommodate, at all levels, where one chooses; the choices for intelligibility are always limited. The second is that there is not just a fiction about Grammar 2; it has a reality, a social reality of its own which we all in practice acknowledge and rely on. The accommodation view of le Page and Tabouret-Keiler is a serious attempt to make sense of the linguistic units which act in some way as norm providers. But it is nevertheless the case that (even) within a speech community individuals relate, linguistically, more easily to some members than to others; and this is not entirely determined on attitudinal grounds.

There are also linguistic reasons. An English-speaking Scot may relate to Gaelic speakers easily enough in one variety or other of English, or of Scots, but he has no way at all to accommodate to them in Gaelic. Furthermore, speech communities typically contain one or more (at least one) standard languages and it is the standard language which seems to provide the answer we are seeking; the paradigm case for our native speaker combining with another native speaker is a Grammar 2.

Defining the Speech Community

At least three definitions of the speech community have been offered:

(1) a group of people all of whom speak the same language;
(2) a group of people who share critical attitudes about linguistic communities; and
(3) a group of people who exist in the mind of any one individual.

The first of these is a summary statement of the view that speech communities and other communities are homogeneous. This is not only untrue to experience but also to language because it would mean that language could never change. After all, for language change to occur it is necessary for people to be different and for each of their Grammar ls to be different. Equally, it is necessary for individual Grammar ls to change over time. It is this language variation within and between individuals that allows for and reflects language change. I take this for granted and yet at the same time acknowledge a homogeneity that is just not true to reality. However, as long as I recognise that this homogeneity is an appeal to the Standard Language, and as long as I also allow that the Standard must change, then I can bear the over-simplification of the first assertion.

Alternatively, it means that a speech community is made up of only one person which negates the idea of community. Curiously, such an interpretation of the first definition indicates a very close similarity to the third definition. The definition of the latter assumes not a given homogeneity (as in the first) but a constructed homogeneity wherever and whenever intended. Such an assumption about human interaction is not true to the common lack of understanding and sameness in that it is frequently just not possible to communicate with others when we wish to do so. Communication is sometimes claimed to be facilitated by intent, by wanting to communicate. But to define intention solely by success is no way out of the dilemma because it ignores both those who wished to communicate but failed and the successes who may not have had the intent to start with. The third definition leads to a community of one person locked in solipsism into his/her own world, since s/he cannot contemplate any alternative views to his/her own. Such a view is likely in philosophy, politics or religion to lead to megalomania or despair. Now while this stark view of life may be supportable in language it will not serve as a denial of the common sense of the speech community and is of value only as an addition to and a commentary on the acceptance of the notion of speech community.

So I am left with the second definition and indeed this, with all its vagueness, seems the most useful. Communities of all kinds are made up of people who share one or more qualities, views or attributes. Communities of scholars share an interest in and a respect for scholarship; communities of soldiers share an agreement to fight and the discipline that this requires. Communities of a nation normally accept a common attitude towards the law and to the culture(s) of the state. Similarly with language(s): what makes a speech community a community, apart from its geographical unity (which is usual if not essential), is a common acceptance of which language/ code and so forth is to be used for which purpose. This does not mean that every member of the community is capable of controlling all the relevant codes, rather that they acknowledge which is which. Indeed this is tantamount to saying that a speech community is a sociolinguistic entity defined in terms of the basic sociolinguistic questions: who speaks which language to whom and when. Or to saying that the object of study of sociolinguistics is the speech community.

It is not the case that speech communities are fixed. They do not have the basis of a legal contract; members may come and go at will. However, the absence of a legal contract certainly does not mean there is no basis for the existence of the speech community. Indeed there is and it is a linguistic one. And linguistic conventions (we shall use the general term norms to cover both conventions and attitudes as well as rules) are just as firm as laws and carry just as powerful sanctions even if they are not legally enforcable.

Standard Language and Other Norms

A speech community is therefore built up on the attitudes and norms of its members; and we can summarise these norms as being concerned with

language	standard/ dialect
accent	stratification of language use
discourses	appropriate registers
prestige	appropriate pragmatic forms
rhetorics	appropriate conversation styles

Now as I will show shortly, these norming categories approximate very closely indeed to those which I will want to attribute to standard languages. This is not at all surprising given the role of a standard language in the definition and life of a speech community. I wish then to claim that a speech community requires at least one standard language.

Standard language and the concept of norm

I have assumed that the object of my Grammar 2 search is the standard language. So let me now consider to what extent the standard language does represent Grammar 2 and how closely this may relate to any definition of the native speaker I may reach. In so doing I will need to give close attention to the concept of the norm as a defining feature of the standard language.

Saussure, as we saw earlier, provided an explanation for what he regarded as being the goal of linguistics. This was to define the scope of linguistics as being concerned with the system of language, thereby getting away from the obsession of philology with sound change (and hence variation) and, in so doing, to secure for linguistics the (scientific) qualities of stability and structure. Saussure was therefore interested, above all, in system. Saussure put forward his famous trinity of categories: *language* (everything that goes on linguistically in the speech community); *langue* (the system employed) and *parole* (the speech of any one individual). I think it is fair to say that Saussure was more interested in the atypical monolingual community than in multilingual communities. For him langue is what people share – the average of their individual speech differences. Langue for Saussure is, therefore, the linguist's object of attention.

Now the problem seems to have been that Saussure was intending, by *langue*, to mean both system and norm, in other words to argue for *langue* as a norm carrier (exactly what I have been suggesting for Grammar 2) but also as a linguistic system (and therefore, in our terms, also catering for Grammar 3.

This is not strictly possible, as Bartsch (1988) shows. Norms are crucial to any concept of standard language; Bartsch helpfully clarifies a distinction between norms and rules and conventions and we propose to follow her argument. I will also suggest that Saussure's argument is not as vacuous as Bartsch suggests and that a norm definition of standard language will do very well indeed for the *standard* language part if not for the language part.

Correctness

It is refreshing to find that if we follow Bartsch we can account for Grammar 1 becoming Grammar 2 by the establishment of a standard language and then argue that the speakers of Grammar 1 do, in fact, agree to a surrender of their idiolectal individuality by acceptance of a set of norms. Bartsch (1988: 4) states: 'norms are the social reality of the correctness notions ... In this way correctness concepts which are psychic entities have a social reality'. The correctness notions are the 'how to behave notions', similar to all other forms of learnt behaviour: how to ski, drive, play an instrument, dress and so on. What distinguishes language from these other skilled behaviours is that in addition to the psychic entities (knowing whether or not you are doing it well, right and so on) there is the social reality which carries and provides sanctions. The rules which are attributed to language by linguists, those which are constructed for Grammar 2, are, therefore, in part an acknowledgement and a working out of the intricate normative system acquired in taking on a standard language.

And it is important to remember that for Bartsch (and for us) correctness is not restricted to a few shibboleths such as in English: *it's I/me; who/whom; will/shall,* however frequently they may occur in teaching programmes, in primers and as examples of the uselessness of the whole notion of correctness put forward by libertarian descriptivists. Correctness for Bartsch includes the basic means of expression, lexical items, syntactic form, texts, semantic expression and pragmatic correctness. There is no argument here for triviality and no want of indication of the importance for language acquisition of correctness.

Norms are established in terms of central models in speaking and writing; and those models may be individuals or, more likely, élite groups. There is often indignation that this should be the case. The point surely is not that it is this group or that group which provides the models: the point is that some group inevitably will provide them because that group is seen to be desirable to imitate or because it has power. When alternatives are offered they are always from alternative groups who wish to take power from the existing élite and take their place as a new élite. This is the explanation for the advocates of Black English in the USA (also known as Afro-American and Ebonics) and of working-class English in the UK as much as it is of Hindi instead of English in India or of Marathi instead of Hindi in Bombay (and Konkani instead of Hindi in Goa etc.).

Observers of such scenes do occasionally offer a further alternative and that is that instead of there being one standard language or even two, three or four standard languages there should be none and that instead all norms should be individual norms. This is liberty turned into ranterism; and a recipe for total anarchy because in its laudable attempt to replace authority (and self-stigmatising by those who are excluded from standard language membership) by autonomy what it does is to destroy communication. Its show of emancipation is a pretence. Most societies provide some educational means (however inadequate) to give access to the standard language and to that extent they permit an open society, while acknowledging the privileged position of those in the élite. To forego any attempt at a common standard language by abandoning common norms is to give up on community while not improving the lot of those already weak. The applied response in such cases is surely always to improve existing provision towards a greater and more equal unity.

The law analogy

Bartsch uses law as an analogy for language in terms of norms and social acceptance. As she points out, a major difference is the heayy sanction attached to law but more important for our present interest is the fact that it is not necessary to obey the law to acknowledge its authority. Nor is it necessary to know what the law is and, therefore we can break it in ignorance. The law still binds those who break it and those who are ignorant of it because they, too, are part of the community.

The religion analogy

But an even more apposite analogy with language might be that of religion. Let us assume for the argument that religion (some type of religious view, of any kind) is quite basic to human nature. It is after all the case that religion manifests itself in one way or another in most, if not all, human societies. We can argue then that the analogue to the speech community is the religious community (using this term now in a special way) and that the religious community exists not at all because those who belong to it share the same religion but because they understand and share attitudes towards features of religious practice and belief. Examples of viable religious communities might be Catholics and Protestants in Germany or Muslims and Hindus (and Christians and Buddhists) in India.

Like speech communities, religious communities can break down because they cease to share common attitudes and respect, as is seen in some parts of India (Sikhs and Hindus) and in Northern Ireland (Catholics and Protestants).

Analogous to the standard language there is the church, mosque, temple or other religious institution which is set up to carry out and allow for the religious behaviour of its members. Now it is not at all the case that any one church, mosque or temple is homogeneous: all such institutions contain within themselves great differences and yet as long as they survive intact they still maintain a boundary between themselves and other religious bodies. Sometimes they cannot contain the differences: hence the Protestant Reformation and the various subsequent breakaways. Hence, too, the modern schism in the Catholic Church (Archbishop Lefebvre), and the continuing Shiite–Sunni division in Islam. Hence again the concern of the Anglican church for its own stability in face of the increasing demands for the ordination of women including, most recently, into the episcopacy.

Each church exists to represent the beliefs of its adherents and at the same time to cause them to conform. If they do not conform then at times churches have dealt ruthlessly with them; they can be declared heretic; or they can just leave. And as I have shown, in leaving, what they have often done is to establish an alternative church (for example, Methodism from the Church of England). Many such examples have emerged in central and eastern Africa since colonialism. But no church can possibly exist without norms which, in religion, usually have to do with correct beliefs, appropriate rituals and conforming social behaviour. Membership of a church means conforming to its norms in exchange for the communication it provides through shared membership with people whose religious beliefs and valued practices are not too different from one's own. When they are, then tensions do indeed arise and conflict (schisms) occurs or overt sanctions (for example the Inquisition) are brought into play.

There are further comparisons between religion and language. If the church is the standard language and the church member is the native speaker then the priest/minister/lama/rabbi ... the professional holy person is the norm-maker (or at least interpreter for his/her church). The priest in a church then takes on the role assumed for the Standard Language by the teacher, writer, academician and lexicographer. Of course there are differences where the comparisons do not work, largely in the member–native speaker comparison. Native speakers, after all, learn their behaviour very early; church members perhaps later. But, as we shall see, it may be that we will need to revise our ideas of who a native speaker is and of at what stage one can acquire native speakerness. And further it is also the case that in many religions children do, in fact, absorb the religious experience and ambience from their earliest years. And so perhaps even here there is another close relationship.

We do well to ask whether church members need their priests or whether they can act as their own norm interpreters and renewers. The answer surely has to be yes: we have already established that not having academicians (specially appointed members of the Academy as in France and some other countries) does not mean that English lacks norms: others take on the role or are given it part-time as it were. In other words the community itself (speech, religious) can provide support for its members in preserving and adhering to its norms. And there are examples of religious communities (for example the Quakers) where there are no priests but which provide a very strong community structure both in the spiritual and in the social life of its members.

It is interesting (in terms of our earlier discussion of the danger of handing over to every native speaker, every member, the responsibility for his/her own norms) to note the same danger in religion. As long as individuals are prepared to establish para norms with one another, that is by establishing a consensual standard language, then such freedom works for language; and it works equally well and equally so for religion. But what this means is a standard language (a church) with a set of non-professional norm-givers (priests) who, in practice, maintain a shadow standard language (a shadow church). What is out of the question is for individuals in religion or in language to negotiate afresh with every new member, and with every old one at each new encounter, how communication is to be achieved, how worship is to be performed. Where the analogy no doubt does break down is that religion, unlike language, can be practised alone as eremites and desert fathers have shown. No doubt it would be equally possible for a native speaker to communicate always in her/his way only with God, but even then it is surely true that individual religious experiences are viewed as somehow atypical. They are seen as peculiarly mystical rather than religious and it does seem that religion is always viewed as an activity to engage in with one's fellows, in a social context.

I have noted that there is always difference within a standard language as within a church and perhaps in some cases more internal than external difference. For example it is likely that some High Anglicans are more like some Catholics than they are like Evangelical Anglicans. Similarly with standard languages: it is probably the case that some creolised speakers who claim membership of standard language A are closer to speakers of standard language B than they are to some speakers of standard language A. (For example a speaker might claim to identify as an Urdu speaker and yet know little or no Urdu and be linguistically closer, say, to Bengali.) It must be remembered we are here more concerned with attitudes and identities than with linguistic features.

Norm acceptance

I would maintain that the norms of the standard language are not distributed equally, that is not everyone performs them equally well and some will know them very little. This leads inevitably to misunderstanding, to sanctions, to stigmatising and so on. But there is also present a good deal of give and take, meaning that members do, in practice, give permanent importance to membership and accept that within membership there will be variation. Variation can then be regarded as acceptable, eccentric, lovable, human or whatever, but somehow tolerable as long as that variation is not used as an excuse for abandoning the norm or for setting up new ones. (Australia provides an example of such a difference between the reality of continuation of the anglo-celtic cultural tradition and the myth of multiculturalism). Native speakers in this regard behave in a sensibly ethnomethodological way, 'adhocking' with one another as far as possible and assuming (with good faith) serious intentions to communicate, guessing at or predicating meanings and making every common-sense effort to seek to understand. To this extent it is indeed my assumption that native speakers do recognise one another and they do this through an explicit and demonstrated acceptance of and regard for the norms, however faultily they may be applied.

Language norm accepters choose to identify with the norms. In some cases the acceptance may be largely symbolic. I would cite the Celtic languages especially after the nationalist revivals of the 1960s and 1970s. For example in the Census for 1971 for Scotland and Wales the answers to the language question:

Do you speak Welsh?
Do you speak Gaelic?

showed an increase of monolinguals, which was surely counterintuitive. Increases in the number of bilinguals, Welsh–English or Gaelic–English, were certainly explicable because of the identification of nationalism with language, especially in Wales. But it did not make sense that there had been a monolingual switch from English to Welsh or from English to

Gaelic on such a scale. What the 1971 Census returns showed then was not a falsification of the figures but a demonstration of loyalty to Welsh and to Gaelic rather than to English (HMSO, 1971).

Norm transience

Bartsch writes relevantly of norm beneficiaries and norm victims and the West Indian Antiguan writer Jamaica Kincaird in *A Small Place* (1988) writes with appropriate passion of her inability to describe the crime of colonial history except 'in the language of the criminal who committed the crime'. A related example is that of Hindi–Urdu. These two languages are essentially politico-religious names given to the same language, now of course slightly differentiated by Sanskrit loans in Hindi and Persian/Arabic loans in Urdu and, more importantly, differentiated by the use of two distinct scripts, Nagari for Hindi and Arabic for Urdu. It is therefore loyalty to the implied norms of one or the other language which makes a speaker claim to be a Hindi speaker or an Urdu speaker. I have suggested that norms will diverge in the due effluxion of time and that divergence will be increased by the use, in the case of Hindi–Urdu, of the two classical languages as sources of new vocabulary and of the separate scripts.

But the Hindi–Urdu divide also reflects a strong need to identify separately. This may suggest that in other situations of political (or other ethnic) conflict, such as the former German political division into the two Germanies, there is less need or wish to demonstrate such a division perhaps because, apart from a possibly transient political division, there is no potent ethnicity (like religion in the Hindi–Urdu case) to appeal to as a strong reason for attaching to it a further linguistic divide.

Growth of nationalism

Brass (1974) notes in all situations of emerging nationalism the importance of the existence of one central symbol which can be appealed to (religion in Hindi/Urdu, language in the Celtic societies). To this other symbols can then attach themselves in order to make the case for autonomy and separation stronger (language now in Hindi/Urdu; culture perhaps for the Celtic societies but nothing for the former two Germanies or indeed the two Koreas, the two Vietnams).

Brass further points to the importance of a mobilising élite who will take over the leadership, give direction and encourage the emergence of a separate set of norms (state, religion, language). When existing norms no longer serve the interaction purpose for which they were intended, then they are abandoned for new norms:

> norms come about when certain recurrent problems of adjusting actions between partners in interaction emerge. Norms provide solutions to these problems. (Bartsch, 1988: 104)

Standard Language as an Ideal

We have argued that a standard language exists more as an idealisation than as a detailed description. 'This is how to do it, isn't it?' is the typical appeal to membership. It is the case that descriptions (grammars, dictionaries, etc.) do follow on but they are always out of date. Hence the stock answer to the question: 'How does one say A?' 'Can you say X?' is 'Let's look it up'; 'I'm not sure, I think it can be said in different ways'; or 'I think you can say X or Y'. The standard-language adherent, in other words, is a member who belongs to the standard-language club, plays its game well or badly but rarely has any idea what its rules or norms are, even though s/he can usually perform the ones that are relevant with some degree of success.

Criticism has been levelled at standard languages (Rosen & Burgess, 1980; Trudgill, 1975; Bex & Watts, 1999; but see Honey, 1997, and Davies, 2000) on the grounds of improper discrimination against those from non-élite (and non-standard) backgrounds. As we have noted before, this argument is usually fallacious since it wishes to exchange one standard language for another and not really to give power to individuals. Nevertheless the argument about discrimination against the powerless is worth treating seriously. This is not, however, an issue of making life better for the disadvantaged, because that is not in question. Rather it is a question of whether any language change can bring about such amelioration. What is surely important is for all groups to be given as much access as possible to the standard language. At the same time consideration must be given on structural grounds as to just how necessary the standard language really is for all functions including education. 'Obviously' says Bartsch (1988: 122) 'for many occupational functions fluency in the standard language is not necessary.'

However, it is just not possible to dispense with a standard language and therefore with norms:

> Successful communication is only possible when people agree in means of communication and their use. Presupposing that all members

of a linguistic community always agree in this way is a simplification which leads to mistaken reality. (Bartsch, 1988: 130)

Norms which are imposed rather than assumed are prescriptive: a standard language is obviously more readily acquired if the norms have been assumed. But where there is fierce loyalty either to a dialect (for example Black English Vernacular) or to a first language (for example Polish), the norms required for acceptance for Standard English or Russian may simply not be acceptable. Then conflict arises.

What is needed is to give authority, validity, to dialects and treat the standard language as essentially a stylistic shift rather than as in any way a cognitive change. But, as is well known, this is more easily said than done.

However, it is too easy to give way to the feeling that nothing can be done, that identities are somehow permanently locked into opposition. No doubt some of the long-term conflicts (Lebanon, Palestine/Israel, Northern Ireland) give support to that view. However in the case of language, as Bartsch (1988: 147) points out,

> language not only serves human action and interaction ... it is also subjected to human action and control, as far as specific linguistic norms are concerned. To this extent language is manageable. This insight is the basis for all language planning.

Indeed it is possible to act upon language in such a way that norms can be shifted, if only marginally. The current interest in language and gender is a case in point (see Chapter 4 and also Zuengler, 1989).

Language evolution

There is no reason to view language as different from other human behaviours: it, too, is subject to the processes of evolution. As such it can be argued (see, for example, Dawkins, 1986) that development in language (including presumably deliberate development, through language planning) is selective in terms of producing more efficient systems. This does not mean more suitable for one environment, because such species typically become over selected, rather it means a more robust selection for more general use. In language terms this is likely to advantage languages which are more easily adaptable to writing and to speaking; to printing and to script; to electronic and to manual production; to transmission orally across distance and through noise and at speed. Such selective criteria are likely to be to the advantage of the more rather than the less general, the less rather than the more specific, the more syntactic and the less morphological and so on.

What is surely at issue is language change, one of the central concerns of linguistics. Because this is inevitable (without regard to the direction of that change) and happening at all times, language is necessarily in a state of imbalance. This is another way of repeating that all Grammar Is are different and therefore it is necessary for there to be implicit tacit agreement as to a common language, that is an acceptance of the norms of the standard language.

Implicit (standard) languages[1]

If it is the case that standard languages are not all official, well known and, usually, those associated with writing, such as Chinese, Sanskrit, Greek, Latin, Arabic, English, then it must also be the case that an implicit (standard) language exists even when there is no codification (Haugen, 1966). It is difficult to provide evidence for this assumption since, by definition, it is only those (standard) languages for which codification exists that can be regarded as standard languages. But there are even today non-written 'languages' which occupy the role Jespersen accorded to common languages: in other words, the fact of their commonality means that their users agree implicitly on norms for their use. And this is the clue to what so far has been a missing element in our whole argument: the status and acceptance of dialects. It must surely be the case that dialects, although not formally standardised, do in fact draw on a set of norms, however vague, for dialect members. There will exist no norms for writing and probably none for public speaking since it is often a major distinction between (standard) language and dialect that a dialect becomes a language through standardisation in order to take on the public and formal roles of writing and speaking to non-intimates. This is why it is just not possible to develop public (that is permanent, objective, accountable) activities like education, science or research without a standard language. It also helps explain why, when there is a non-written oral tradition, the language acceptable for such activities is very conservative since 'How to do it' is enshrined only in the memory of those who are the professional tellers. And presumably we see the influence of this tradition on holy books like the *Quran* and the *Vedas*. This conservative tradition has also influenced attitudes to the languages as a whole.

When a language, whether it be officially standard or not, loses speakers it can start to decay or die (for example many Australian aboriginal languages, the Celtic languages or the languages of the American Indians). In such situations what tends to happen (and the case of Welsh is very clear here) is that structural and functional loss take place without compensation within that language, since compensation is, in fact, occurring in other codes. Thus a Welsh speaker who may find s/he can cope with close family interaction in Welsh will feel ignorant about how to communicate in Welsh in more public situations but may be able to cope in those public situations perfectly satisfactorily in English.

Role reversal

Where there is such function loss for individuals there is a sense of shame in their command of the language and this can lead to curious role reversal.

Case Study 1

For example I know of a highly educated Indian whose English is native-speaker-like and who says English is his best language. He also says, however, that his first language is a version of Hindustani and is very much a family code. However, since he is himself Moslem, it is to Urdu that he turns in his search for a code model. He finds increasingly in non-family situations where Urdu is being used that even though his dialect approximates to Standard Urdu he feel inhibited and foolish and somewhat ignorant if he makes use of his own code. And so he tends to interact in such situations in English.

Given the continuing role of English in India it so happens that in such situations his interlocutors will, in fact, also be as much at home in English as they are in Urdu. And this may be, in part, the clue. Since Urdu is so symbolically tied to Islam and religion and non-Hinduism the norms its adherents accept are heavily prescriptive towards themselves and to one another. Deviation implies a negative attitude towards Urdu and cannot be tolerated. Now in the case of English this is not so. English does not stand (or no longer stands) for a particular symbolic position and therefore is much more tolerant of Englishes, however non-standard or of different standards.

No doubt my informant would be hoist with his own petard were outsiders to attempt to learn and use his family's version of Hindustani since that too would be making a statement about membership this time of a small and exclusive group; and it would not be tolerated. Small (and declining) language groups are quite intolerant of attempts to learn their language, which is seen as a claim on membership. Learners are often rebuffed by native speakers with incomprehension. The surface explanation is that only native speakers speak this language; but the deeper explanation must be that outsiders are not welcomed into membership of exclusive groups. Which must mean in such tightly knit groups (like the Hindustani-speaking family) that language and culture are indeed quite closely associated with one another. The example of our informant raises again the issue of semilingualism but in this case the resolution seems clear. My informant does indeed lack proficiency in Urdu (and his version of Hindustani may also be lacking, at least functionally so since he uses it for a narrow range of purposes) but he is not semilingual since what he cannot do in one code (Urdu or Hindustani) he does in English. In any case, if semilingualism exists, it must involve speakers who are incompetent overall without compensation, and we have argued that no such state is possible on logical grounds, except for pathological states.

Semilingualism?

Now the case of language loss in the individual which is compensated for by another code is common. The problem is the individual's and, while s/he no longer has a capacity in his/her declining language, s/he could recover it since there is a continuing speech community in which that code (in our example Urdu) is in full use. It would be possible for my informant to acquire that code and become fluent and therefore productive in it.

But there is also the other case of language loss in which, like the examples I quoted earlier (such as Australian aborigines) the number of speakers declines to a point at which not just the speaker but the language itself is no longer productive. Nobody, for example, knows how to borrow and nativise a new term or how to create exponents of grammatical categories such as in English where the extremely productive less as in coffee-less can be attached to any noun. This sort of automatic knowledge would disappear in addition to the large-scale functional disappearance of everything but the close familial. Dressler and Wodak-Ledolter (1977) describe the process of language decay and language death for disappearing languages with clarity. In such cases it becomes increasingly difficult to recover productivity, although there is a logical problem as to why this should be so as long as there remain at least two speakers.

It is interesting, therefore, to observe attempts at reproductivising a language. The case of Finnish is sometimes referred to, but it appears that Finnish vitality in rural areas never disappeared. A better example is that of Hebrew. No doubt, once the attempt has begun (and Hebrew is such a special case that it may not be a useful precedent for deliberate action) and a new generation is rising for whom this 'artificial' code is their only language, then what happens is that for all productive uses they, the new generation, take over.

This is the explanation for the way in which, in a creole continuum, development beyond the basilect towards an acrolect takes place. It is always the next generation who regularise their language and, as it were, take over from their parents and move the basilect on to some more comprehensive system. And in this way children influence their parents who then adopt the new systematizations made by their children (Bartsch, 1988: 201).

But to return to language loss in the case of Australian aborigines, we must once again ask the semilingualism question. And once again the answer must be no: apart from the very rare and remote examples of people who have no contact outside their moiety and who are left to die off without outside contact, and for whom it may be the case that their linguality declines and shrinks through lack of use (though my logical problem still remains). Apart from that, in all other cases there is language shift: speakers have overlapped with and into other codes.

Case study 2

Let me then once again consider the particular case of semilingualism. And again let us quote an example from another Indian informant, a woman. Here, as in the first case study, my informant's own English is native-speaker-like. She too has adopted English which is, without question, her language of choice and her best language.

This time my informant is from Goa, from a Portuguese-speaking family. Her family adopted English when she was a child and she has one younger sister who has no Portuguese. But Portuguese was for the rest of the family their familiar language. The local language in Goa is Konkani; and our informant always spoke Konkani as a child but only with servants and other 'inferiors'. It was the language of the streets and the bazaar but never of any formal or 'superior' activity. To that extent at that time (my informant is now in her mid-forties) Portuguese and Konkani were in a diglossic (High–Low) relation with one another. As an adult living in Delhi my informant finds that when she uses Konkani with neighbours (all Goan) who tend to be immigrant Goans who came to Delhi for work and have no Portuguese, they invariably reply in English, not in Konkani.

How can this be? The answer has already been given; they regard Konkani as the language of servants and although they may have come to Delhi as servants, they have now become socially mobile and as a mark of mobility have abandoned Konkani, not just with our informant, in public situations, but also with their own families. There they have switched to English. The fact that such Goans are also typically Christian may have a bearing on this choice of language. That is, if not Konkani, which Christians in Goa may use, then certainly not another Indian language (for example Marathi, Hindi, Gujerati) which would indicate some kind of non-Christian allegiance. This parallels our other informant and the Hindi–Urdu distinction. The informant says:

> My neighbours' problem is that their English is quite unsatisfactory, inadequate both structurally and functionally. Their children know no Konkani, since they live in Delhi and have received no parental input, and their English is limited, since again the parental input in English can only be partial. These children are semilingual.

Let me consider both parents and children. First, the parents. Are they semilingual? Does this not take us back to the situation of the first informant and his inadequate Urdu? Aren't these Konkani-speaking parents (with inadequate English) in the same position? They may not use Konkani but they could if it were necessary if, for example, they were to visit Goa. (The situation is no doubt complicated by the number of generations they have been away.) And when they think, inasmuch as thinking is language based, which language do they think in? We would expect it to be Konkani. It is also likely that when the parents speak to one another they do so in Konkani, even though they may never address their children in Konkani. Such mismatches in bilingual situations arevery common. I must conclude that the parents are not semilingual. Remember what semilingual means (Skutnabb-Kangas, 1981; Martin-Jones & Romaine, 1986). It means that the individual has inadequate linguistic resources.

What about the children? Are they semilingual? They have little or no Konkani. I will ignore what in their case may be important, which is that living in Delhi it is very likely that from other children they will acquire one or other Indian language, Hindi, Marathi, Gujerati. But I will just assume that their only alternative to Konkani is English. It is indeed difficult to visualise a setting in which there is no other code used locally or in which the target language, in this case, English, is not used locally. I seem to have got myself into a logical dilemma which may be the answer to my question.

But still, for the sake of the argument, let me continue to assume that these non-Konkani-speaking children's only alternative is English, and indeed in certain confined situations this may be possible. Are they semilingual? There are three answers to the question:

(1) The first is the creole continuum answer which we have already dealt with and which points out that the children themselves regularise

their language, the creole. That creole may not be Standard English but it is a language. And they are therefore not semilingual.

(2) The second is the typical acquisition-from-peers answer by which these children, who will certainly be attending school in English, acquire English from peers and teachers. No doubt in some cases this may be building on the basilect which is what they bring from home (although even then their creole continuum process of regularisation will surely have begun). But it is English that they are acquiring, whether creolised or not. Again it may not be Standard English, but it is English and a language. And they are not semilingual.

(3) The third is the one I have already rejected – that they are also acquiring the codes in their neighbourhood and so gain a proficiency in at least one of these before their English starts to take off. Again then they have at least one language and are not semilingual.

These children do indeed have a problem which shows up in terms of educational disadvantage, that is true. It may also be the case that they have inadequate English (for it is their English that is pointed to as the problem). What is called a linguistic and cognitive problem is, in fact, an educational problem (see Scribner & Cole, 1981). And what is called semi-lingualism is, in fact, an inadequate command of formal and public English in a situation where what is required is Standard or (standard) English. Again then we have a situation comparable to that of our first informant, the Hindustani/Urdu speaker. His Hindustani has the same sort of stigmatised relation to Urdu that these children's English has to Standard English.

Standard Language and (Standard) Language

I propose that a standard code of some kind can be found in all societies, whether literate or not. Such a code – let us call it 'a (standard) language' – provides the norms that make an organised society (including patterns of interaction) possible. A Standard Language is then simply a codified (standard) language. This codification includes the classical processes of selection, elaboration and acceptance. Lack of acceptance produces conflict over norms and uncertainty as to action; but however that may inhibit individual decision, there is always a Standard language available for use. In the cases of both a (standard) language and a Standard Language but particularly in the latter case, as we have observed before, the variety of choices is more apparent than real. We are here thinking both of choices among parallel options and of choices that are too far outside the average for the Standard Language to have so far absorbed them. This is obviously the case in terms of two or more competing Standards (say British and American English) where it may not be clear to a speaker of one whether or not a feature is governed by the others' norms.

In the case of putative standards, say Scottish English and English English, the solution sometimes taken is precisely to claim an alternative Standard, for example Scottish English, and insist that this has its own set of discrete norms. Such a claim will have implications if accepted, in various applied ways such as examinations, publishing, international communication (which one to use). But in the case of Scottish and English English or British and American English the reality is that that the norms shared are so all embracing and those not shared so few that there is really no danger of loss of intelligibility in either spoken or written English; even in writing it is not a problem to read a text which conforms to the norms of a standard which is not one's own except of course in terms of assumed background knowledge (and possible negative attitude). But that can equally well be a problem with an unfamiliar text written in the standard to which one conforms. Which probably means that there is a composite English Standard which combines with a flexible enough degree of tolerance all the Englishes reckoned to be old Standards: British, including Scottish, Irish, American, Canadian, Australian, New Zealand (Quirk, 1987). There is, in fact, a range of standard use which is acceptable: and this is true also for the alternative case where individual (or small group, such as a family, like my informant on Hindustani) use is outside the usual set of choices. It is then surely a matter of degree of difference: and the tolerance of Standard Languages for the amount of difference that can be allowed within the normal range is likely to differ markedly. As we have seen: very far for English, very little for Welsh.

As well as a range of acceptance, a Standard Language also has a model to which it attaches itself, sometimes one individual and his/her own language use, sometimes a small group, an élite. Sometimes an alternative informal standard may be promoted by some disadvantaged group who are excluded from participation in normal society. Such groups may create their own social and linguistic norms. Giles and Powesland (1975) have claimed that there are in the UK working-class youth language norms based perhaps on some pop group model; young blacks in the US and gay societies also show similar norm creation which is not far from the creation of a secret language. All Standard Language members are therefore nearer to or further from the model but all are accepted as members. When, therefore, a member is asked the obvious question: 'How do you say this in English?'; the answer is often 'This is what I (think I) say' or 'Let me ask my friend, colleague, wife, husband'. This is just what Daniel Jones (1917) said he did with his *Pronouncing Dictionary*, that he used his own speech and when in doubt he asked his brother. There is nothing to be ashamed of in our dependence in this way on role models: after all they exist elsewhere in cultural patterns. And what I am referring to here is that chimera of intuition, because what the inculcation, the full acceptance, of norms really means is that the speaker is able to make judgements about whether or not items are acceptable and grammatical.

But is it only the Standard Language for which this is true? This intuition is indeed about Grammar 2 (that is the Standard Language) but there is a sense in which Grammar 1 can be subsumed within the Grammar 2 range. Intuitions then are also available for those areas of Grammar 1 that overlap with Grammar 2. But what about other parts of Grammar 1, is intuition available there too? Again, the answer must be yes, but always subject in some sense to group accord, thus: 'Yes I think I can say that but I'm not sure, I'll ask my sister'; 'Yes I can say that but I doubt if you can'; and so on. And in nearly all such responses the appeal is to the group, the individual informant is saying that such and such a use is grammatical or acceptable in a Standard Language or a (standard) language.

But there are examples where the informant has no range on which to call, where the example is only his/hers, where idiolect stands alone. Does intuition play a part here too? The answer again must be yes; that in terms of the rules of Grammar 3 there are regular possibilities which any Grammar 1 is likely to follow. What the informant in such a case is doing (if his/her imagination or conceptualisation can be prodded thus far) is to do precisely what it is we have decided creole continuum children do, they regularise their language. And so where there is a gap, if the informant can be given the necessary means of explaining or performing, there is a way to indicate how the gap might be filled. Of course the reality of parallels still exists in that two such informants might well close the gap in different ways. But that simply adds a further dimension to the notion of Standard Language range.

Intuition and the Standard Language

Where does this intuition come from? Two sources suggest themselves: the first is the norms of Grammar 2 to which we have already referred. The second is the resources of Grammar 3 and although we do not wish to commit ourselves at all in the argument as to the reality of universal grammar, nevertheless there is no doubt that the existence of a language faculty with which all humans are born would go a long way to explaining just how it is we can have intuitions about our own idiolect in addition to those we have about the Standard Language. However, we do need to retain our common sense about the 'adhocking' of all Standard Languages and (standard) languages. What Standard Languages do (just as with law and religion) is to provide a commonality but not a homogeneity. This is why it makes sense to speak of norms rather than of rules which the Standard Language member accepts.

The exclusive concentration on rules, while it would seem to allow individuals greater licence to use their own norms, would not in fact be possible since

(a)   it would lead to non communication; and
(b)   it assumes, through complete identity of rules, a homogeneous speech community once again.

In other words (as with Le Page & Tabouret-Keller, 1985) the attempt to escape homogeneity brings me right back in a full circle. As Bartsch (1988: 293) points out, the importance in community of norms must not be trivialised and deflected by foolish or tendentious concentration on particular vacuous and unimportant examples:

> that sometimes minor norms are the object of undue attention should not be used to discredit the basic attitude and the whole endeavour of language cultivation at which a linguistic community as a whole works and for which some people feel more responsible that others, and for which even a great number of people are appointed and paid by the community.

A language community is not given but, like other communities, has to be created, worked at and maintained. There are no given rules for such communities (certainly no inherent ones): but there are norms and these, like laws, must be upheld and, when describable, can be changed. Those who accept the norms of a Standard Language as members must, as with other organised activities, accept the responsibility of membership. We have argued that, again as with other types of membership, it is in the interests of everyone that members should seek conformity that is, in this case, mutual understanding though not necessarily agreement.

Further, we have argued that members are prepared on the basis of their 'membership' to give the benefit of the doubt to other members, to guess and predict and generally take in good faith what is said as serious or potentially meaningful. Given such an in-good-faith approach, given the power of such an ethnomethodological-like approach to the business of communicating (the basic assumption of which is: what s/he is saying is meaningful unless I find overwhelming counter evidence) why then does intra Standard Language communication ever go wrong? Because of course it does. We list some of these problems (following Bartsch, 1981: 326) but would comment that in most of these cases it is not so much the actual code that is the problem but rather something else which is triggered by a norm violate which would in all other situations probably be ignored:

(1) A norm conflict and misunderstanding can arise in an interaction between a native speaker and a learner usually triggered by lack of similar cultural assumptions. For example:

> **Native speaker:** 'I like your coat'
> **Learner:** 'Please take it; it's yours!'

(2) A norm conflict can arise because the participants are in an unequal power relationship for example in an interaction between immigrant parents and their foreign born children. For example:

> parental advice being ignored by teenage child where the cultural norm for the parent but not for the child is that advice is equivalent to a command.

(3) A norm conflict can arise in a situation where the 'same' community using the 'same' Standard Language may have quite distinct norms in some areas of life. A currently much discussed example would be the attempt by females to gain success in careers which have been male dominated. For example:

> the Anglican Church provides an interesting paradox over the disputed inclusion of women both in the priesthood and in language use. The paradox is that the male-dominated language is held by conservatives as really meaning both sexes; but in terms of indicators of priesthood to refer to males only. To hold both views must be illogical. To hold the second but not the first could be held to be obscurantist The paradox however remains.

(4) A conflict can arise because the strategies attached to the same norms are just different and may be opposed, for example, politeness may be realised in different ways by different strata in the community. For example:

> The English person's 'Would you mind not smoking?' might be regarded by some Scots as hypocritical while the Scottish equivalent, 'Don't smoke!' might be thought rude.

(5) Conflict may arise when (as in writing or public speaking) the audience may be composed of a variety of the subgroups previously included. It is difficult to cite a case which will be multiply ambiguous but perhaps a narrowly ritualised utterance might be, perhaps something connected with sport or the pub. What this suggests is that the more restricted/ritualised the more narrow the shared community.

In all these cases while it is indeed norms that are being violated it is also the case that the reason for triggering their violation is external to the language itself:

> We have, at least presently, no method to decide whether two speakers of a language have the same linguistic competence, in the sense that they have reconstructed the same competence grammar. But we know what it means that a social rule or norm is the same for two or more speakers ... We merely have to study their practice. (Bartsch, 1988: 182)

Relevance to Applied Linguistics

The applied linguistics relevance of Chapter 7 is again very clear. It is to the continuing debate on norms, rules and correctness in first language (L1) English teaching. (The fact that we refer to English solely here is because it has recently aroused so much controversy and debate; but the argument holds good for all languages.) The criticism of contemporary English teaching must be placed in the more general attack on standards of English. Responsibility for maintaining standards is sometimes allocated to an academy. As we have seen English has no academy. And so the obvious social institution to blame is education. What is claimed by the critics of present day standards is that they have fallen. No evidence other than anecdotal is cited. The Assessment of Performance Unit (APU, 1984) which was set up by the Department of Education and Science in the 1970s to monitor standards over time could find no evidence that standards (usually measured in terms of literacy) were worse than they had been (Bex & Watts, 1999). They also had no way of showing that they had improved: hence the felt need to set up such an organisation. The criticisms, however, continued about English standards and two committees set up in the 80s reported their findings on the state and needs of English teaching in England and Wales (DES, 1988a, b, 1989).

What the discussion in Chapter 7 suggests is that linguists have not always been as sensible in their pronouncements about education as they might have been, hence opening themselves, and linguistics, to cheap attacks (Honey, 1985, 1997; Davies, 1984b).

It must be our position, from an applied linguistic point of view, that native speakers need encouragement and improvement in their control of their own standard language. They do not learn it by growing, like Topsy. And for the skills of the written standard they need special skills and training. Some of the reported linguists' remarks seem to suggest that there is no consensus about a standard and that a standard does not matter. This, in our terms, is an abandonment of Grammar 2 for Grammar 1 and is a recipe for social chaos!

We therefore have a curious clinical situation. The diagnosis is correct, the critics are correct. But they always were correct. It is not that standards are lower now than they were. Rather that standards were always low. Of course they need to be improved, they always did. There again the critics are wrong. For it is not because the children lack grammar that their standards are low. What is lacking is a proper education in the rhetoric, registers, discourses and resources of the language, that is the norms and how to break them. If grammar, overt, explicit, is needed at all it is the teachers who need it. This is where the critics are right but this is not what they mean.

Summary

In this chapter I have argued that the native speaker's relation to language is similar to the native cultist to culture. Knowledge is observed in automaticity of behaviour, whether linguistic or cultural. Again, in a similar way, language is made up of varieties just as culture is made up of subcultures. The speech community we noted is in part made up of groups who share a set of common attitudes and norms to one or more standard languages. Norms are crucial both to the speech community and to the standard language in that they are shared by members whose acceptance of norms leads to the creation of a standard language. Norms are importantly symbolic in the sense that members accept them even without using or applying them. I argued that native speakers always create a (standard) language even where there is no official Standard Language. The native speaker also recognises when norm violation occurs to his/her Standard Language. We also argued that semilingualism is not acceptable as a concept linguistically or psychologically.

In Chapter 8, I consider the politicisation of the concept native speaker and, in particular, the arguments from post-colonialism and from the research into World Englishes. I conclude that hegemony of the standard language is decided as much by those who regard themselves as oppressed as by their oppressors. This, of course, is the nature of hegemony but it needs to be seen as a matter of perception.

Note

1. By (standard) language I mean a prestige, but non-codified, dialect. See Bloomfield (1927), and p. 186 below.

Chapter 8
Losing One's Language

The art of losing isn't hard to master. (Bishop, 1983)

The telling has not been easy. One has to convey in a language that is not one's own the spirit that is one's own. One has to convey the various shades and omissions of a certain thought movement that looks maltreated in an alien language. I use the word 'alien'; yet English is not really an alien language to us. It is the language of our intellectual make-up – like Sanskrit or Persian was before – but not of our emotional make-up. We are all instinctively bilingual, many of us writing in our own language and English. We cannot write like the English. We should not. We cannot write only as Indians. (Rao, 1938: vii)

Négritude

Individuals and groups in transition occasioned by migration, colonialism or demographic disaster are threatened by the loss of their community language(s). As Fishman (1967) demonstrates, speech communities need a stable language situation. Such stability can be found in multilingual speech communities, just as much as in monolingual ones (if any exist). What matters is that form and function are clearly linked. Uncertainty as to which language or dialect to use in which situation is unsettling and eventually impeding to communication and threatening to a sense of identity. It is, therefore, not surprising that transition is commonly treated as a temporary state and a switch to the dominant code in the new situation is a common choice. But that choice, whether taken or simply contemplated, carries a cost. For making that choice may imply the loss of the home language. Not necessarily a complete loss: the old home language may be, often is, retained by individuals and families but it cannot have the status and the significance it once had – not public use, not easy neighbourhood (including shopping and other routine transactions). Altogether, there is guilt and sorrow at leaving the old (ways, country, culture, language); above all a poignant sense of loss. It is to this sense of loss that post-colonialism speaks. This sense of loss is widespread, extending from nationalist sensitivities in the older colonies of England — Scotland, Wales and Ireland — to the ethnic minority migrants such as Sikhs, Kurds, Berbers for whom partial maintenance of two home languages may be the choice they make or the choice they would like to have when facing the daily imperative of mastering the host language, English, German, French, Arabic, Persian etc.

The anguish of loss that Aimé Césaire (1956: 115) and his fellow francophone 'négritude' writers expressed was primarily a response to what they saw as the theft of their identity as African or Black:

> Ma négritude n'est pas une pierre, sa surdité ruée contre la clameur
>   du jour
>   ma négritude n'est pas une taie d'eau morte sur l'oeil mort de la terre
>   ma négritude n'est ni une tour ni une cathedrale
>   elle plonge dans la chair rouge du sol
>   elle plonge dans la chair ardente du ciel
>   elle troue l'accablement opaque de sa droite patience.
>   'Cahier d'un retour au pays natal'

This angry distress was, it appears, not directed at the language take-over; their primary complaint was not that the French language had replaced their own mother tongues, but that they had lost something more profound. After all, through French they had become citizens of France, 'assimilé and évolue'. There is a paradox here; they were, it seemed, content to declare their négritude in standard metropolitan French, no Ngugi-like return to an indigenous mother tongue for them (see later). And they were highly successful products of the French civilising mission (the mission civilisatrice) and so had become French in a way that was never possible for an anglophone African (indeed for any non-white colonial) to 'become' British. Leopold Sédar Senghor, first President of the independent Senegal, had been a member of the Senate of France and legal draughtsman of the Third Constitution of the French State. And yet they felt this loss of négritude, it was more a loss of identity than of language (see Chapter 4). With hindsight we may speculate that part of their sense of anomie was linguistic. But it remains paradoxical (or just human) that in their successful acceptance of Frenchness there co-existed a profound regret for losing something fundamental to their sense of themselves. No doubt it was a yearning for lost innocence, a romantic longing. Perhaps it had never existed, but it had been their heritage and what in part they wished to assert was that they now had a new heritage of which it was right to be proud. They were people between two worlds.

Abiola Irélé (1964: 11) writes:

the capital point about the movement [négritude] [is] its ideological implication. The black poet's descent into himself is an effort to disalienate his being and to re-establish a concordance with a distinct essence. For this reason he reconstitutes this essence as much as he can from the remains in him of the African heritage.

Again a paradox: while, as Irélé also notes, the act of writing for these poets required them to carry out a systematic reversal of values 'beginning from the very vehicle of expression through which [they] were obliged to transmit their experience: the French language' (p. 10), their ideological need to create a sense of Africanness compelled them to seek a vehicle of expression that linked them across the continent and left no option of an African language for that purpose. There was really no choice but to make use of one or other colonial language: French, English or Portuguese.

How unlike the early African anglophone writers! When asked about his concern for négritude, Wole Soyinka, the Nobel laureate, replied that he was not concerned, for him there was no loss. Can a tiger, he asked, lose its tigritude? Later (as we have mentioned) losing became salient, notably with the writer James Ngugi (Ngugi wa'Thiong'o) who decided in mid-career that he would switch from writing in English to writing in Kikuyu, his first language: 'The bullet was the means of the physical subjugation. Language was the means of the spiritual subjugation' (Ngugi, 1986: 9; quoted in Punter, 2000: 17).

It has been argued that Chaucer's decision to make English his medium (in, for example, *The Canterbury Tales*) in place of the Latin and Norman French he had previously used was instrumental in the acceptance of English as a language for public affairs in 14th century England. Perhaps Ngugi's decision will affect Kikuyu in the same way. The numbers who read Kikuyu are small but then the number in Chaucer's day who could read English were also small. What the francophone and the early anglophone writers tell us is that language is a means and not an end, but they do this in different ways. For the francophones the fact that they were writing in French did not seem to matter — what mattered for them was identity. For the anglophones to write in English had nothing to do with their sense of Africanness, of négritude. For them, it seems, language and identity were distinct — the same conclusion as the francophones but for a different reason. Or, as the Caribbean writer George Lamming said, 'English is a West Indian language'. And the same relaxed attitude allowed the faux naïf writer Amos Tutuola to produce his remarkable novels *The Palm Wine Drinkard* (1952) and *My Life in the Bush of Ghosts* (1953).

Indeed, it permitted Tutuola to write in an idiosyncratic non-standard English, use of which may have been part of his appeal, but it certainly did not prevent him from being applauded and published by a major publishing house, surely an unlikely outcome for a parallel francophone writer.

Later Anglophone writers may have been less relaxed about the language, taking on the view that English controls and indeed imprisons them. Punter (2000: 75) comments:

> the language used to recount the story is haunted by the languages in which the protagonists might have told the tale, had they their own language, at their disposal.

A strong sense of loss permeates the work of Kincaid (1988: 43), the sense of having to think and work in borrowed clothes. And it is there that we find the connection with being/not being a native speaker:

> what I see is the millions of people, of whom I am just one, made orphans: no motherland, no fatherland, no god ... and worst and most painful of all, no tongue ... For isn't it odd that the only language I have in which to speak of this crime is the language of the criminal who committed the crime?

And yet there seems to be a development from the strong anomic experience of loss to a kind of reconciliation, from 'my mother tongue has been stolen, I am forced to work through others' words' to 'this new hybrid mixed variety is my own. I am fully proficient in it, indeed I am a native speaker of it'. This must be how Creoles shape and develop and how mature Creole speakers come to regard the Creole as their mother tongue and themselves as its native speakers. But the New Varieties of English (the NVEs) are not Creoles, as we see later.

Owning English

Udaya Singh takes an extreme view of the question of ownership of English:

> Anglisticians like Braj Kachru ... make fantastic claims (such as: although linguistic systems such as 'Indian English' (IE) or 'South Asian English' (SE) are varieties of English, their speakers are not native speakers of English) ... This exclusive native of their club is what is on attack now from those who wish to gatecrash into the club by virtue of their speech habits, length of association with the language and/or culture, creative achievements, if any, etc. (Singh, U.N., 1998: 16)

The critique of 'linguistic imperialism' (Phillipson, 1992) condemns the influence of western anglophone polities on the indigenous languages with which they have come in contact. English (and a similar attack could be made on French or any other colonial or ex-colonial language within this argument) not only destroys other languages by compelling or seducing its speakers to use English for an increasing range of functions but it is also used as a deliberate instrument of centralising authority by the west.

When a language is under threat, in decline, facing death, being marginalised, when groups or individuals are pressured or compelled into language shift, when children are educated in the medium of a language other than their home code, we are accustomed to being told that their identity is at risk (Cummins, 1984; Pattanayak, 1998). In other words, that the change that they are experiencing is not only difficult — so much is obvious — but that it is also destructive of their personal identity, their basic sense of self.

If identity is so important then all symbols of identity are likely to be highly valued. As Brass (1974) points out, language is one such symbol, along with race, colour, gender, religion, historic tradition, all in fact criteria of group membership.

> Four requisites are essential to the successful transformation of an objectively different group of people into a subjectively conscious community — the existence of a 'pool' of symbols of distinctiveness to draw upon; an élite willing to select, transmit and standardise those symbols for the group; a socially mobilising population to whom the symbols of group identity can be transmitted; and the existence of one or more other groups from whom the group is to be differentiated. (Brass, 1974: 43–4)

Identity does seem to be connected to language, but it is not obvious it relates exclusively to the first learned language, the language of which one is a mother-tongue speaker, the language of which one is a native speaker.

The anthropological uses of the term identity are ambiguous, relating both to self-identity and to individuals' sense of group solidarity which distinguishes ethnic identity. As Barnard and Spencer (1966: 292) state: 'Individuals' identities are ... emergent properties of their categorical memberships'.

This marries well with the earlier view put forward by Barth (1969) who treated ethnicity as a form of organisation maintained by inter-group boundary mechanisms, based not on possession of a cultural inventory but on manipulation of identities and their situational character (Barnard & Spencer, 1996: 192).

Barth himself, contends: 'The features that are taken into account are not the sum of "objective" differences, but only those which the actors themselves regard as significant ... (Barth, 1969: 14).

This ascriptivist view of identity fits well with what Honderich (2001: 23) calls the most extreme philosophical view of personal identity, the view that we proceed through identity stages which are somehow linked together: 'To describe it again ... the crucial questions of personal identity do not have to do with identity over time but with the persons we are, the persons we have been, and the connections between them.'

Such a fluid sense of identity fits easily into current post-modern views of impermanence and is, in a sense, an extension of Barth's model of the boundary as being the categorical feature of ethnicity. What post-modernism (and Honderich) do is to take the boundary and comment that just as the content within the boundary is fluid, negotiable, so is the boundary itself. What was my ethnicity then need no longer be my ethnicity now – or indeed yours. But there is a danger that such a very relativist position disintegrates into solipsism and anomie, the threat of what happens to those who lose sight of their cultural norms (or in the medieval version abandon God).

Anomy, heinous sin of the medieval Christian church, defined the individual's rejection of, alienation from God. Taken up by Durkheim and later Robert Merton and now spelled in the French manner as 'anomie', the term moves from the psychological to the sociological, embracing a state of affairs where there is social anarchy, no norms, no conventional ways of behaving and of relating. It has particular resonance for the alienation experienced by the uprooted, immigrants and refugees.

> Anomie represents the polar opposite of morality, it is, in Durkheim's words, 'the contradiction of all morality'. Human nature is anomic, irrational, insatiable and egoistic, whereas society is the source of norms, rationality, contentment and altruism. (Orru, 1987: 58)

Robert Merton (1938) extended anomie as a social malfunction, seeing it as a condition of imbalance within the social situation since, unlike Durkheim, he wanted to implicate society in the onset of anomie. Social deviance takes place in settings in which the approved social goals are not achieveable for those who lack the economic (or other) resources. Only certain privileged groups can succeed in such situations. 'The true conformist will be the person who has access to both the legitimate means and the approved goals' (Marshall, 1994: 16). In the absence of this privileged access, anomie occurs, Merton argues, as the disjunction of means and goals.

As far as language learning is concerned a sense of deprivation may be experienced when learners set themselves a false goal (say of becoming native speakers of British or American Standard English). Such a goal is generally not achievable by most foreign learners because they lack the opportunities of privilege (education in an English medium, long-time exposure to English native-speaker peers and so on). A chastening example of such a false goal is provided by immersion language education. In that large-scale project research demonstrates that the intense exposure provided by immersion exposure (in various models) has not succeeded in turning groups of learners into native speakers (Swain & Lapkin, 1982).

The global expansion of English in the 20th century has been widely discussed and analysed (Crystal, 1997; Holborow, 1999; Graddol, 1999). It has been seen in both a favourable and in a critical light. Those who regard the expansion favourably (Fishman, 1977; McArthur, 1998) comment on the empowering role of English, the values of openness it brings, the access it provides both to knowledge and to markets. Those who regard the expansion negatively discuss the hegemonising of the weak by the strong, the ways in which English is used by the powerful west and their allies to dominate through globalisation, much as they dominate through economic and military means. They also point to the loss of choice, first linguistic and, then, inevitably it is suggested, cultural. What the spread of English does, it is argued, is to squeeze other languages into less and less central roles, eroding their functions until eventually they are marginalised to the private and the home and finally lost. This, it is suggested, is what is happening in a society such as Singapore where English is now the only medium of instruction for all Singaporeans. It is what has already happened in Guyana. And this destruction of the local language(s) is not confined to the Third World, to poor countries which do not have the resources at hand to combat the rise of English. It applies equally to the developed world where it remains for the present possible to operate a language policy of the local language + English, in countries such as Denmark, The Netherlands and Sweden. Such countries are often held up as models of successful language learning and teaching: successful because they succeed in acquiring the foreign language, English, and becoming proficient in it while at the same time not losing their first language, Danish, Swedish, Dutch and so on.

But the picture of easy (and stable) bilingualism in these western countries is queried by observers such as van Els (2000), who take the view that English in these settings could well be the cuckoo in the European nest, meaning that in another couple of generations, these local languages could be in terminal decline. This is the problem with the argument from function: if language is primarily a matter of functional distinction and adequacy, then once a world language such as English starts to encroach on the local language functions, there is really nothing to stop it from taking over all functions. Except sentiment of course, except the sense of distinctness, except the concern that it is possible to be truly oneself (a Dane, a Swede, a Singaporean) only in the local language or in one of the local languages (Holborow, 1999; Ngugi, 1986). At the back of such a sentiment is the two-fold awareness of language in (personal or group) identity. On one side there is the central role accorded to language as the transmitter and carrier of the sense of self, both in-group inclusiveness and exclusively through distinction from others who are seen to belong to other ethnicities. On the other side is the meaning attached to the local language itself, meaning that derives from its cognitive and psychological importance in the onto-genetic growth of cognition and other aspects of 'normal' development. The first of these concerns what you do with language, its sociolinguistics, the second with what language does to you, its psycholinguistics.

Both have to do with the sense of self which is, or seems to be, bound up with the language(s) in which one grew up as a child, one's first language, one's mother tongue. The sense of self, one's personal identity is, on this basis, closely associated with the power that being a native speaker gives. Such power may not be attainable or, at its least, is very hard to attain in any additional acquired language.

And this identity is threatened by the sense of not being valued for one's self (one's language is perceived as not good enough), of someone else's language being presented not just as different (so much is obvious) but as better than yours, and of the pervading feeling that whatever you do you will never achieve 'proper' command over the incoming language, that 'inferiority complex' of which Medgyes (1994: 10) wrote.

One's personal sense of identity is bound up with one's language: this is true both for the social aspects − sharing being a native speaker with others (and the opposite, not sharing it with those who do not belong); and the psycholinguistic aspects − mapping one's way through the BICS and the CALP that are claimed to be necessary to effective cognitive development (Cummins, 1984).

This being so, or rather if this is so, then we would expect the growth of English to be condemned as an aspect of post-colonial imperialism because it erodes the pride of native speakerness appertaining to local languages and never somehow replaces it with the achievement of becoming a native speaker in the acquired language. Here, the attitude of the ex-colonialists themselves, native speakers of for example English, is not dissimilar to the attitude the British took in their colonial heyday: the attitude that allowed the 'natives' to remain native, that accorded them large measures of local autonomy (indirect rule) but which took for granted that it was never going to be possible for the colonised to become British.

Literary Models

Rejecting the old colonial model is not easy, if only because models are necessary (Bloomfield, 1927). Kramsch (2000) charts the move away from literary models in language teaching towards colloquial language use. Those literary models themselves rejected the earlier all-European model of literature in Greek and Latin. For us what is of interest is the veneration of creative literature as especially emblematic of the true, the best native-speaker models. As Kramsch points out, this changes over the 20th century. The change was gradual, but already early on in the century Wyld (1934) was extolling a different native speaker model, that of the 'regular British army officer'.

Kramsch (2000) does not discuss what the creative writer as role model of native speaker means for New Varieties of English (NVEs). There, the creative writer has a difficult choice. If s/he uses an old variety (OVE) the charge will be of renegade, traitor. If s/he uses a NVE, then all too easily s/he is condemned for non-standard performance. The tightrope walked by Chinua Achebe, between the metropolitan French of Leopold Sedar Senghor and the local/idiosyncratic English of Amos Tutuola, is a precarious one (Punter, 2000).

The classical traditional literature model carries an aura of refinement, of uncontaminated origin, a sense of purity. Not surprising therefore that support for the 1913 foundation of the Society for Pure English (SPE) in the UK came from writers and academic critics as well as from linguists. Thus among the Society's founders were:

> Lascelles Abercrombie, Robert Bridges, Walter de la Mare, G. Lowes Dickinson, Henry Elroy Flecker, Edmund Goss, Thomas Hardy, Desmond Mccarthy, Gilbert Murray, Henry Newbolt. Arthur Quiller-Couch, Walter Raleigh, George Saintsbury, Logan Pearsall Smith, Hugh Walpole, Mrs Humphrey Ward, Arnold Bennett, E.M. Forster, Percy Lubbock, J.C. Squire. (SPE *Tract* 1, 1919: 13, 15)

The vast majority were men: in our short list there is only one woman! What price the chances of the Bronte sisters, Jane Austen or George Eliot?

The issues of the journal (known as *Tracts*) of the Society for Pure English (SPE) were published between 1919 and 1937. The term 'tract' has an interesting resonance, especially in the Oxford connection with the High Church Anglican revival under the Tractarians; which suggests that the SPE had, albeit implicitly, a missionary purpose.

The founders of the SPE were circumspect about the harnessing of the term 'Pure' in the name of their Society:

> In calling itself the Society for Pure English, it was not overlooked that the work Pure might carry a wrong suggestion. [It does nor imply] that words of foreign origin are impurities in English; it rather assumes that they are not; and the Committee, whether wisely or unwisely, thought a short title of general import was preferable to a definition which would misrepresent their purpose by its necessary limitations. (p. 3)

While we are not told just what was meant by 'pure', we are told that 'the ideal of the society is that our language in its future development should be controlled by the forces and processes which have formed it in the past; that it should keep its English character, and that the new elements added to it should be in harmony with the old' (p. 6).

Pure English, it would seem, means tradition and stasis; it means an Old Variety of English, preferably British English.

English: A Special Case?

Underlying many of the remarks by post-colonial apologists is their failure to acknowledge that English in the world at the start of the 21st century is a special case. This denial of a special status for native speakers of English is surely ideological, belonging to an argument about the role of English in a world filled with World Englishes, where there are more ESL than L1 speakers of English. In this context there is a political point to be made in opposing the privileged position of the OVE native speaker/user. Rajagopalan (1997: 229) maintains: 'the quest for the pure native is part of a larger agenda that in other epochs manifested itself – and in some quarters still does – as the quest for the pure race'. Since there are no 'viable and fool-proof criteria for identifying a native' (p. 228) then all that is left is the 'myth of nativity' (p. 229). Is this peculiar to English?

Are such sentiments specific to English? Or are they generalisable? Would these critics make the same point about Welsh or Basque or Menomini or Kikuyu? Clearly they are making a political point and an understandable one, given the inequities of the world. It is worth remembering that English is not itself a cause of those inequities; rather, it is a correlative. There are, after all, countries and societies with high levels of English (e.g. Kerala) which remain very poor. But that said, if native speakers' privilege is controlled, is it still the case that there is no special status to be accorded to native speakers of English? Graddol (1999:68) writes of the 'decline of the native speaker' and asks the 'tantalising question: ... large numbers of people will learn English as a Foreign Language in the 21st century ... But will they continue to look towards the native speaker for authoritative norms of usage?'.

It is this question of authority that worries Greenbaum (1985) when he writes of the inherent instability of a NVE: 'what is in dispute is the acceptance of the national characteristics and their institutionalisation'.

Where does this leave the Singapore native speaker/user of English? Tay (1982) and others maintain that there is good documentary evidence for the existence of Singapore English. Surely, the answer is that it leaves Singapore English exactly where it leaves, say, Glasgow English. Singapore is, in fact, in a stronger position: it has statehood and therefore a centralising force for language planning and norms). We might speculate on what would be the position of English if Scotland became independent. Would there be a deliberate scot-ising of norms? Or would Scotland go the way of Ireland. There, the rich vein of creative writing in English has never been supported by – or itself supported – the demand for the development of a Standard Irish English. True, there has been research into and discussion of Hiberno-English (Harris, 1985) but little sign of different norms for education and publishing and the media (as in the USA, Australia). Perhaps Ireland – the oldest British colony – has had enough confidence not to insist on making that difference explicit. Or perhaps the presence of the Irish Gaelic language has provided a sufficiently separate identity and taken up the space that a Standard Irish English movement might have filled.

The theoretical debate about native speakers may be unresolved, but in the daily practice of language teaching and testing resolution is necessary and agreement on a model and a goal required. Even so Leung *et al.* (1997) argue for flexibility: 'Little development of such an expanded pedagogy is possible without the displacement of conventional notions of the "native speaker" of English (what we here label the "idealised native speaker")' (p. 1). While this approach makes sense for individuals it is hard to see how it would lead to a language teaching policy for whole populations. Cook (1999b) proposes that the second-language (the non-native speaker) model should replace the native speaker in order to counter the harmful effects of privileging an inappropriate communication model in countries such as Japan.

What both Rajagopalan (1999) and Canagarajah (1999a, b) helpfully do is to argue strongly (as Medgyes (1999) does) for the valorising of the L2 teacher of English while at the same time reassuring professional colleagues that in teaching English as a Foreign Language (or indeed ESL) they are not acting as instruments of linguistic imperialism. This needs to be said by those who, it has been claimed, are victims of this globalising process. Rajagopalan (1999: 202) attacks the 'alarmist thesis that the teaching of English to speakers of other languages is an outrageous act of aggression'. And Canagarajah (1999b: 3) – who yields to no-one in his critique of the power of English in the periphery – makes very clear that scholars and teachers in the periphery are not dupes, that they are perfectly capable of operating 'subtle forms of resistance to English', appropriating from it what they need. And he puts a question mark against the absolutist strategy advocated by Ngugi: 'there are many reason why [his] oppositional strategy may be ill conceived ... this is not a solution to the ideological challenges, but an escape from it (Canagarajah, 1999b: 177). This is the argument presented by Agnihotri and Khanna (1997: 50) following their survey of young people in India's views on 'the space of English in tomorrow's India'. What they conclude is that English is indeed an Indian language and needs to be problematised in the Indian contexts, that it must be accorded its proper role within the 'complementarity' of the English language' (p. 139). But what they do not do is to raise the question of what model of English is appropriate in India.

Proposed Solutions

The loss of identity as a native speaker of one's own language through domination by English attracts four kinds of comment. The first is that of the attack on the cult of the native speaker, usually as teacher of his/her L1. This reminds us of the Paikeday (1985) argument and is presented typically by those who have suffered from discrimination on the grounds of themselves not being regarded as native speakers. The second comes from the special case of so-called World Englishes, the term used to legitimate the Englishes spoken in the British non-white colonies (Indian English, Malaysian English, Kenyan English and so on). The position taken up here is again one that complains of discrimination against users of World Englishes by those who are native speakers of metropolitan English varieties (British English, American English and so on). The third concern with identity takes the World English critique further. It presents the linguistic imperialism argument which states that English (and by implication any world language) rides roughshod over all local languages with which it comes in contact and particularly those in the ex-colonies: so now the critique is not just of the attitude of native speakers of metropolitan English to new Englishes but also to all other languages. These three attacks are all on the sociolinguistic side, claiming that belonging to desired groups is made difficult by the loss of or denial of native speaker status. The fourth attack takes on the psycholinguistic argument and concerns the claimed need for all normal development to take place in the language of the home. This is the argument from child development (of a Piagetian variety) and is closely associated with the work of Jim Cummins (1984) who has argued that unless early socialisation takes place through BICS, later cognitive learning (by means of CALP) is not possible. So this is an argument for the rewarding of first-language importance in child development and therefore may be regarded as a claim not just for the fact of native speaker status but for its pre-eminence.

Commentators take up very different positions on the issue of native-speaker power. But we can, I think, postulate that they separate into those writing from the foreigner perspective and those writing from the 'other-native' perspective. The foreigner view is of two kinds, − 'traditional' and 'revisionist'. The traditional view is that native speakers have special advantages but that these advantages are not unfair, just given; and in any case it is possible for non-natives working in professions such as language teaching to gain high levels of proficiency and to use their own learner background to deploy particularly relevant pedagogic skills. Medgyes (1999) provides an excellent summary of this type of view, as do several of the contributors to Braine (1999) such as Connor, Kramsch and Lam, and Li and Medgyes again. They argue that being a non-native-speaker teacher of English is a powerful position to be in.

The traditional foreigner

Medgyes looks for cooperation: 'The ideal NEST [Native English Speaking Teacher] and the ideal non-NEST arrive from different directions but eventually stand quite close to each other' (Medgyes, 1999: 74). Or as Kramsch and Lam (1999) make clear from the title of their chapter ('Textual Identities: The Importance of Being Non-native') being a non-native has advantages. This is an appealing view, given the fact that by far the majority of the world's language teachers are teaching what is to them a foreign language. A supportive view, though not directly concerned with the language of teachers, is found in Mohanan (1998). Mohanan who is himself an 'other-native' rather than a foreigner with regard to English, takes a very traditional line: 'For a given speaker, a non-native system is one that s/he has acquired after the acquisition and stabilisation of some other linguistic system' (Mohanan, 1998: 50). And he challenges those who argue the issue from the position of righting social justice: 'the plea for "endonormative" standards as a means of preventing social injustice contains a logical contradiction. We should be willing to abolish all standards or to accept exonormative standards' (p. 53).

What Mohanan is drawing our attention to here is how what is endonormative to a distant exonormative standard (say Singapore English to British English) has the tendency to become exonormative to some marginalized groups in Singapore. And Annamalai makes a similar point with regard to the relation between Telugu and Tamil in India and ponders whether bilingual speakers of both may be regarded as native speakers of Tamil: 'Nativity ... is a shifting construct and is correlated with political perceptions' (Annamalai, 1998b: 154).

Holborow (1999: 79) offers a similar argument from a Marxist perspective. 'Often attempts to revive and impose a former national language can be a nationalist cloak under which new rulers' interests are hidden' (Holborow, 1999: 79).

The revisionist foreigner

Observing the sense of deprivation of which Medgyes writes, Barbara Seidlhofer (2000) takes the bold step of recommending the abandonment of the traditional native-speaker model, echoing Kramsch (1993: 49) who suggests that it is time to 'take our cues not from monolingual native spealers ... but from the multilingual non-native speakers that constitute the majority of human beings on the planet'. The problem with such boldness is that it takes learners into a setting without maps. For indeed the state of mind she describes among non-native speakers of English as a *lingua franca* is surely one of anomie. Seidlhofer quotes Medgyes: 'We suffer from an inferiority complex caused by glaring defects in our knowledge of English. We are in constant distress as we realize how little we know about the language we are supposed to teach' (Medgyes, 1994: 10). (Sceptics among us might wonder how far this lament applies to native speakers also.)

And so Seidlhofer recommends that attention be given to the variety of English used by speakers of English as a Lingua Franca (EliF) communicating with one another. She claims that the appeal to the native speaker (NS) as model for all English is not appropriate now that the numbers of EliF speakers far outnumber the English first language (L1) speakers, especially since the L1 model is neither desired by nor relevant to the kind of communication between EliF speakers 'it is important to realise that native-speaker language use is just one kind of reality, and not necessarily the relevant one for *lingua franca* contexts' (Seidlhofer, 2000: 54). So it is English as a *lingua franca* that needs to be investigated and described, now that EliF is spreading 'with a great deal of variation but enough stability to be viable for *lingua franca* communication' (ibid: 54).

Seidlhofer (2000: 65) proposes a research project which works towards 'mapping out and exploring the whole spectrum of Englishes across the world'. Such a project may be thought timely now that the methodology exists for the compilation of a corpus of English as a *lingua franca*. Indeed, work on such a corpus ('the Vienna EliF corpus') has already begun. The end point of the research is to provide a description of EliF use which 'would have potentially huge implications for curriculum design and for reference materials and textbooks'. Seidlhofer's ambition is both limited and huge: limited in that she is concerned with interactions solely among non-native speakers of English; huge because the range and variety of such interactions is boundless.

It is understandable that Seidlhofer should wish to overturn the native speaker model. 'There is', she claims, 'really no justification for doggedly persisting in referring to an item as "an error" if the vast majority of the world's L2 English speakers produce and understand it' (p. 65). As she points out, this iconoclasm is widely shared in the linguistic imperialism English post-colonialist literature (Phillipson, 1992; Canagarajah, 1999a, b; Medgyes, 1994; Paikeday, 1985).

The other native

The 'other native' view is very well represented in both the Braine (1999) volume and in R. Singh (1998). A number of the contributors to the Braine volume are involved in teaching English in North America where they have met with prejudice about their lack of native-speaker status. And so the prevailing theme of the book is critical, protesting at not being accorded the same status as native speakers. This was, it will be remembered, the complaint of Thomas Paikeday, pointing to the experience of job discrimination. But it is worth noting that such discrimination is typically found in mother-tongue English settings (or, exceptionally – see Kandiah [1998] – in other situations where private schools advertise teaching by native speakers). In the great majority of situations where English (or any language) is taught, the teachers are not native speakers but members of the local community who themselves have acquired the language they teach as a foreign language. The exceptions are the NVE settings, those former non-settler countries (so Nigeria, India rather than Australia and New Zealand). Even to draw such a line is an ambiguous gesture: on which side do we place South Africa which is both settler and non-settler? Or indeed India? Much of the argument, and the anger, that we find in, for example, R. Singh (1998) comes from those who have a connection to that subcontinent. There the exposure to English has been long; there English has official status; there too some families (it is unclear how many) have adopted English as their first home language. So if we say, as is sometimes argued (Greenbaum, 1985), that a language needs a continuing body of native speakers for the sake of vitality, then on those grounds alone India qualifies as the home of a native variety of English, unless we add that such native speakers need, on the whole, to be monolingual and therefore dedicated as it were to that language.

But of course the argument about NVEs is not primarily about whether there are native speakers, though as we have seen there are always likely to be some. What the argument is really about is whether language use in a NVE setting which involves English and no doubt other languages as well provides participants with sufficient exposure to English to make them native users and furthermore in so doing to give them everything that the traditional native speaker has acquired in absorbing the language from childhood. Clearly such native users – this is agreed – speak a different variety of English, a NVE, but this is in no way inferior to the variety spoken by those brought up in the UK or in any other setting Kachru has called the inner circle. And it therefore follows, so the argument runs, that there should be no discrimination (in teaching or in any other occupation) on the grounds of group membership of such NVEs.

This is the argument that R. Singh (1998) puts forward. It is the post-colonial argument. It is the argument that says that American English is different from British English but it is not regarded as being full of errors because of that difference. Therefore, Indian English (etc.) should be considered different not inferior. It is an argument that appeals to social justice (as Mohanan (1998) points out). So much is clear. But is it an argument that convinces in applied linguistic terms?

Let us examine what R. Singh says. He tells us that in an earlier publication he had made his position clear:

> I insisted ... that whereas it made eminent sense to speak of English in India or Indian English, it made less eminent sense to speak of Indian English as a non-native variety of English. A non-native variety of a language was, I said, something of a contradiction in terms. (p. 26)

He takes issue with Trudgill who, in an earlier publication, had commented that 'non-nativeness does not inhere in the variety but in the speakers' (Trudgill, 1995). Trudgill's text shows that 'everyone who has grown up and spent all their life in Dover is clearly and unambiguously a native speaker ... Trudgill insists ... that there is a real and vital difference between native and non-native speakers but what does that have to do with the fact that Trudgill is a native speaker of English English and Mohanan is a native speaker of a particular variety of Indian English? They are both native speakers of their respective varieties.' (p. 34).

It turns out that Rajendra Singh is primarily responding to what he regards as the appropriation of the whole NVE/NNE debate by those prominent in the World Englishes movement. He is offended on professional linguistic grounds by what he regards as the unsustainable claims of WEs that, for example; 'although systems such as IE and SE are varieties of English, their speakers are not (native speakers of English.' (p. 28). So what we have here is, at least in part, yet another incident in the so-called linguistic wars (Harris, 1993), suggestive of a religious-like disagreement: Singh describes the WEs response to views such as his on the native speaker as 'ritualistic repetitions of the articles of the "N/NNE" faith' (p. 29).

We may ask why it matters so much. The answer is that it matters because it speaks to closely to the questions of power and of identity. Whose English is it anyway? Who owns my English? Who decides whether the English I deploy is correct? Whose norms do I appeal to? These are the questions at issue. Singh refers approvingly to the article in the volume by Ikome: 'Ikome begins with the observation that "native speaker" is foremost a political designation for social empowerment or for peer recognition' (p. 37); and to the article by Kandiah: 'For him the important questions is "what we mean when we say that people know, use and view a language in a manner that allows them to see themselves and to be recognized and accepted as native users of it"' (p. 37). Kandiah's article discusses the case of English in Singapore. In it, Singh tells us, Kandiah provides an 'illuminating analysis ... that is important for the entire field of linguistics' (p. 37).

Let us turn now to Kandiah's (1988) analysis. His stance is very obviously political, as the title of his chapter makes clear: 'Epiphanies of the Deathless Native User's Manifold Avatars: A Post-colonial Perspective on the Native Speaker'. His onslaught is wider than that of Singh, attacking 'the mainstream discourse on the native speaker [which] can be seen to be a strongly normative discourse that is heavily invested ideologically against considerable numbers of people on our globe' (p. 92). He insists that 'it ought not to be necessary to repeat here the demonstration that these varieties of English (the NVEs) are the equal of any other variety of the language, being not mere hodge-podges of errors, mere deviations from the norms of the "mother" language, but viable rule-governed systems in their own right which sustain and are sustained by speech communities of their native users' (p. 93). And he refers to earlier examples of his own work which provide the evidence for this statement. As he admits himself, the argument is not fundamentally about what distinguishes one variety from another, nor about whether a variety of native users (rather than native speakers), maintained by a speech community largely made up of non-monolingual speakers of English whose English has not necessarily been acquired as their first childhood language, should be regarded as 'the equal of any other variety'. What the argument is about is whether the boundary between the NVE and the OVE is seen to be a real boundary by the NVE native users. This is the appeal to the Barth social boundary theory (Barth, 1969) and ultimately is about the attitudes of native users to their own NVE.

> The critical feature of the group then becomes self-ascription and ascription by others on the basis of features, signs, signals, value orientations and standards which the actors themselves regard as significant and by which they judge themselves and expect others to judge them. (Barth, 1969: 96)

Barth's model of ethnicity (which we have met before in this chapter) is helpful here since what it does is to emphasise, as Kandiah realises, membership before content. This is the conclusion that Medgyes (1994) comes to, quoting Davies: 'membership, as I see it, is largely a matter of self ascription, not of something being given ... [but] those who claim native speaker status ... do have responsibilities in terms of confidence and identity' (Davies, 1991a: 8).

Medgyes is concerned with the status of an individual near-native speaker, unlike Kandiah whose concern is for group membership. The confidence Medgyes refers to applies equally to both. But while the Medgyes individual near-native needs to identify with the norms of English, both in a linguistic and a cultural sense, which in his case means the norms of OVEs, the identity Kandiah is concerned with is identity with the NVE group; and confidence for him means asserting that the English variety which his NVE members speak relates to the norms of their own NVE. This is the post-colonial imperative, that just as the Australian native speaker of English no longer admits allegiance to the norms of British English, similarly the NVE native user (say of Singapore English) no longer takes account of the norms of British English.

How far the norms differ is an empirical question, but it seems likely that as far as the written language is concerned, the differences are minimal. I remain therefore of the opinion I expressed in 1991 (Davies, 1991a), which is presented in Chapter 4 of this volume:

> on linguistic grounds Singaporean English does not exist, but nor of course does British English ... what does exist is the individual speaker. If a speaker identifies him/herself as a native speaker of Singaporean English then that is a sociolinguistic decision. (p. 69)

Which means, of course that it is a decision about identity.

To an extent the argument between Singh and, say, the Kachrus is much less substantial than that between, say, Kachru and Quirk or Greenbaum. The latter argument is about the viability as a norm-bearer of NVEs while the former seems almost to be about what you call the speakers of a NVE. Mohanan who is basically on Quirk's side takes the view that NVEs do not have their own coherent norms:

> the term 'non-native variety' refers to a perfectly legitimate concept in linguistics as a domain of inquiry. The term 'new variety' is either the same as 'non-native variety' or does not refer to any coherent concept ... the plea for 'endonormative standards' as a means of preventing social injustice contains a logical contradiction. We should be willing either to abolish all standards, or to accept exo-normative standards. (p. 53)

So for Mohanan the view is rather like that of Medgyes, the foreigner view not the other native view. The question no doubt that remains — as it does increasingly in critical applied linguistics — is whether we should/ can take account of social justice in our categories and in our definitions. For example, would it be justifiable to label someone as a native speaker of language X on the grounds of inclusiveness and equity, whether or not the claim to be a native speaker can be substantiated on linguistic grounds?

A final word is necessary with regard to the neurolinguistic evidence. Paradis (1998: 217) is sure that there are clear distinctions between a native and a non-native speaker of a language and he lists some of these. But for the kind of individual Medgyes describes, the pseudo native speaker and for the groups that Singh *et al.* portray, the members of NVEs, the distinction disappears; it disappears for the Medgyes individual because they have reached 'ultimate attainment' (Birdsong, 1992); and it disappears for the NVE members because they are indeed native speakers/ users of their own NVE.

Relevance to Applied Linguistics

For applied linguistics the issues discussed in Chapter 8 relate particularly to the tension between local identity formation through a NVE and wider communication through an OVE. Underlying this issue is the more fundamental question of what determines replacement of one code by another — and how far such replacement is amenable to political planning. For the applied linguist, decisions as to which standard language to propose as the institutional model (for education and so on) cannot be avoided.

Summary

Chapter 8 evaluates the challenge to the concept of the native speaker from post-modernism and, in particular, post-colonialism. The question is raised of the centrality of language to a sense of loss of identity, expressed powerfully in the 1960s and 1970s in the appeal among francophone writers to the concept of négritude. How to cope with the intrusion of the new world language is the applied problem, found in societies wishing to participate in the global economy. How they do so ranges from the insistence in NVE contexts on the status of a local standard to the valorisation in foreign language contexts of the non-native speaker teacher. What matters in all cases, it is agreed, is that the community should be confident in choosing its own solution.

Chapter 9
Assessment and Second Language Acquisition Research

There are two types of judgements relevant to these discussions about the L2 learner in relation to native speaker status. The first type concerns judgements of identity, the second judgements of language.

The kinds of judgement discussed in this chapter are those arrived at in a formal setting where informants are asked through questionnaires and other elicitation tasks to make judgements.

However, the applied issue is that of proficiency and I want first to observe that informal judgements are being made in interaction all the time – and they can be wrong. This is the force of the Gumperz examples in the 'Interethnic Communication' chapter of *Discourse Strategies* (Gumperz, 1982). One of the examples he uses there is of an interview where the interviewer is a British female native speaker (B) and the interviewee an Indian male (A). Here is a small part of the text. (N.A. indicates 'not audible'.)

19.	A:	Um, may I first of all request for the introduction please
20.	B:	Oh yes sorry
21.	A:	I am sorry
22.	B:	I am E
23.	A:	Oh yes ... I see ... oh yes ... very nice ...
24	B:	and I am a teacher here in the Centre
25.	A:	very nice
26.	B:	and we run
27.	A:	pleased to meet you
28.	B:	different courses, yes, and you are Mr A?
29.	A:	(laughs)
30.	A:	N.A.
31.	B:	N.A., yes, yes I see. Okay that's the introduction.
32.	B:	(laughs)
33.	A:	Would it be enough introduction? (Gumperz, 1982: 175)

As Gumperz's discussion shows, the final question: 'Would it be enough introduction?' indicates that there is something seriously wrong, in spite of all the earlier signs that the two speakers were, in fact, fully understanding one another and that the Indian speaker's English was very proficient. The reply 'very nice' is also unfortunate in the context (and could be interpreted as impolite) but as Gumperz shows is almost certainly a direct translation of the Urdu formulaic 'buhut uceha', 'OK, go on'. The Indian speaker's apparent proficiency is inadequate in a British English setting where the expectations of the interviewer and of the interviewee are different. The interview is consequently full of miscommunication. The fundamental question of what the interview is for is never addressed by either party. It is in the context of this interview that Gumperz speaks of 'parallel tracks which don't meet' (Gumperz, 1982: 185).

Purpose of Assessment

Arguments about the purpose of assessment can be reduced to the issue of what to use as the criterion (or norm) for judgements. On the one hand is the view that judgements should be made on the basis of ranking population abilities. In this way everyone being assessed is placed in a ranked order, with the most able placed at the first rank. This is sometimes known as norm referencing. On the other hand, there is the view that it is not helpful (and may indeed be unethical) to judge people against one another. Instead, so the argument goes, we should judge individuals against an achievement yardstick. And so those being assessed are judged as reaching or not reaching achievement level on the yardstick or not: those who have are scored as Passes, those who have not as Fails. It is, of course, possible to be more sophisticated such that there are more than two outcomes, thus a Good Pass as well as a Pass, and so on. This type of assessment approach is sometimes known as criterion or mastery referencing. An analogy for both types can be found in athletic jumping, in the long jump, where the level to reach (and supersede) is set by the last leading contestant: this resembles norm referencing; and the high jump, where a level of success is set (and when appropriate, changed) on the basis of what height should be reached in order to show mastery: this resembles criterion referencing.

Debate between the two views has, at times, been fierce; this is particularly so in the field of language assessment, perhaps because where there is less to agree on, content or knowledge-wise, arguments about what should count as the norm or criterion are fundamentally arguments about what counts as language.

In reality the dispute is more shadow than real (Wood, 1991). What the two views represent is not two philosophies but (perhaps) two methodologies, two ways of determining a scale (a point Bialystok [1998: 502] makes in her discussion of language proficiency: 'the two theoretical approaches have simply defined the problem differently'). And, of the two, norm referencing is probably the point of departure because we can set a criterion yardstick (the bar on the high jump) when we know what those being assessed are capable of, how high the best jumpers can jump. We can set the level (which becomes criterion referencing) and then we can determine not just how the most able perform but also how most people perform; and then, if we wish, we can set a lower level of performance which we may wish to describe as level of mastery. The point we are making here is that rank ordering and criterion ordering do not represent different philosophical or political positions even though they are often presented ideologically.

A similar distinction — and an equally false opposition — can be made with regard to the norm (or criterion) of attainment in language learning, language teaching and language acquisition. Should the norm be, as is often claimed, the native speaker or should it be some yardstick of language proficiency? As with our jumping analogy, our view of proficiency is constrained by the kind of performance we observe among native speakers, both the 'mastery' kind — what most native speakers are capable of — and the high-level kind where we recognise superior levels of language skill among gifted native speakers. Our analogy to assessment does, however, break down: the continuum between criterion and norm referencing in assessment does not hold for proficiency and the native speaker, because the native speaker is a developmental as well as an attainment concern. In other words, however close the match between our modelling of proficiency and the native speaker may be, we can never be sure that there is a complete match.

Defining Language Proficiency

However, defining language proficiency is just as elusive as defining the native speaker. It makes sense to provide a range of definitions:

(1) a general type of knowledge or of competence in the use of a language, regardless of how, where or under what conditions it has been acquired;
(2) ability to do something specific in the language, for example proficiency in English to study in higher education in the UK, proficiency to work as a foreign language teacher of a particular language in the United States, proficiency in Japanese to act as a tour guide in Australia; or

(3) performance as measured by a particular testing procedure. (Some of the procedures are so widely used that levels of performance on them (e.g. 'superior', 'intermediate', 'novice' on the FSI Scales) have become common currency in particular circles as indicators of language proficiency.)

In its more portmanteau sense of general language ability, proficiency was widely used in the 1970s and early 1980s under the label general language proficiency, synonymously with unitary competence hypothesis. Proficiency has since come to be regarded as multifaceted, with recent models specifying the nature of its component parts and their relationship to one another. There is now considerable overlap between the notion of language proficiency and the term communicative competence. Debates about language proficiency have influenced the design of language tests and language testing research has been used in the validation of various models of language proficiency (Davies *et al.*, 1999: 153).

The attempt to encapsulate proficiency in a language test raises acutely the question of which norms of English are appropriate. This is particularly so in the case of high stake contexts, e.g. TOEFL, TOEIC, IELTS [International English Language Testing System] (Spolsky, 1993; Clapham, 1996; Criper & Davies, 1988). What is at stake here is whose norms are to be imposed. Bhatt (1995) upbraids Quirk for discrediting the use of non-native varieties of English as pedagogically acceptable models since these varieties are not adequately described. While agreeing that this is the case, Bhatt (1995: 247) continues:

> Quirk argues that in non-native contexts only the 'Standard' (the 'native' model) must be used in the teaching of English, and further, that non-native teachers must be in constant touch with the native language. The implications of this argument are quite unfortunate and backward. (Bhatt, 1995: 247)

Norms of English

Nelson (1995) condemns 'the monocentric, probably ethnocentric view that a particular form of English is "correct" and "right" and that other forms are, then, by definition "wrong"'. And Davidson (1994: 119–20) comments on

> the prevalent imperialism of major international tests of English … Several large English tests hold sway world-wide; tests which are clear agents of the English variety of the nation where they are produced.

These tests maintain their agency through the statistical epistemology of norm-referenced measurement of language proficiency, a very difficult beast to assail.

Hill and Parry (1994) complain about the conservatism of those responsible for English language examinations in the face of these new World Englishes (see Chapter 8) challenges. 'One question', they remark, 'that [educators] continually face is the degree to which non-native learners in a particular country should be tested on local as opposed to metropolitan varieties of English' (Hill & Parry, 1994: 2). Lowenberg (1993: 95) makes a similar point about the conservatism of the language testing profession:

> in language testing, an implicit (and frequently explicit) assumption has long been that the criteria for measuring proficiency in English round the world should be candidates' use of particular features of English which are used and accepted as norms by highly educated native speakers of English.

Lowenberg's (1993) analysis of the TOEIC test leads him to the following conclusion:

> the brief analysis presented in this paper is sufficient to call into question the validity of certain features of English posited as being globally normative in tests of English as an international language, such as TOEIC, and even more, in the preparation materials that have developed around these tests. Granted, only a relatively small pro-portion of the questions on the actual tests deal with these nativized features; most test items reflect the 'common core' of norms which comprise Standard English in all non-native and native-speaker vari-eties ... But given the importance usually attributed to numerical scores in the assessment of non-native language proficiency, only two or three items of questionable validity on a test form could jeopardize the ranking of candidates in a competitive test administration. (p. 104)

And for that reason he challenges 'the assumption held by many who design such English proficiency tests ... that native speakers still should determine the norms for Standard English around the world'.

Lowenberg offers no empirical data for his claim that the items he analyses are discriminatory. Indeed, there is a remarkable absence of empir-ical evidence to substantiate cries of bias (Coppieters, 1987; Birdsong, 1992). ETS (Educational Testing Service) has over the years produced a number of research reports on the conduct of TOEFL (e.g. Clark, 1977) which have shown that performance across national and linguistic groups varies systematically. But that does not of itself support the bias case since it might well be that the group differences that are found are reflections of the groups' true scores, just as a tape measure which shows that men are, on the whole, taller than women is not biased in favour of men.

One way to avoid using the global norms to which Lowenberg objects is to investigate to what extent local norms are appropriate both locally and beyond the local. Such an investigation is reported by Hill (1996) and Brown and Lumley (1998), both referring to the development of an English Proficiency Test for Indonesian teachers of English. Hill (1996: 32) comments:

> the majority of Indonesian learners will use English to communicate with other non-native speakers within South-East Asia. For this reason it was decided the test should emphasize the ability to communicate effectively in English as it is used in the region, rather than relate proficiency to the norms of America, Britain or Australia ... this approach also aims to recognize the Indonesian variety of English both as an appropriate model to be provided by teachers and as a valid target for learners.

Brown and Lumley (1998) claim that in developing the Indonesian test they had several aims in view. These aims, they maintain, were all fulfilled. They were:

- the judicious selection of tasks relevant to teachers of English in Indonesia;
- the selection of culturally appropriate content;
- an emphasis on assessing test takers in relation to regional norms; and
- the use of local raters, i.e. non-native speakers of English (whose proficiency was nevertheless of a high standard) (Brown & Lumley, 1998: 94).

Kenkel and Tucker (1989) mounted one of the few research studies in this field. They noted that 'international students ... have spent much of their lives acquiring and using their regional variety of English. These students bear some similarities ... to speakers of Black English in the US' (p. 202) and they concluded from their analysis of written essays by Nigerian and Sri Lankan students that the 'errors' in their work should more accurately be called deviations from the native-speaker norm. Recent empirical work that has attempted to marry the two approaches, the international and the local, has been carried out by Hamp-Lyons and Zhang (2000). They report:

on an investigation into the behaviour of raters of university-led examination essays, focussing on the rhetorical patterns found in EFL test essays ... specifically at how raters' judgements of the essays interact with their perceptions of the culture-specific or nativized rhetorical features. Issues are raised regarding the raters' degree of tolerance for rhetorical diversity, the appropriacy of "non-nativelike" rhetorical patterns in university students' written work, the selection and training of essay writers, and the implications of the study for English language writing assessment in localized and international contexts. The question of which English(es) should be privileged on tests is particularly problematic and interesting in academic contexts where traditionally 'standard' forms of English are the only ones accepted.

The Problem in Language Proficiency Testing

During the last 30 years there appears to have been a loss of nerve about the native-speaker goal among language testers. Robert Lado (1961: 93–4) was certain that the true criterion of a test's validity was the native speaker.

When the (test) items have been written and the instructions prepared the test is ready for an experimental administration to native speakers of the language ... Items eliciting the desired response from native speakers 95% of the time or better should probably be kept.

But 30 years later, Lyle Bachman (1990: 248) was less sure:

there are serious problems in determining what kind of language use to consider as the 'native speaker' norm, while the question of what constitutes a native speaker, or whether we can even speak of individuals who are native speakers, is the subject of much debate.

These are indeed serious problems, as Bachman reminds us, and the solution, that of delineating the language proficiency continuum from zero to ultimate attainment in terms of the native speaker, is, as he indicates, now in doubt. In doubt, therefore, are scales such as the Foreign Service Institute (FSI), now the Inter Agency Roundtable (ILR) and the Australian Second Language Proficiency Ratings (ASLPR) and the like, which typically fix a criterion of native speaker ability, thus:

- *FSI Level 6*:   Native pronunciation, with no trace of 'foreign accent'

- *FSI Level 6*:   Understands everything in both formal and collo-
                      quial speech to be expected of an educated native
                      speaker
- *ASLPR Level 5*:   Able to use the second language as effectively as
                      native speakers ('there is nothing about the way I
                      speak that suggests I am not a native speaker').

The Critical Period Hypothesis

If we accept that 'to be a native speaker means not being a non-native
speaker' (see p. 208), then we are taking it for granted that there are
categories of native speakers and of non-native speakers, even if defining
them eludes us. The temptation – still very much alive – to fall back on
early childhood acquisition (or at least on a critical period hypothesis –
CPH) is very strong. So strong indeed that we could use scholars' position
on this issue to label them as taking a 'psycho' or a 'socio' approach to
language learning and the native-speaker. Those who favour a psycho
approach argue vehemently for an absolute distinction between native
speakers and non-native speakers, that the critical period (in one or other
variant) exists; those who favour a socio approach are prepared to coun-
tenance that the appropriate social context can bring about native-speaker
capacities even after the onset of the critical period. What this means is that
the psycho party have complete faith (akin to a religious belief) in the
rightness of the early child learning view; while the socio party are
sceptical and reckon that there is no such thing as absolute biological
constraint on second language-learning. The CPH to the socio party is
meaningless. It is not that they do not accept maturation. They do, as
in other developmental areas. But they cannot accept in blind faith that a
second language is categorically different for learners from a first
language. And if it is they want evidence.

Surveying the field, Hyltenstam and Abrahamsson (2000) occupy a half-
way position. Their careful study of the evidence leads them to state: 'To
our minds the Second Language research on the topic of the Critical Period
Hypothesis, together with data from first language development under
both "normal" and atypical conditions (cf. Gleitman & Newport, 1995)
clearly provides stronger evidence for than against the existence of maturational constraints. However, a number of questions remain.' (Hyltenstam
& Abrahamsson, 2000: 159–60). What Hyltenstam and Abrahamsson are
saying is that while there is evidence for maturation the CPH may need to
be rejected. 'Many aspects of the CPH would be seriously questioned,

although, at the same time, there would be strong support for the existence of maturational constraints' (p. 163).

But before we rush to the view that Hyltenstam and Abrahamsson have
become converts to the socio view, we need to ask ourselves just what is
meant by maturational constraints. And, indeed, what Hyltenstam and
Abrahamsson are really proposing is a flexible CPH. In other words, the
distinction native speaker–non-native speaker is still biological, but we
cannot be sure when the development trigger kicks in for individuals.
Which is not really different for other areas of development, for example
the menarche.

This is the conclusion that Singleton (2001: 84–5) comes to in his survey
article on the effect of age on second-language acquisition. He maintains:

> Few L2 researchers challenge the proposition that those L2 acquirers
> whose exposure to the L2 begins early in life for the most part attain
> higher levels of proficiency than those whose exposure begins in
> adolescence of childhood ... The more closely we study very early L2
> beginners, the more we realise that, at the level of subtle detail, they
> too differ from monoglot native speakers.

> It seems that, as Grosjean (e.g. 1992) and Cook (e.g. 1995) have been
> arguing for years, what makes the difference is the very fact of know-
> ledge of another language.

But Singleton does not stop there: he is (rather like Hyltenstam &
Abrahamsson) prepared to move a little from the extreme psycho position
that language is wired into the brain and is unaffected by social context.
He does, after all, accept that, as he says himself, the truth is rarely pure
and never simple and ends his survey:

> the notion that L2 age effects are exclusively neurologically based,
> that they are associated with absolute, well-defined chronological
> limits, and that they are particular to language looks less and less
> plausible. (Singleton, 2001: 85)

This is a big step from the kind of extreme position that Cook occupies.
For him there can be no overlap between native speakers and non-native
speakers:

> The indisputable element in the definition of native speakers is that a
> person is a native speaker of the language learnt first; the other
> characteristics are incidental, describing how well an individual uses
> the language. (V. Cook, 1999b: 187)

What we need to ask ourselves – and what Cook does not do – is just what that first learning of a language means cognitively and behaviourally. What is it that Cook's native speaker knows and can do with that first learned language that no late acquirer can ever do?

Temple (2000) agrees with Cook. Researching into learner speech production she concludes:

> speaking is a highly skilled activity, requiring a complex system of parallel processes and storage requirements and which functions mainly in automatic mode. In native speech, working memory is generally involved only in planning and monitoring, with lexical choice and appropriacy, in particular, receiving controlled attention. Foreign language learners reveal in their nonfluency a quantitatively and qualitatively different operation. (p. 296)

But Bongaerts *et al.* (2000: 305) take a different view. Their research concludes that 'it is not impossible for post-critical period learners to achieve a native-like accent in a non-primary language, in spire of the alleged biological barriers'.

The extreme psycho position has been seriously questioned in recent second-language acquisition (SLA) research. And it is interesting that those querying it belong to a psycho rather than to a socio tradition. We refer later to comments by Birdsong (1992), Bialystok (1997) and to White and Genesee (1996). Birdsong, it should be noted, was a firm upholder of the critical period until he examined his own data which compelled him to change his mind.

SLA research has always been more interested in the native speaker than in language proficiency. In particular it has compared native-speaker behaviour and that of various second-language learners, asking the question: What does the second language learner know and to what extent does this differ from what the native speaker knows?

Long (1983) sets the scene with his paper on 'Linguistics and Conversational Adjustments to Non-Native Speakers'. He notes that Native Speakers (NSs)

> react to a combination of factors when they make linguistic/conversational adjustments to non native speakers (NNSs). These include the comprehensibility of the NNS's interlanguage, the interlanguage's linguistic characteristics, and the NNS's apparent comprehension of what the NS is saying. (p. 188)

Long concludes that there is sufficient evidence to suggest that adjustments by NSs are necessary (and may be sufficient) for acquisition to take place. In other words, Long is challenging the view that all that is necessary for acquisition to take place is comprehensible input; he is also accepting the view that Foreigner Talk (Ferguson, 1971) plays as important a part in second-language acquisition as Caretaker Talk does in first-language acquisition. Gass and Varonis (1985) make much the same point but concentrate on the NNS's comprehensibility rather than on the interaction of NSs and NNSs. Much of the research has to do with the issue of 'ultimate attainment' in a second language, the extent to which there is an absolute distinction between NSs and NNSs who acquire the target language after the so-called critical or sensitive period. Ioup *et al.* (1994) argue that there are two important differences between successful and unsuccessful second-language learners with regard to ultimate attainment: these are attention to form and language aptitude. They maintain:

> even if language learning talent involves continued use of the first language acquisition system in adulthood, talented adult language learning differs from child first language acquisition in one very significant respect. For some yet to be discovered reason, talented adults, unlike children, appear to require conscious attention to grammatical form. (Ioup *et al.*, 1994: 93)

Whether or not attention to grammatical form is necessary, White and Genesee (1996: 261) report results that show that 'adult learners can achieve linguistic competence which is indistinguishable from native speakers'. They recognise that adult learners are typically less successful than younger learners but point out that it is important to determine just what is the locus of the effects of age on learning. They accept that their findings are at odds with those of many other researchers although they are in accordance with Birdsong's (1992) conclusions. They attribute the greater success of their adult subjects to their careful subject sampling and to the design of the tasks used in their experiment. This claim by White and Genesee is far-reaching indeed: they are not making a case for performance differences or similarities. On the contrary their claim is that there is no principled structural (that is cognitive) difference between NSs and NNSs in their schemata or their procedures. What they propose is that what differences are found are essentially performance differences which may be attributed to the lack of comparability of exposure and opportunity. This is precisely the point that Bialystok (1997) makes. She argues:

> The documented cases of perfect mastery of a second language achieved by late learners are not anomalous exceptions to a biological law or extraordinary facts by rare individuals with an unusual and

prodigious talent. Rather, they are quite ordinary occurrences that emerge when conditions are favourable. (Bialystok, 1997: 134)

In other words, age is just another situational factor which is not itself critical as long as there are other factors that compensate. Bialystok continues:

> In the absence of compelling evidence, it is prudent to assume that successful SLA remains a possibility for all those who have learnt a natural language in childhood and can organize their lives to recreate some of the social, educational and experiential advantages that children enjoy.

The Coppieters' Experiment

Coppieters (1987) reported an experiment which appears to challenge this position. She took a group ($N = 21$) of non-native adult speakers of French who had 'so thoroughly mastered French that it was no longer clearly possible to distinguish them from native speakers by mistakes which they made, or by the restricted nature of their choice of words and constructions' (p. 544). For baseline data she took 20 native speakers, matched as far as possible. She used 107 sentences illustrating a variety of aspects of French and asked her subjects individually for acceptability judgements. She found that the native-speaker group varied between 5% and 16% from the norm (based on the most common native-speaker response) with a standard deviation of 4.1. The non-native speaker group, however, varied between 23% and 49% from the same norm and, using a significance test, Coppieters concluded therefore that they belonged to two different populations with no overlap between, even at the extremes.

Coppieters accepts that there is an argument in favour of the identity theory.

> A speaker of French is someone who is accepted as such by the community referred to as that of French speakers, not someone who is endowed with a specific formal underlying linguistic system.

But for Coppieters such an argument is too strongly sociological and in her view competence must include a psychological dimension. She continues:

> However, it is also clear that the variation between native speakers and non-native speakers cannot simply be subsumed as a special case of the variation among native speakers: that is, non-native speakers have been found to lie outside the boundaries of native speaker variation. (Coppieters, 1987: 545)

Native speakers, suggests Coppieters, on the basis of her data did not need the help of an explicit context. No matter how skilful non-native speakers might be at deriving the appropriate interpretation of a sentence in context, their inability to do so on the absence of an explicit context indicates a fundamental difference between their knowledge of the language and that of native speakers (pp. 566–7).

On the basis of her analysis, Coppieters claims that the differences between native speakers and non-native speakers involve not so much the formal areas of grammar traditionally covered under the term universal grammar 'as those typically addressed by linguists interested in "functional" or "cognitive" aspects of grammar' (p. 565). To some extent this claim underpins the answer she provides to the inevitable question: Why is it that her non-native speakers whose French could not in normal interactions be clearly distinguished from that of native speakers show up on her tests as so very different?

Coppieters' answer makes use of her distinction between functional and formal areas of grammar and implicitly accepts that what is salient in interaction is the formal:

> the interpretive system … tends to take a constructive attitude: it automatically makes amends for many apparent inaccuracies in everyday native conversation … information read from the context of the speech event usually overrides what is directly expressed in a spoken utterance. In such circumstances, native comprehension seems not to distinguish the semantically divergent uses of some grammatical forms that must occasionally occur in a non-native speaker's output, for the most part, from the inaccuracies occurring in native speakers' utterances. (pp. 570–1)

In the terms used in this book Coppieters is appealing to Grammar 2 in her acceptability tests; her findings accord with our view of Grammar 2 being available as a point and as a range: thus for Coppieters (as for Ross, 1979) her native speakers cluster more closely around the point, her norm, while her non-native speakers exhibit a wider range. Such research necessarily makes greater use of Grammar 2 than of Grammar 1 because the subjects, whether native or non-native, typically are educated standard-language speakers. What is of interest of course is to what extent a greater use of different Grammar 2s would show up a wider range for native speakers.

What does seem to be the case is that non-native speakers, who have acquired the target language as a second language after the critical age, can achieve some parts of native-speaker competence, even that shown up by judgement tasks, but are usually not as coherent, as consistent about it as are native speakers, who acquired the language in early childhood. This conclusion seems inescapable. However, we must reiterate what we have pointed out earlier, that such findings are based on what is a kind of engineered homogeneity, that of Grammar 2, the Standard Language. What we do not know is to what extent individuals from a wider range of social and geographical settings would provide such uniformity.

Nevertheless, for Coppieters, such an argument is strongly sociological and, in her view, competence must include a psychological dimension. She continues:

> it is also clear that the variation between native speakers and non-native speakers cannot simply be subsumed as a special case of the variation among native speakers: that is non-native speakers have been found to lie outside the boundaries on native speaker variation. (p. 545)

Native speakers, reports Coppieters,

> did not need the help of an explicit context. No matter how skilful non-native speakers might be at deriving the appropriate interpretation of a sentence in context, their inability to do so in the absence of an explicit context indicates a fundamental difference between their knowledge of the language and that of native speakers. (pp. 566–7)

In view of the idiolectal and dialectal differences among native speakers themselves, Coppieters' claim is a strong one, raising, as Spolsky (1989: 45) notes, 'the interesting possibility that native-speaker-like performance may be based on different underlying competence' (from that of learners). Coppieters's argument for cognitive rather than formal dissonance between native and non-native speakers concerns the grammar of the standard or common language learned before the critical period (Lennerberg, 1967). Even so, this claim has been challenged.

Birdsong (1992) takes issue with researchers such as Long (1990a) who appear to make an absolute distinction between the native speaker and the non-native speaker, i.e. that 'ultimate attainment' for the non-native speaker can never be equal to native-speaker competence. Birdsong re-examined the Coppieters (1987) experiment with learners of French and reports also on his own parallel study. What he concludes is that while as a group his French language learners and the French native-speaker subjects differed significantly, the large amount of overlap suggests that 'this general lack of difference is taken as evidence that ultimate attainment by non-natives can coincide with that of natives' (Birdsong, 1992: 739). Of course those who overlap are, as Birdsong admits, 'exceptional learners';

but the implication here is that 'our attention should turn to the issue of trainability: what can be discovered from exceptional learners that could be applied to improve other learners' chances of attaining native norms' (p. 742).

Birdsong's challenge to the view that ultimate attainment (native-speaker ability) is not possible for exceptional second-language learners has been supported by Bialystok (1997), who has shown that on the basis of her experiments it is not only the exceptional learner who is capable of such attainment. Bialystok accepts that 'the general success of younger learners in acquiring a second language is true' (p. 133) but points out that the evidence does not therefore mean that 'this advantage is the reflection of a sensitive period in learning' (p. 133). She rejects the casuistry of those who wish to add qualifications to the claim that a second-language learner can become a native speaker; as she writes: 'there either is a maturational constraint on second language acquisition or there is not' (p. 134).

And she concludes that it is not in fact only the exceptional learner who can overcome the problems of reaching ultimate attainment after the sensitive period. Indeed it is quite a normal feat:

> it is prudent to assume that successful second language acquisition remains a possibility for all those who have learnt a natural language in childhood and can organize their lives to recreate some of the social, educational and experiential advantages that children enjoy. (Bialystok, 1997: 134)

The fact of the success of these exceptional learners suggests that the native speaker is as much a sociolinguistic construct as a developmental one.

Coppieters represents the strong psychological position, according to which the native speaker is defined by early acquired knowledge. Bartsch (1988) takes a more sociological view, allowing for the importance of attitude and identity. Although both views concern control of the standard language, they are probably not reconcilable. But why should they be? The concept 'native speaker' is used entirely appropriately in these quite different ways. It is probable that what is most enduring about the concept has nothing to do with truth and reality, whether or not individuals are native speakers; what matters most is the enduring native-speaker myth combining both knowledge and identity: in that myth the two views have an equal role.

Bartsch (1988: 4) states that 'norms are the social reality of the correctness notions ... In this way correctness concepts which are psychic entities have a social reality'. The correctness notions are the 'how to behave notions', similar to all other forms of learnt behaviour: how to ski, drive, play an instrument, dress and so on. What distinguishes language from these other skilled behaviours is that, in addition to the pyschic entities (knowing whether or not you are doing it well, right and so on), there is the social reality which carries and provides sanctions.

The rules which are attributed to language by linguists, those which are constructed for the grammar of what Jespersen (1922) called the common language, are, therefore, in part an acknowledgement and a working out of the intricate normative system acquired in taking on a standard language.

And it is important to remember that for Bartsch (and for us) correctness is not restricted to a few shibboleths (such as in English: *it's I/me; who/whom; will/shall*) however frequently they may occur in teaching programmes, in primers and as examples of the supposed uselessness of the whole notion of correctness put forward by libertarian descriptivists. Correctness for Bartsch includes the basic means of expression, lexical items, syntactic form, texts, semantic expression, pragmatic correctness. There is no argument here for triviality and no want of indication of the importance for language acquisition of correctness. Norms are established in terms of central models in speaking and writing ; and those models may be individuals or, more likely, élite groups.

Bloomfield (1927) writes: 'the Menonimi will say that one person speaks well and another badly, that such-and-such a form of speech is incorrect and sounds bad, and another too much like a shaman's preaching or archaic ("the way the old, old people talked")'. Bloomfield notes that though a foreigner he was able to share in these judgements of the Menonimi.

> The nearest approach to an explanation of 'good' and 'bad' language seems to be this, then, that by a cumulation of obvious superiorities, both of character and standing, as well as of language, some persons are felt to be better models of conduct and speech than others. (Bloomfield, 1927: 394, 396)

Standard languages, like religions, provide a commonality but not a homogeneity. That is why it makes sense to speak of norms rather than of rules which the standard-language member accepts.

Judgement Tests (1)

Ross in his paper 'Where's English?' discusses grammaticality judgements. He dismisses the strong hypothesis: English consists of that set of sentences which all speakers agree is grammatical, in favour of the much weaker: Beyond the core there is no single continuum of acceptability (Ross, 1979: 129, 131).

Ross (1979) reports an empirical study of grammaticality judgements of 13 English sentences, selected so as to offer a range of sentences types on what he regards as the continuum of grammaticality. Ross's results, based on the 12 sentences in the Appendix (he discarded one of the original 13), may be summed up thus: 'the sentences of a language seem to be viewed by speakers as falling into three groups, a Core (Sentences 1, 10), a Bog, and a Fringe (Sentences 12, 5)' (Ross, 1979: 156).

He finds general (though even here not universal) agreement about the grammaticality of his Core sentences; there is some variability in consensus that the Fringe sentences are not grammatical, and then comes the greatest variability in agreement about the Bog sentences (all the rest). He continues

> There are fairly clear differences between linguists and normals (the latter view themselves as more conservative than the former, and ... reject more sentences, and with greater confidence than the former do). There are also differences between native and foreign speakers, with the latter tending to reject more sentences than the former do, and also tending to make fuller use of all four grades than the former do. (p. 156)

Ross invited his subjects ($N = 30$) to rate the sentences on the four-point scale as follows:

(1) The sentence sounds perfect. You would use it without hesitation.
(2) The sentence is less than perfect – something in it just doesn't feel comfortable. Maybe lots of people could say it, but you never feel quite comfortable with it.
(3) Worse than (2), but not completely impossible. Maybe somebody might use the sentence, but certainly not you. The sentence is almost beyond hope.
(4) The sentence is absolutely out. Impossible to understand, nobody would say it. Un-English. (Ross, 1979: 161)

I replicated Ross's study (using a slightly localised version of his questionnaire) on a sample of applied linguists, all of whom had had experience as English language teachers (Davies, 2000). The sample ($N = 34$) was made up of staff (faculty) members, research students and Master's course-work students, containing both native speakers (NS, $N = 16$) and non-native speakers (NNS, $N = 18$) of English. The non-native speakers of English were in all cases fluent, highly proficient English speakers. The NS in the sample were mostly speakers of British English.

My results were similar to Ross's on his test. I report here only one feature, the Native Speaker (NS) – Non-native speaker (NNS) difference in terms of the overall sentence acceptance and rejection rate. The results for NS/NNS selection of the four categories for all 12 sentences, ranging from Category 1 ('the sentence sounds perfect') to Category 4 ('the sentence is absolutely out ... Un-English') are given in Tables 1–4.

The two groups are significantly different at the 1% level (t [for independent samples] = 18.5, df = 32). As the Total Sentence Mean and SD for the two groups indicate (Table 3), the NS range is narrower than the NNS range (Mean = 1.99: 2.23; SD = 0.78: 0.85). Not that this means that the NS are more conservative. Indeed, on the contrary, they are more

Table 1 Choices of grammaticality sentences by NNS

NHS	Sentences												Mean
	1	*2*	*3*	*4*	*5*	*6*	*7*	*8*	*9*	*10*	*11*	*12*	
Siswati	1	4	1	1	4	3	3	1	4	1	1	4	2.5
Greek	1	3	1	1	4	3	3	1	1	1	1	3	2.2
Hungarian	1	3	1	1	4	4	4	1	1	1	3	3	2.4
German	1	1	1	3	4	3	3	4	1	1	1	4	2.3
Japanese	1	4	1	1	4	1	4	4	1	1	1	3	2.4
Hungarian	1	3	1	1	4	3	3	4	1	1	1	4	2.4
Urdu	1	1	1	1	1	3	1	1	1	1	1	3	1.6
Japanese	1	3	1	1	3	4	3	3	3	1	1	3	2.4
Korean	1	4	1	1	4	1	3	3	3	1	1	1	2.2
Dutch	1	1	1	1	3	1	4	1	3	1	1	4	2.2
Japanese	1	3	1	1	4	1	4	1	3	1	1	3	2.3
Hebrew	1	4	4	3	4	1	3	1	4	1	1	4	2.8
Chinese (a)	1	3	1	1	1	1	3	3	4	1	1	4	2.3
Chinese (b)	1	4	1	1	4	1	1	3	4	1	1	3	2.3
Kirundi	1	1	1	1	1	4	1	1	1	1	1	4	1.5
Spanish	1	3	1	1	4	1	1	1	1	1	1	1	1.7
Japanese	1	3	1	1	4	3	3	4	1	1	1	3	2.4
Sinhala	1	3	3	1	4	3	4	1	1	1	1	4	2.4
Mean	1.1	3.0	1.8	1.6	3.5	2.5	3.0	2.2	2.5	1.0	1.5	3.3	

Table 2 Choices of grammaticality sentences by NS

NS	Sentences												Mean
	1	**2**	**3**	**4**	**5**	**6**	**7**	**8**	**9**	**0**	**11**	**12**	
ENS 1	1	4	1	2	3	1	2	1	2	1	2	2	1.8
ENS 2	1	2	1	2	3	2	4	1	1	1	2	4	2.0
ENS 3	1	3	1	1	1	1	2	1	2	1	1	2	1.4
ENS 4	2	3	3	2	2	2	4	1	3	1	2	2	2.2
ENS 5	1	3	2	1	3	1	4	1	3	1	1	3	2.0
ENS 6	1	3	4	2	3	1	4	2	3	1	2	4	2.5
ENS 7	1	3	1	2	2	1	3	1	1	1	2	1	1.6
ENS 8	1	2	3	3	1	1	4	1	1	1	3	4	2.1
ENS 9	1	2	1	1	4	4	2	1	4	1	1	4	2.2
ENS 10	1	3	1	2	4	2	3	1	2	1	1	3	2.0
ENS 11	1	2	1	2	4	2	3	1	2	1	1	3	2.3
ENS 12	1	3	2	2	2	1	3	1	3	1	1	4	2.0
ENS 13	1	1	1	1	3	1	4	1	2	1	2	4	1.8
ENS 14	1	4	2	2	4	2	3	2	4	1	2	2	2.4
ENS 15	1	2	1	2	2	2	3	1	2	1	2	2	1.7
ENS 16	1	2	1	1	3	2	4	2	2	1	1	3	1.9
Mean	1.1	2.7	1.6	1.7	2.7	1.7	3.3	1.2	2.3	1.0	1.7	3.0	

Table 3 Means and SDs for NS and NNS on grammaticality sentences

	Sentence mean	**Sentence SD**
NS	1.99	0.78
NNS	2.23	0.85

adventurous, or perhaps we should say they are more tolerant of uncertainty with regard to grammaticality. If they were more conservative than the NNS, their ratings for sentences would focus narrowly in the middle range, with predominant choices of the 2s and 3s (between the perfect 1s and the absolutely out 4s). But in fact what they do (relative to the NNS) is to cluster their choices on the 1s and 2s, giving the benefit of

Table 4 Mean ratings by NS and NNS on grammaticality sentences

	1	2	3	4
NS	4.9	3.6	1.9	1.5
NNS	4.3	2.7	2.6	2.3

the doubt to doubtful sentences. The NNS, however, choose 3s and 4s more frequently. It is they, as a group, who are more conservative, or perhaps here we should say, less aware of possibilities, less wide-ranging in their knowledge of potential contexts of use, more concerned with the risk of being wrong.

The mean choices for the four ratings for the two groups are given in Table 4. At the same time, the two groups are similar. A product-moment correlation between the two sets of sentence means gives an r of 0.88. In other words, in spite of the difference in mean amount (reported in Table 1), in terms of variance the two groups tend to order the sentences in the same way. A Sign Test ($N = 12$; $T = 11$ (one pair identical), $L = 3$) indicated a non-significant result since the obtained value of L is greater than the highest required value of L1 where $T = 11$ (L is the frequency of the less frequent sign and T the frequency of both pluses and minuses). At the same time, since in 8 of the paired values NNS is higher, there does seem to be a suggestion that higher scores are likely to occur for NNS than for NS. But of course we knew this already from the differences already reported between group means and SDs.

In terms of Ross's three categories of grammatical uncertainty (Core: Sentences 1, 10; Fringe: Sentences 5, 12; Bog: Sentences 2, 3, 4, 6, 7, 8, 9, 11), the two groups agreed almost exactly on the grammaticality of the two Core sentences (Tables 1 and 2). On the two Fringe sentences, the NNS were less accepting than the NS. But most disagreement was on certain Bog sentences, notably Sentence 8 (Mean difference of 0.91)

(8)   That is a frequently talked about proposal
      and Sentence 6 (Mean difference of 0.82).
(6)   I urge that anything he touch be burned.

In both cases the differences were in the expected direction. These are extreme examples of the general case to which we have already referred, that the NNS are less likely to accept as grammatical sentences those about which they are uncertain. The NS, however, are either more knowledgeable or they are prepared to give such sentences the benefit of the doubt and it is precisely in what Ross calls the Bog that this difference exhibits itself most acutely.

A crude summary of the NS/NNS group differences then might be that NNs have internalised the same grammatical judgements as NS but do not as a group know as much.

What about their performance as individuals? Does the NNS group contain any of Birdsong's 'exceptional learners'? In a non-linguistic sense they are all candidates for such ascription. They are all fluent adult speakers of English; all are teachers of English, all have studied English for at least 10 years. None of them started acquiring English as a young child.

In order to support my claim that in selected cases NNS individuals, on this evidence, are indistinguishable linguistically from NS, I present here ratings for the 12 sentences for three pairs of respondents having the same or similar total scores. The first pair contains two NS, the second and third pairs have one NS and one NNS. As will be seen, the choices by the pairs of NS/NNS are just as similar/dissimilar as those made by the pair of NS. Since it is the case that all of the NS produce a unique set of ratings and no two profiles are identical, it seems reasonable to argue that, in certain cases, individual NNS cannot be distinguished from what is normal variation within a similar group of NS.

The two NS (both with a mean for sentence ratings of 2.0) agree with one another in five ratings (Table 5); they differ by one level in six cases and by two levels in one case. Similarly, NS/NNS pair 1 (both with a mean for sentence ratings of 1.7) agree with one another in five ratings (Table 6); they differ by one level in six cases and by two levels in one case.

In the second NS/NNS pair (NS/NNS pair 2) while the overall means differ in the expected direction (2.3:2.0) the two members of the pair agree with one another in 7 of the 12 cases and differ by only one level in the other five (Table 7).

Table 5 Comparison of ratings by NS/NS pair

ENS 2	1	2	1	2	3	2	4	1	1	1	2	4	2.0
ENS 12	1	3	2	2	2	1	3	1	3	1	1	4	2.0

Table 6 Comparison of ratings by NS/NNS pair 1

Spanish	1	3	2	1	4	1	2	1	2	1	1	2	1.7
ENS 15	1	2	1	2	2	2	3	1	2	1	2	2	1.7

Table 7 Comparison of ratings by NS/NNS pair 2

German	1	2	1	3	4	3	3	4	2	1	1	4	2.3
ENS 2	1	2	1	2	3	2	4	1	1	1	2	4	2.0

The question which we need to address is what it is that binds the NS together (and, to a large extent, these NNS, who are, after all, near NS) as speakers of what Jespersen called a common language, given that they show such idiolectal variability when presented with grammaticality judgements. And the solution I offer is indeed the common language of Jespersen or, more relevantly perhaps, the Standard Language to which they (like the NNS) have been exposed through the Bartschian norms of education and training. If, therefore, native speakers become native speakers, at least in part, through education and training, NNS can also become native speakers of the target language if they too are exposed to similar education and training.

Judgement Tests (2)

As a further check on the NNS potentiality to become 'exceptional learners', I replicated the Eisenstein and Bodman (1986) study of pragmatic competence in expressing gratitude in English. In their study Eisenstein and Bodman report an analysis of their questionnaire data relating to seven gratitude situations. Their analysis shows that native and non-native speakers of English varied in their responses. They emphasise the importance of those differences: advanced non-native speakers of English had considerable difficulty adequately expressing gratitude in the target language. Some problems were pragmalinguistic in nature, exhibiting divergence from native use on lexical and syntactic levels. Learners were often unable to approximate native idioms and routines. In our judgement, socio-pragmatic limitations were more severe, because the sociocultural incongruities they revealed created the potential for more serious mis-understandings (Eisenstein & Bodman, 1986: 176).

In Table 2 of their article (p. 173; reproduced in the Appendix) they summarise the results for all non-native students. In spite of their general conclusion, quoted earlier, that the differences between native and non-native speakers were considerable, what this Table reveals is that their sample contained a substantial number of 'exceptional learners' who were not distinguishable in this highly sophisticated communicative competence area from native speakers. Their Table 2 provides columns for the following categories of response: No Response; Not Acceptable; Problematical; Acceptable; Perfect; Not Comprehensible; Resistant.

Summing across responses by non-native speakers gives a total mean for Perfect + Acceptable of 51%. If we exclude Acceptable ('clear and appropriate language, but containing small errors which do not interfere seriously with native speakers' understanding') we still retain a total mean for Perfect of 31%. In other words of the 67 non-native speakers of American English in the USA, 'in advanced-level ESL classes', 20 were producing native-speaker responses. Eisenstein and Bodman stress the limitations of their data, pointing, in particular, to the lack of fit between the respondents' written responses to what were presented as situations requiring oral expressions of gratitude. But of course the same lack of fit existed for their native-speaker subjects whom they used as a control.

In a partial replication (slightly localised to the UK context) of the Eisenstein and Bodman investigation ($N = 32$; 16 native speakers of English; 16 non-native speakers of English) I collected responses to three of their gratitude situations (the $5 loan, the dinner invitation; the sweater gift: see Appendix). These were all analysed in three categories, from 'Bald' to 'Bald plus Expansion' to 'Elaborate' expressions of gratitude. Thus, an example of a Bald response to the offer of the loan would be 'Thanks a lot!'; of a Bald + Expansion 'Thanks very much. I really appreciate this'; and of an Elaborate response (in this case with a promise and/or a comment) 'Are you sure this is OK? Thanks very much. I'll give it back on Monday, definitely.'

Table 8 NS/NNS gratitude expressions in three categories

		NNS	NS
Loan	Bald	5	2
	Bald + Expansion	3	4
	Elaborate	8	10
Sweater	Bald	0	0
	Bald + Expansion	7	6
	Elaborate	9	10
Dinner	Bald	0	1
	Bald + Expansion	7	6
	Elaborate	9	9
Totals	Bald	5 = 10%	3 = 6%
	Bald + Expansion	17 = 35%	16 = 33%
	Elaborate	26 = 54%	29 = 60%

Across all four situations the differences between native and non-native speakers were minimal: non-native speakers had slightly more Bald + Expansion and slightly fewer Elaborate responses (Bald + Expansion: native speakers = 16; non-natives = 17; Elaborate: native speakers = 29; non-natives = 26).

In terms of Eisenstein and Bodman's 'Perfect' category, across all four of my situations, 56% of NNS responses could be regarded as 'perfect'. No doubt what counts as 'perfect' is a matter of interpretation and the figure of 56% refers to responses rather than to individual NNSs. Even so, a check of individual total responses indicates that at least three of these NNSs had completely 'perfect' responses. It is, therefore, hard to avoid the conclusion that several of these NNSs of English were pragmatically 'exceptional learners'.

Operationalising Language Test Data to Describe the Native Speaker

Morton's fork,[1] offered two equally unpalatable choices. Is that where we are with the native speaker? If the native speaker still seems problematic as a goal is that, as I have suggested, because we remain doubtful whether learners can ever reach that goal or is it because we are no clearer about how to define the native speaker?

Can we avoid both choices by instead using second-language test data to help describe the native speaker? After all, the measurement question will not go away, since we still need to demonstrate how it is we describe the attainment of these exceptional learners.

There are several ways of demonstrating this. The first is to take examples of performances on tests by the kinds of second-language learners who find careers in international agency interpreting or, of course, spying. It does not have to be test data. It could equally well be examples of writings (writings rather than speeches because of the distraction of accent) by such well-known learners as Nabokov, Senghor, Becket or Narayan. But such demonstration is perhaps supererogatory because we all know that learners can − in exceptional cases − reach such ultimate attainment. And if it is then countered that these are always limited tasks or domains, that there are other areas of native-speaker control that are not within the demonstration, then the answer must be that this is true also of subgroups of native speakers.

A second way of demonstrating is to use test descriptors to describe exceptional learners' attainment in order to examine to what extent they fail to reach ultimate attainment. For example, the descriptors on a test such as the Italian Teachers' Proficiency Test (see later) purport to describe what a second-language learner is required to achieve. But what is intriguing about performance at the highest level (Level 3) on these scales is how difficult it is to distinguish what is expected of the learner from what is assumed of the native speaker (Elder, 1994).

'Certificate of Proficiency for Language Teachers: Italian'

Description of Test Performance: Level 3:
> In performing the range of test tasks the speaker demonstrated communicative abilities and strategies which were highly appropriate for the classroom context. The tone of voice, intonation, phrasing and pace of delivery and level of language used reflected a high degree of confidence and audience awareness. In explaining student error, the speaker was able to articulate the rules of Italian grammar and phonology in a clear and accurate manner with judicious use of specialist terminology.

A third demonstration is to use test data to chart language separation, that is performance on a test (like writing in a code) which illustrates a late stage of acceptance within a speech community of a new standard. In other words what is needed are answers to an EFL test (e.g. TOEFL) which would not receive a high mark from an American or British judge but would do so from a compatriot. Such evidence would support the claims of New English writers that the standard they are modelling is now localised.

Exceptional learners are needed for all three demonstrations: in the first and second cases (joining the target standard) they indicate individual ability. In the third case (here we would call them prestige speakers) they show how individuals can influence the direction of a social group. Lowenberg (1995:64) argues that 'diversification on a societal level is clearly a significant variable that can no longer be ignored in the measurement of English proficiency'. Interesting as such an argument is, it seems to me quite unlikely that any international language proficiency test would build in local variation in this way. What is more likely is the development of localised proficiency tests.

The fourth type of demonstration is to establish an acceptable local foreign language level of attainment as the norm. This issue has been considered in relation to a teacher proficiency test for Indonesian teachers of English (Brown & Lumley, 1995:122–8). What this test sets out to do is:

- to assess English language proficiency as relevant to teachers
- to base its content on topics and situations relevant, familiar and hence accessible to people in Indonesia; to emphasise assessment of the ability of inhabitants of the region to communicate effectively in English with each other, rather than relating their proficiency to metropolitan norms; to rely entirely on local Indonesian teacher trainers as raters.

The top level of performance on this test could, in essence, represent, in a reportable way, an approximation to native-speaker proficiency.

Relevance to Applied Linguistics

Language proficiency has been referred to in many places in this book. In Chapters 9 and 10 the judgement issue raises in its sharpest form the actual differences between native and non-native speakers. I have in the course of the book proposed various explanations for the asserted differences, in proficiency, in communicative competence and in linguistic competence (of which judgements are a special part). In all cases I have claimed that while of course there are differences on each of these parameters it must be the case that there is overlap. That is to say that non-native speakers can become native speaker like in the target language in terms of proficiency, communicative competence and linguistic competence. I would also specu-late that these three parameters represent a gradient of difficulty such that proficiency is easier of attainment than is communicative competence and communicative competence is easier to achieve than is linguistic com-petence. Further that within linguistic competence the most difficult aspect for the learner is that of judgements of grammaticality.

Whether or not this is so, the message of this chapter for applied linguistics is that there is no substitute for proficiency, that for learners of second languages the native speaker must represent a model and a goal. Of course it is the case that successful second-language learners can choose native-speaker membership. That is a different issue. The goal and model for the second-language learner remains a chief preoccupation and for that the developing interest in testing language proficiency through more refined and carefully analysed tests, through a better understanding of proficiency and through an awareness of the articulation of levels of accept-able language proficiency is to be encouraged and applauded (Hughes, 1989; Bachman, 1990; Spolsky, 1989; McNamara, 1990; Davies, 1990a; Alderson *et al.*, 1995).

Summary

A standard language needs as its 'members' those who uphold its norms by taking on the responsibility of being its native speakers. Native speakers represent standard languages: it is the standard language they are native speakers of. What exceptional learners tell us is (1) that native-speaker attainment is achievable in the target standard language and (2) that an alternative standard is possible when such learners are accorded the status of prestige speakers of the alternative standard. What we saw with both the Ross replication and the Eisenstein and Bodman replication was that, both in grammaticality judgements and in pragmatic selections, in certain cases, individual NNSs are indistinguishable from NSs; these are exceptional learners.

The native speaker is a fine myth: we need it as a model, a goal, almost an inspiration. But it is useless as a measure; it will not help us define our goals. So, in spite of my firm agreement with Birdsong and my conviction that there is a continuum between native speakers and non-native speakers, nevertheless, I recognise that for language teaching purposes what is crucial is the description of adequate partial proficiencies. It is to language tests that we look for these partial proficiency descriptions, but that is the subject of another book. This is what the second-language learner can tell us about the native speaker which the native speaker's lack of boundaries cannot.

Note

1. John Morton (1420–1500) was Archbishop of Canterbury and a minister of the English King Henry VII. As a way of raising forced loans he would apply his 'fork' – the argument that if people were obviously rich, then they could afford to pay, and if people looked poor, then they were obviously holding something back and so could also afford to pay. An early form of Catch 22.

Chapter 10

Conclusion: Who is the Native Speaker?

As we saw in Chapters 2 and 4, Singapore provides an interesting case study in discussions about the New Englishes and the issue of just how acceptable internationally these Englishes are for using as an international language. Crewe's (1977b) valuable paper is now out of date but the examples he gives of various formal styles of Singapore English point up the problem. For example among the examples he quotes from Goh Poh Seng's novel *If We Dream Too Long* (1971) he includes the following:

> They waited by the bus-stop and then *alighted* the STC bus together.
>
> I don't suppose you *would* be surprised if I tell you.
>
> At the hospital they were told their father had *come into* consciousness.
>
> The day after his decision, his father was *boarded out* of his job.
>
> I wish *I've* read more, Kwang Meng said. (Crewe, 1977b; 109–10; emphasis in original)

Crewe's comment (quoted in Chapter 7) about the difficulty of classifying non-native errors as error because they can so often be found in native-speaker dialects holds good here too. At the same time there is a sense in which these examples would not be regarded as 'correct' in a formal context by native speakers. But by which native speakers? 'Under which King? Bezonian, speak or die', as Falstaff demanded of Justice Shallow.

Before we bring together the arguments set out in this book, we review the kinds of judgement relevant to our understanding of the native speaker. These judgements are of two kinds: judgements of identity and judgements of language.

Judgements of Identity

The issue is whether native speakers and second-language learners make the same or different judgements about one another. We have called this a question of identity, that is the judgements are being made about people, but, as will be obvious, it is difficult to separate judgements of people from judgements of language. In fact it may always be a matter of identity, that is to say that when judgements are elicited about people or about their language what is obtained is some view of the people themselves. In other words all sociolinguistic judgements are essentially identity ones. However, these are typically distinguished from judgements about language on its own, as far as is possible decontextualised in terms of identity. Such judgements are not sociolinguistic ones: I deal with that issue later.

In the case of identity judgements the question is whether native speakers and second-language learners make the same or different judgements about language use. Judgements may be made at a variety of levels and in different situations: pronunciation (including segmental, intonational, stress, rhythm), grammar, semantics, pragmatics, discourse, style alone or in combination. The common assumption (Gardner, 1985) is certainly that native speakers are judged differently in a variety of ways from second-language learners, that they are reckoned to be more/less kind, resourceful, attractive, sincere and so on; that native speakers and second-language learners make different judgements about one another, even though it is common to find native speakers being given greater prestige both by themselves and by second-language learners (Giles & Powesland, 1975).

However, it is the case that such studies typically make use of stereotyped second-language learners, in most cases clearly unlike native speakers in one or more ways and that the native speakers chosen are themselves representative (above all in terms of accent) of a privileged élite group who would receive similar attribution of status from other native speakers (see, for example, Giles & Powesland 1975).

An equally interesting question is whether native speakers and second-language learners invariably recognise one another: this is not a question about location in either case nor whether the native speakers can determine the provenance of the second-language learners or *vice versa*. Rather it is a question only about the boundary between native and non-native speakers. Now here there are serious problems about how to collect the evidence: even the question to be asked is difficult to formulate. Is it, for example, 'Is this person a native speaker or not?' for this assumes an unlikely awareness among the judges. Better perhaps to ask: 'Is this person a second language learner?.' What is of interest is which features of a spoken/written performance cause judges to make their decision.

But there is important evidence that native speakers and non-native speakers fail to recognise one another if the non-native speakers are very proficient. Evidence of this sort is produced by, for example, the Lambert attitude studies (Gardner, 1985), in which group stereotyped language attitudes are investigated by way of the matched-guise technique. Typically these studies show that the judges, who in this case were both francophone and anglophone Canadians, fail to detect that the stimulus voices are in only half the cases anglophones speaking as francophones, in the remaining half of the cases, francophones speaking as anglophones. Now it may be true that this is the paradigm case of 'true' bilingualism to which we have already referred, that is of people who are native speakers of two languages Lx and Ly and that they cannot therefore be regarded as evidence for failure to detect second-language learners. Gass and Varonis (1985), Eisenstein and Bodman (1986), Thomas (1983) and Wolfson (1981) among others, have all shown that native speakers and second-language learners behave differently, notably in the discourse and pragmatic areas.

What I seek is the trigger to the 'Aha!' of recognition, of difference or sameness and it may well be useful to consider this against the social psychological accommodation theory of Giles (1984) and shift even though attitudes may. In the second case the language itself moves towards the other's in a formal sense.

Native speakerness raises expectations, both others' expectations and our own, in us all, which suggests that we judge decisively and intolerantly. We rarely give an alter the benefit of the doubt; our judgements are of the inclusive/exclusive type. We are not interested in being kind about other group membership, the reason being those expectations which native speakers take for granted in one another. These judgements then have to do with such characteristics as the following ones.

Flexibility of expression

This means having a wide range of syntactic and semantic alternatives so that

(a) native speakers can/do vary what they are saying; and
(b) they can repeat a message in another form for the sake of clarity or to disambiguate.

Avoiding avoidance

Native speakers normally do not give up on comprehension or on production; they assume that what is said to them (by a native-speaker alter) can be understood by them in principle and they also assume that what they wish to say they can say. Normal native speakers therefore do not get frustrated because they cannot encode their ideas: yet this is precisely what gives adult second-language learners so much frustration since they find they cannot put into the target language the ideas which they know so well how to encode in their L1.

Expecting interaction between native speaker–native speaker to be intelligible

Native speakers assume that what they say will necessarily be intelligible and that the same is true of the interlocutor. They do not, however, expect to understand or to be understood in the sense of comprehending the message.

Actually there are probably distinctions among native speakers in this regard in that those with less experience of variety (less mobile, more rural, more restricted socially and culturally) may more frequently expect to be understood, arguing from the notion of restricted codes, since they are based on a situation in which all interaction takes place among dialectal or subcultural in-group members.

Native speakers also expect non-native speakers to be intelligible in the dyad native speaker–non-native speaker and are surprised and frustrated (Janicki, 1985: 10) when intelligibility is low or non-existent. This is an extension of the earlier point about native speaker–native speaker and understanding where there is no intelligibility problem. In other words what counts as *understanding* for a cross-dialect group of native speakers is equivalent to *intelligibility* for a native speaker–non-native speaker interaction.

In the straightforward case of native speaker–native speaker and intelligibility, since both parties expect full intelligibility in normal settings, they assume that any problems are caused by channel noise and therefore what is needed is to have recourse to redundancy, usually by repetition or, possibly, by switching to another medium (for example speech to writing). When such repetition takes place (for example, 'Say that again please!' or (on the telephone) 'Speak more slowly!' or (in a lecture/public meeting) 'Please speak up!' 'Speak louder!' etc. then the typical speaker reaction is to concur not object, the assumption being that it is the channel that is under criticism, not the message nor the speaker.

Fluent spontaneous discourse

Pawley and Syder (1983) suggest that this is the reflection more of stem (repeated elements) routines than of the composition of grammatical sentences. Non-native speakers exhibit an inadequate control over the processing capacity while native speakers demonstrate a command of 'chaining' whereby they show their 'one clause at a time facility': pauses tend to occur, therefore, for native speakers at clause boundaries unlike second-language learners who also pause medially (for example after articles, prepositions). Pawley and Syder are enthusiastic about the idea of the linguistic memory as containing a large stock of lexicalised sentence and clause patterns which can be called on at will. The suggestion is that, in addition to a generalising capacity which is essential for acquiring competence, the native speaker also gains a facility in a processing capacity, not unlike the operation procedure of a computer.

Whether or not this is so, the fact of native speaker fluency (in 'normal' settings) is well attested as is the claim that much of what is said by native speakers is repetitious and routinised (Firth, 1957). Hence the typical concern of non-native speakers that they cannot understand what native speakers are saying to one another and cannot themselves participate in it, because the context of such interactions is often empty; what the non-native speakers are missing is not the *what* but the *how* of ritual.

Strategies of performance

Native speakers take it for granted that they share performance strategies, even though they also know that strategy control is not equal. Thus interruption, circumlocution, silence and so forth are assumed as are more stylistic features of irony, sarcasm, ambiguity and jokes, against the background of the cultural assumptions which native speakers associate with their first language. English has a special problem because as it extends its range of first- and second-language users so it becomes increasingly difficult to rely on expectations and assumptions. It also raises the interesting question of the possible status as a language of International English – since it is not clear how a natural language without some cultural basis is possible. Advocates of International English avoid this problem in some case by using a different terminology (such as English as an International Language, for example Smith (1983), or World Englishes (see Chapter 8).

Paralinguistics

In addition to their linguistic expectations about one another, native-speakers also have strong expectations of their native speaker alter's paralinguistic behaviour. While they can again be confused and sometimes mistaken by subgroup paralinguistics, their expectations are usually confirmed: with regard to such features as facial expression, head and arm movements, body posture and distance. What all such features indicate very strongly is membership: native speakers take for granted, as members of all groups do, that membership is an acceptance of and an agreement to use certain norms of behaviour.

Membership too can lapse after disuse and there is general acceptance for the view that native speakers can cease to possess the language as native speakers after longish periods among non-native speakers, in at least three ways. First, they lose out on contemporary uses, for example slang, new coinages and idioms. Second, they lose some of their generative capacity and tend to become fixed in the locutions of their time of exile, and third, they become increasingly prescriptive and less tolerant of change.

Foreignness

As Janicki (1985: 10) points out, foreignness is relative to the situation:

> a 'linguistic foreigner' may be defined as a speaker whose language either is totally incomprehensible to other participants or its integrative function is perceived as foreign by the remaining participants of interaction.

Native speakers act in a proprietorial way towards their L1, as the 'personal possession hypothesis' (Marton & Preston, 1975) suggests, and they regard any assumption of native-speaker rights by non-native speakers (the use of slang, obscenities, informal pronunciation) as 'linguistic thieving'. Janicki (1985) offers three types of sociolinguistic deviance:

(1) forms which do not exist in the target language;
(2) forms which are inappropriate to the situation; and
(3) forms 'reserved' for native speakers, such as those we have just mentioned.

Janicki points out that non-native speakers are prone to error in their use of all three types. Native speakers do not employ forms which do not exist in the target language; they cannot, by definition, employ forms reserved for native speakers; and while forms which are inappropriate to the situation may be used by native speakers and cause disagreement with other native speakers about their appropriacy, this is not the case with some uses by non-native speakers which will be rated as deviant by all native speakers. Examples might be swearing or obscenities in public settings.

Janicki puts forward the interesting conjecture of there being perhaps three main categories of non-native-speaker situation:

(1) native speaker–non-native speaker (context L1 of native speaker),
(2) native speaker–non-native speaker (context L1 of non-native speaker) and
(3) native speaker–non-native speaker (context L1 of neither)

and argues that the native speaker will in all cases be governed by some form of 'accommodation' and as a result is likely to be influenced by the particular culture in which the interaction takes place.

Studying the foreigner's language means being able to distinguish what one means by the native speaker's language. Again I have a boundary distinction. Janicki refers to a number of areas which repay investigation with regard to research in this area, for example sex, time, social roles, relationship, topic, schema, sociolinguistic rules, formality, directness, politeness, conversational analysis, speech act analysis. He also notes the difficult balancing act of the non-native speaker: 'the better the foreigner's command of grammar and pronunciation, the more likely it is that sociolinguistic deviance on his part will evoke the native's negative attitude' (Janicki, 1985: 40: a factor we considered in the 'Why bother?' story in Chapter 6). The native speaker is always likely to react strongly to non-native speaker language in terms of irritation, amusement, acceptance and appreciation. What is significant here is that such reactions are common in the native speaker–non-native speaker context but rare in the native speaker–native speaker context, although, of course, they do occur there and when they do they illustrate the thin partition that lies between dialect differences and language differences between the native and the non-native speaker.

I have argued that the term native speaker refers to at least three types of knowledge or capacity: First, speaking one's own dialect: in other words everyone is a native speaker of his/her own language; this type or category therefore is meaningless and can be regarded as empty except for the important boost it gives to everyone's sense of self-worth, since it indicates that being a native speaker of one's own idiolect is part of being human. Second, being attached to a group whose idiolects share certain unspoken and non-formalised norms: I have labelled this type of attachment (standard) language in order to emphasise that norms exist even when they are not codified. It would, of course, be rash to think otherwise since this is exactly the situation for most cultures. They are clearly norm-based since we all belong to groups and act as members, whether conforming or not, but the norms are typically uncodified. That is to say it is just not possible to consult any reference material for a culture comparable to reference materials such as grammars and dictionaries for a language. There are, it is true, books on etiquette and sometimes guides to being a foreigner in a society but, apart from the world of anthropologists, these are at an informal level. Nevertheless such books are not to be dismissed and their attempt to codify should be recognised.

The third category is being attached to a group whose idiolects show certain formal and codified norms: this is the case of the Standard Language. We have further suggested that while a Standard Language or indeed a (standard) language necessarily has what Bartsch calls a *point*, a model to be imitated, aimed at, judged by and so forth (and this model may be one person or an élite group or indeed a particular, often sacred, text), it also has a *range*, ensuring that a considerable and wide tolerance of idiolects is permitted. All Standard Languages are therefore likely to include some (standard) languages and of course many idiolects. All (standard) languages do not, however, belong to Standard Languages since they may either fall outside the range of particular Standard Languages (as in the case of creoles) or there may be no relevant Standard Language for them to be attached to (such as Konkani). All idiolects, however, belong to a (standard) language which may or may not be part of a Standard Language. Identity then is crucial to the sense of native speakerness. Belonging to a group marked by shared norms and with whom intelligibility is possible is what membership of a (standard) language group or of a Standard Language group means. Note that in all cases the (standard) language membership must facilitate interaction; that is everyone is socialised into some primary group. But it is clearly possible for some members of a (standard) language group to claim membership of a Standard Language group solely on ideological grounds of identity and for that claim to be largely symbolic, in that verbal communication is not facilitated. (Spoken Arabic or spoken Chinese may well provide illustrations of this phenomenon.)

Judgements of Language

We have briefly considered judgements of language in Chapter 9. Much of the literature on second-language acquisition and interlanguage concerns such judgements, judgements often comparing native speakers and second-language learners. In most cases these judgements differ and, in particular, what they show is that native speakers are, in terms of everything but pronunciation, more tolerant than second-language learners and that second-language learners are very normative indeed in their judgements on all areas.

What this literature also shows, however, is that while on other comparisons non-native speakers can demonstrate equal competence with native speakers (for example in multiple choice grammatically correct form selection tests), judgements about acceptability are more sensitive to underlying competence differences. Such an argument does, of course, support the strong position of Felix, Cook, Greenbaum etc. – see Chapters 2 and 9) on the difference between native speakers and non-natives in the sense that the ability to make judgments is acquired early or not at all.

Reprise

Are there, then, differences between native speakers and non-native speakers? The question is not unlike another question: are there differences between men and women? But not quite. It may be (though this is disputable) that the roles of men and women are only social and that through socialisation each would accept the other's role (including the whole social psychology of the presentation of the self) or there could be neutralisation. This is possible. But there remain the genetic differences which produce different biologies (and by some are said to lead inevitably to differential role function). Again I know that sex change is possible through chemistry and surgery (and courage) but even then there remains the generating difference: as yet, only women can have babies.

The native speaker–non-native speaker distinction is hardly as dramatic: and it does not contain the crucial genetic difference. Indeed that it does not do so has been the burden of our argument since we have accepted the principles and parameters model of Universal Grammar. According to this model, different languages are the same languages (or set of principles) but with different parameter settings. From this point of view it has been maintained that languages differ essentially in terms of vocabulary. I can express the argument as follows. A child draws on Universal Grammar (our Grammar 3) to construct his/her L1 (our Grammar 1) on the basis of input from parents or other caretakers using their L1 (Grammar 1 and Grammar 2). The child is then socialised into a Standard Language or a (standard) language, that is his/her Grammar 2. Parameters are set and reset at all points. The same procedure applies to the adult L2 learner who both regresses to Universal Grammar (Grammar 3) and exchanges one L1 for another L1 through resetting of parameters.

Even so there are similarities between the two constructs of language and sex: socialisation into the other sex role is no doubt easier the earlier it starts; and I have argued that the native speaker may be a native speaker of more than one L1, as long as the acquisition process starts early and necessarily pre-puberty. After puberty, as I have shown (following, for example, Felix, 1987), it becomes difficult – not impossible but very difficult (Birdsong, 1992) – to become a native speaker. The great pubertal divide, since it is fundamentally sexual, changes totally the other sex role learning possibility, making hormonal treatment essential for later imprinting to take place. Indeed this is also probably the case at puberty even when a male baby has been brought up as female and *vice versa*. The native speaker–non-native speaker differences therefore are not innate but learnt but they need to start being learnt very early. The male–female differences are innate and it seems to be the case that they can never be completely reversed.

I conclude that the concept of the native speaker is not a fiction but has the reality that 'membership', however informal, always gives. Therefore the native speaker is relied on to know what the score is, how things are done, because s/he carries the tradition, is the repository of 'the language'. The native speaker is also expected to exhibit normal control especially in fluent connected speech (though not of course in writing), and to have command of expected characteristic strategies of performance and of communication. A native speaker is also expected to 'know' another native speaker, in part because of an intuitive feel, like for like, but also in part because of a characteristic systematic set of indicators, linguistic, pragmatic and paralinguistic, as well as an assumption of shared cultural knowledge.

The native speaker who remains a learner but who is able to balance that role with the proper authority role necessarily attained can only be a valued resource. McCawley (1986) notes the difference between the native and the non-native speaker as learner since the native speaker has to combine this with also being the authority. Indeed, we might hazard that a non-native speaker can claim that s/he has achieved the steady state of being a native speaker in the second language when s/he is prepared to accept the fragility of the knowledge s/he has so carefully acquired. Adulthood as a native speaker is no different from being an adult in any other field.

In this book I have emphasised the role of the Standard Language (or the (standard) language) which we have discussed in terms of what I have labelled Grammar 2. Individuals have no choice of a Grammar 1, which is theirs by virtue of the idiolect into which they are socialised. But I have argued that there is a sense in which they do have a choice in terms of Grammar 2 and that choice is a reflection of the group they identify with. Membership therefore, in our view, determines behaviour, in this case, adoption of a Grammar 2, the Standard Language, rather than the other way round of behaviour determining membership (Barth, 1969).

Such a stress on identity relates this view of the native speaker to the work in social identity theory of Henri Tajfel. It is fitting to close with a comment of his on the typical majority–minority situation: 'minorities are often defined on the basis of criteria originating from, and developed by, the majorities. They are different from something which, itself, need not be clearly defined' (Tajfel, 1981:317). There is a relief in this saving comment that allows us to conclude that our failure to define the native speaker may indicate that, like other majorities, native speakers define themselves negatively as not being non-native speakers. To be a native speaker means not being a non-native speaker. Such a conclusion reminds us of the central importance to all discussions of language behaviour of the non-native speaker.

The Argument So Far

Let me at this point summarise under the following five heads the position I have reached on the Native Speaker:

- Everyone is a native speaker of his/her own unique code. I have therefore rejected the idea of semilingualism as illogical.
- Everyone accepts and adheres to norms of a Standard Language, either an informal (standard) language, which might be a dialect, or a codified Standard (typically called a language). The relation between an informal (standard) language and a codified Standard is that the codified Standard is typically flexible enough to permit a good deal of tolerance to the informal (standard) language, with, however, many situations in which for extraneous cultural, political or religious reasons there is norm conflict leading to misunderstandings and refusal to communicate.
- Because the preceding argument represents both a range and a point (Bartsch, 1988) those near the point (the centre or model of the Standard Language) are favoured and advantaged. They suffer less from insecurity, are less likely to practise hypercorrection and, above all, have less of a learning problem in using the Standard Language for public purposes (for example in education). Meanwhile those near the extremes are disfavoured and disadvantaged, more likely to feel insecure and to have their version of the Standard Language stigmatised as well as to stigmatise it themselves (as with our informant's Hindustani and Urdu, see Chapter 7). In public uses

(such as education) they have more of a learning problem. It is possible (though this is quite unclear) that they may also have a cognitive problem because they have learnt to think in their own remote variety of the Standard Language, a difficulty compounded by possible lack of intelligibility of input by teachers whose Standard Language may be nearer the point. Nevertheless, this is the situation of social life and of a non-homogeneous community and it is possible, if difficult, for those disadvantaged initially by their own L1 to accumulate and gain full access to a more central version.

This is not to say that they must redesign themselves and deny their own past, though Sutcliffe (1982) provides a counter argument here, rather it means that they have the opportunity, if they choose to take it, to expand and extend themselves. The assumption behind these remarks is, of course, that full account is taken of the disadvantage (the linguistic difference) from which they start and that they are given every incentive, opportunity and informed help to add to their own version the more central version of the Standard Language.

• Native speakers all do indeed have intuitions about their Standard Language but in those cases where there is tolerance but flexibility it is likely that their knowledge of and performance in those norms will be shaky. And where they are uncertain they will guess, admit ignorance or fall back on some basic Universal Grammar principle. What this means is that intuitions are learnt not innate: the grammar of the Standard Language is not built into the head of the child any more than is the grammar of his/her own individual idiolectal version of the Standard Language.

• All native speakers have access to some kind of language faculty, which may be called Universal Grammar (UG) and which has to operate at a very high level of abstraction. I have already made reference (Chapters 2, 5 and 9) to aspects of second-language acquisition but it is worth noting here that the apparent polar arguments seeking to explain acquisition, whether the learner moves across from an L1 (some version of the old contrastive analysis model) or regresses to the primary UG state and then moves forward again into an L2, are in a serious sense non-arguments since both must be true. Since the L1 grammar is a version of UG and underlying it is UG, then it is a matter of generative arrangement how I draw the connection between L1 and L2 since UG must occur there somewhere.

I have discussed the question of whether an L2 learner can become a native speaker of a target language and have agreed that this is possible though difficult. I have separated out the question of childhood bilingualism, pointing out that since age of acquisition seems criterial the two languages acquired early can both be L1s. We turn our attention now to post-childhood L2 learners and their status as native speakers of their L2. We will also give some attention to the feelings and attitudes of L2 learners about their own status in the target language and to what extent being or not being native speakers of the target language is of importance to them.

Characteristics of the Native Speaker

We have referred in the course of our discussion to a number of qualities of the native speaker, taking account of the age of acquisition, the grammatical intuition of the native speaker and the discoursal, creative and translation facilities of the native speaker. Let us summarise briefly our position on just what the native speaker is according to our deductions so far. Unless we do that it is just not possible to determine whether or not an L2 learner can become a native speaker of a target language. What does the native speaker know, what can the native speaker do?

The native speaker (and this means all native speakers) can be characterised in the following six ways:

(1) The native speaker acquires the L1 of which s/he is a native speaker in childhood.

(2) The native speaker has intuitions (in terms of acceptability and productiveness) about his/her Grammar 1.

(3) The native speaker has intuitions about those features of the Grammar 2 which are distinct from his/her Grammar 1.

(4) The native speaker has a unique capacity to produce fluent spontaneous discourse, which exhibits pauses mainly at clause boundaries (the 'one clause at a time' facility) and which is facilitated by a huge memory stock of complete lexical items (Pawley & Syder, 1983). In both production and comprehension the native speaker exhibits a wide range of communicative competence.

(5) The native speaker has a unique capacity to write creatively (and this includes, of course, literature at all levels from jokes to epics, metaphor to novels).

(6) The native speaker has a unique capacity to interpret and translate into the L1 of which s/he is a native speaker. Disagreements about an

individual's capacity are likely to stem from a dispute about the Standard or (standard) Language.

An L2 Native Speaker?

To what extent can the L2 learner become a target-language native speaker? We will consider this question in relation to L2 learners in general. Let us again consider the six criteria:

(1) *Childhood acquisition*: No, the second-language learner, by our own definition, does not acquire the target language in early childhood. As I have noted, if s/he does then s/he is a native speaker of both L1 and the target language (TL) or in his/her case of L1x and L1y.

(2) *Intuitions about idiolectal grammar (Grammar 1)*: Yes, it must be possible, with sufficient contact and practice for the second-language learner to gain access to intuitions about his/her own Grammar 1 of the target language (although, as I will show, this makes an important assumption about criterion 1, childhood acquisition).

(3) *Intuitions about group language grammar (Grammar 2)*: Yes again, with sufficient contact and practice the second-language learner can gain access to the Grammar 2 of the target language. Indeed in many formal learning situations it is exactly through exposure to a TL Grammar 2 that the TL Grammar 1 would emerge, the reverse of the L1 development.

(4) *Discourse and pragmatic control*: Yes, this may indeed be a descriptive difference between a native speaker and a non-native speaker but it is not in any way explanatory: that is to say it in no way argues that a second-language learner cannot become a native speaker.

(5) *Creative performance*: Yes again, with practice it must be possible for a second-language learner to become an accepted creative writer in the TL. There are, of course, well-known examples of such cases – Conrad, Becket, Senghor, Narayan – but there is also the interesting problem of the acceptability to the L1 community of the second-language learner's creative writing; this is an attitudinal question but so too is the question of the acceptability to the same community of a creative writer writing not in the Standard Language but in a (standard) language.

(6) *Interpreting and translating*: Yes again, this must be possible although international organisations generally require that interpreters should interpret into their L1. (It remains of course unclear what judgements

are made of an applicant for an interpreter's post; no doubt proficiency tests are carried out but it would be difficult to deny a claim of an applicant that s/he is a native speaker.)

All except (1) are contingent issues. In this way the question 'Can a second language learner become a native speaker of a target language?' reduces to 'Is it necessary to acquire a code in early childhood in order to be a native speaker of that code?'. Now the answer to this question, and this is where the circularity lies, is to ask a further question, what is it that the child acquires in acquiring his/her L1? But I have already answered that question in my previous criteria (2)–(6), and so the question again becomes a contingent one. But we do need, in (2) and (3), to ensure a cultural dimension since the child L1 acquirer does have access to the resources of the culture attached to the language and particularly to those learnt and encoded or even imprinted early. Still, having said that, what of sub-cultural differences between, for example, the Scots and the English; of different cultures with the same Standard language (for example the Swiss, the Austrians, the West Germans and the East Germans); or of different cultures with different Standard languages (for example the British and the American)? What too of International English or, as I prefer, English as an International Language or of English as a *lingua franca*?

Given the interlingual differences and the lack of agreement and norms that certainly occur among such groups it does appear that the second-language learner has a difficult but not an impossible task to become a native speaker of a target language which can contain such wide diversities. The answer to the question of L2 learners evolving into native speakers of the target language must therefore be 'Yes': but the practice required, given the model of the child L1 acquirer who for five to six years spends much of his/her time learning language alone, is so great that it is not likely that many second-language learners become native speakers of their target language. The analogy that occurs to me here is that of music where it is possible to become a concert performer after a late start but the reality is that few do. The more exact analogy of learning to play the piano as a child and switching to, say, the cello later on is common and is not the relevant comparison I wish to make.

In discussing judgements about language, I referred to Coppieters' (1987) results which indicate that the confirmed difference native speaker–non-native speaker repeats the elaborated–restricted code difference which Bernstein (1971–5) reported. For in exactly the same way what holds back the non-native speaker (like the speaker of a restricted code) is the early acquired generalising capacity.

I concluded that it is difficult for an adult non-native speaker to become a native speaker of a second language precisely because I define a native speaker as a person who has early acquired the language. However, the limitations imposed by the later acquisition, when it is very successful, are likely to be psycholinguistic rather than sociolinguistic. The adult non-native speaker can acquire the communicative competence of the native speaker; s/he can acquire the confidence necessary to membership. What is more difficult is to gain the speed and the certainty of knowledge relevant to judgements of grammaticality. But as with all questions of boundaries (for the native speaker is a boundary that excludes) there are major language differences among native speakers. Native speakers may be prepared to make judgements quickly about grammaticality but they do not necessarily agree with one another. And so I am left asking to what extent it matters. If a non-native speaker wishes to pass as a native speaker and is so accepted then it is surely irrelevant if s/he shows differences on more and more refined tests of grammaticality. This may be of interest psycholinguistically but for applied linguistic purposes I maintain that it is unimportant.

For the distinction native speaker–non-native speaker, like all majority–minority power relations, is at bottom one of confidence and identity. What this means, as Tajfel (1981) points out, is that we define minorities negatively against majorities which themselves we may not be able to define. To be a native speaker means not being a non-native speaker. Even if I cannot define a native speaker I can define a non-native speaker negatively as someone who is not regarded by him/herself or by native speakers as a native speaker. It is in this sense only that the native speaker is not a myth, the sense that gives reality to feelings of confidence and identity. They are real enough even if on analysis the native speaker is seen to be an emperor without any clothes.

The differing positions of the psycho and the socio (as we saw in Chapter 9) are probably irreconcilable. For the psycho no test is ever sufficient to demonstrate conclusively that native speaker and non-native speaker are discrete: when non-native speakers have been shown to perform as well as a native speaker on a test, the cry goes up for yet another test. For the socio there is always another (more) exceptional learner who will, when found, demonstrate that (exceptional) non-native speakers can be equated to native speakers on ultimate attainment. The problem is that we cannot distinguish the non-native speaker from the native speaker except by autobiography. So Cook (1999b) is right. But he is also wrong, very wrong. Making the cut by biography shows only some problems and hides away the exceptions, the bilinguals, the movers away, the disabled intellectually, the exceptional learners. The fact is that mother tongue is not gender, it is not a given from the womb. It is, classically, social, just as culture is. We cannot distinguish them because our premises are inherently flawed, as Hyltenstam and Abrahamsson (2000) point out.

Our searches for the native speaker have returned, again and again, to the question of the standard language. If British English, Singapore English or indeed English as an International Language can claim to be standard languages, then it makes sense to regard a speaker of one of those codes as a native speaker. The debate about the native speaker will go on. In this debate it will continue to be necessary to distinguish between the two senses of native speaker, the flesh and blood and the ideal, the reality and the myth.; and if others choose to problematise, as I have, the flesh-and-blood native speaker, I believe they will still have a use for the ideal. That indeed is a myth but a useful myth.

In addition to the mythic or idealised definition of native speaker, that product of the homogenised, error-free linguistic Eden, there are different flesh-and-blood or reality definitions. They include:

(1)   native speaker by birth (that is by early childhood exposure),
(2)   native speaker (or native speaker-like) by being an exceptional learner,
(3)   native speaker through education using the target-language medium (the *lingua franca* case),
(4)   native speaker by virtue of being a native user (the post-colonial case) and
(5)   native speaker through long residence in the adopted country.

It is clear that definitions (2)–(5) are all ways of compensating for not being definition 1. But they are not parasitic on 1. Indeed they help clarify what it is that (1) means and they challenge us to specify what it is in functional terms they lack that (1) has.

Relevance to Applied Linguistics

An area in which applied linguistics has been attentive to particular non-native speaker needs in recent years has been that of International English (Kachru, 1985; Smith, 1983; Davies, 1989a). The question which arises for applied linguistics is whether International English means a special variety of English with its own norms which are distinct from any national official standard English, or whether it means a use of English in a number of international conferences, settings, for example the United Nations, academic conferences, trade missions, business negotiations. My own view is that International English usually means using one or the other Standard English in international settings. Therefore, from an applied linguistic point of view it is appropriate to designate the activity as English as an International Language rather than as International English. The emphasis is then firmly put on the use of English and not on its separate language form.

Summary

In this chapter I brought together my arguments on who the native speaker is and noted that all characteristics except that of early childhood exposure are contingent ones. I considered the extent to which the contingent characteristics can be acquired without the substantive early exposure and concluded that it is possible but difficult and rare. I have argued that it is in judgement data that the most intractable differences between native and non-native speakers are to be found. I now end by concluding that the fundamental opposition is one of power and that in the event membership is determined by the non-native speaker's assumption of confidence and of identity.

Appendix

J.R. Ross (1979), Grammaticality Sentences

1. Under no circumstances would I accept that offer
2. Nobody who I get along with is here who I want to talk to
3. We don't believe the claim that Jimson ever had any money
4. The fact he wasn't in the store shouldn't be forgotten
5. What will the grandfather clock stand between the bed and?
6. I urge that anything he touch be burned
7. All the further we got was to Sudbury
8. That is a frequently talked about proposal
9. Nobody is here who I get along with who I want to talk to
10. The doctor is sure that there will be no problems
11. The idea he wasn't in the store is preposterous
12. Such formulas should be writable down

(NB: Sentences (11) and (12) in this list were (12) and (13) in Ross's. I omitted Ross's Sentence (11) in my study for the reason Ross himself gives:

> I have omitted from discussion the results of the eleventh questionnaire sentence, where some additional questions of a semantic kind, were asked, because the variation among the respondents was so overwhelming as to defy analysis. (Ross, 1979: 134, fn 2)

Eisenstein and Bodman's Gratitude Situations

(Original numbering: the three used in my study are asterisked.)

1.* It's Friday. You look in your wallet and notice that you only have $2.00. Your good friend at work notices this and hears you say 'Darn, I'll have to go to the bank.' Your friend asks if you need money, and you say that you forgot to go to the bank. Your friend says: 'I have plenty. How much do you need?' You say: 'Could you lend me $5.00? I'll pay you back on Monday.' Your friend says 'Sure. Are you sure you don't need more than that?' You say you don't. Your friend gives you the $5.00.

3.* It's your birthday and you are having a few people over for dinner. A friend brings you a present. You unwrap it and find a blue sweater.

4. You work for a large company. The Vice-President of Personnel calls you into his office. He tells you to sit down, You feel a little nervous, because you have only been working there for six months. The Vice-President says 'You're doing a good job. In fact, we are so pleased with you that I am going to give you a $20.00 a week raise.'

7. You find yourself in sudden need of money – $500.00. You mention this to a friend. Your friend immediately offers to lend it to you. You are surprised and very grateful. Your friend writes out a check for $500.00 and gives it to you. At first you say: 'Oh, no, I didn't mean for you to lend it to me. I couldn't take it.' Your friend says: 'Really, it's all right. What are friends for?' After your friend insists again, you take the check.

9. Your friend suggests going out to lunch. You say that you'd like to go, but you only have $2.00. Your friend says, 'Ah, don't worry. I'll take you today.' Your friend takes you to a very nice restaurant – a much more expensive one than the ones you usually go to. You have a wonderful meal. Your friend pays and you get up to leave.

10. You have just gotten a new and better job. A friend at the office tells you she has organized a farewell party for you.

14.* You have been invited to the home of a rather new friend. You have dinner with him and his wife and a few other friends of theirs. The food was great, and you really enjoyed the evening. As you leave, your hosts accompany you to the door.

Eisenstein and Bodman (1986: 173)

Table 2 Summary of results of all students on individual questions

Q.	Q. topic	No Resp	Not accept	Prob.	Accept	Perf	NotComp	Resist
1	$5.00	5 7.5%	3 4.5%	9 13.4%	9 13.4%	39 58.2%	1 1.5%	1 1.5%
3	Sweat	2 3.0%	3 4.5%	19 28.4%	14 20.9%	29 43.3%	0 0%	0 0%
4	Raise	5 7.5%	10 14.9%	16 23.9%	14 20.9%	18 26.9%	1 1.5%	3 4.5%
7	$500	9 13.4%	3 4.5%	14 20.9%	15 22.4%	21 31.3%	1 1.5%	4 6.0%
9	Lunch	5 3.0%	11 16.4%	22 32.8%	9 13.4%	14 20.9%	1 1.5%	5 7.5%
10	Farewell	14 20.9%	7 10.4%	21 31.3%	11 16.45	13 19.45	0 0%	0 0%
14	Dinner	7 10.4%	2 3.0%	34 35.8%	23 34.3%	11 16.4%	0 0%	0 0%

References

Agnihotri, R.K. and Kanna, A.Y. (1997) *Problematizing English in India.* New Delhi: Sage.

Aitken, A.J. (ed.) (1973) Lowland Scots. *Association for Scottish Literary Studies Occasional Paper 2.* Edinburgh: Association for Scottish Literary Studies.

Alderson, J.C., Clapham, C. and Steel, D. (1997) Metalinguistic knowledge, language aptitude and language proficiency. *Language Teaching Research* 1 (2), 93–121.

Alderson, J.C., Clapham, C. and Wall, D. (1995) *Language Test Construction and Evaluation.* Cambridge: Cambridge University Press.

Alderson, J.C. and Urquhart, A.H. (1983) The effect of student background discipline on comprehension: A pilot study. In A. Hughes and D. Porter (eds) *Current Developments in Language Testing* (pp. 121–127). London: Academic Press.

Allwright, D. (1988) *Observation in the Language Classroom.* London: Longman.

Altmann, G.T.M. (1997) *The Ascent of Babel.* New York: Oxford University Press.

Altmann, G.T.M. (2001) The language machine: Psycholinguistics in review. *British Journal of Psychology* 92 (1), 129–70.

Annamalai, E. (1998) Nativity of language. In R. Singh (ed.) *The Native Speaker: Multilingual Perspectives* (pp. 148–57). New Delhi: Sage.

Ashcroft, B., Griffiths, G. and Tiffin, H. (1989) *The Empire Writes Back.* London: Routledge.

APU (Assessment of Performance Unit) (1984) *Language Performance in Schools* (1982 Secondary Survey Report). London: Department of Education and Science

Atkinson, J. M. and Heritage, J. (eds) (1984) *Structures in Social Action.* Cambridge: Cambridge University Press.

Atkinson, P. (1985) *Language, Structure and Reproduction: An Introduction to the Sociology of Basil Bernstein.* London: Methuen.

Bachman, L.F. (1990) *Fundamental Considerations in Language Testing.* Oxford: Oxford University Press.

Baker, C. and Jones, S.P. (1998) *Encyclopedia of Bilingualism and Bilingual Education.* Clevedon: Multilingual Matters.

Barnard, A. and Spencer, J. (eds) (1996) *Encyclopedia of Social and Cultural Anthropology.* London: Routledge.

Barth, F. (ed.) (1969) *Ethnic Groups and Boundaries.* London: George, Allen and Unwin/Bergen: Universitets Forlaget.

Bartsch, R. (1988) *Norms of Language.* London: Longman.

Bereiter, C. and Englemann, S. (1966) *Teaching Disadvantaged Children in the Pre-school.* Englewood Cliffs, NJ: Prentice-Hall.

Bernstein, Basil (1971-5) *Class, Codes and Control* (Vols 1-5). London: Routledge and Kegan Paul.

Bex, T. and Watts, R.J. (eds) (1999) *Standard English: The Widening Debate*. London: Routledge.

Bhatt, R.M. (1995) Prescriptivism, creativity and World Englishes. *World Englishes* 14 (2), 247–58.

Bialystok, E. (1997) The structure of age: In search of barriers to second language acquisition. *Second Language Research* 13, 116–37.

Bialystok, E. (1998) Coming of age in applied linguistics. *Language Learning* 48 (4), 497–518.

Birdsong, D. (1992) Ultimate attainment in second language acquisition. *Language* 68, 706–55.

Bishop, E. (1983) One art. In *Complete Poems* (p. 178). London: Chatto and Windus.

Bloomfield, L. (1927) Literate and illiterate speech. *American Speech* 2, 432–9. Reprinted in D. Hymes (ed.) (1964) *Language in Culture and Society* (pp. 391–6). New York: Harper and Row.

Bloomfield, L. (1933) *Language*. New York and Chicago: Holt, Rinehart and Winston. Reprinted in 1984 by The University of Chicago Press, Chicago.

Blum-Kulka, S., House, J. and Kasper, G. (eds) (1989) *Advances in Discourse Processes Vol. 31: Cross-Cultural Pragmatics: Requests and Apologies*. Norwood, NJ: Ablex.

Bongaerts, T., Mennen, S. and van der Slik, F. (2000) Authenticity of pronunciation in naturalistic second language acquisition: The case of very advanced late learners of Dutch as a second language. *Studia Linguistica* 54 (2), 298–308.

Braine, G. (ed.) (1999) *Non-native Educators in English Language Teaching*. Mahwah, NJ: Erlbaum.

Brass, P.R. (1974) *Language Religion and Politics in North India*. Cambridge: Cambridge University Press.

Brown, A. and Lumley, T. (1995) How can English proficiency tests be made more culturally appropriate? A case study: The assessment of English teacher proficiency. In S.K. Gill (ed.) *Intelec '94: International and English Language Education Conference: National and International Challenges and Responses* (pp. 122-8). Kuala Lumpur: Language Centre, Universiti Kebangsaan Malaysia.

Brown, A. and Lumley, T. (1998) Linguistic and cultural norms in language testing: A case study. *Melbourne Papers in Language Testing* 7 (1), 80–96.

Brumfit, C. (ed.) (1983) *Language Teaching Projects for the Third World* (ELT Documents 116). Oxford: Pergamon Press in association with the British Council.

Burchfield, R. (1985) *The English Language*. Oxford: Oxford University Press.

Burling, R. (1981) Social constraints on adult language learning. In H. Winitz (ed.) *Native Language and Foreign Language Acquisition* (Annals of New York Academy of Sciences 379) (pp. 279–90). New York: New York Academy of Sciences.

Burt, M.K. and Kiparsky, C. (1972) *The Gooficon: A Repair Manual for English*. Rowley, MA: Newbury House.

Cameron, D. (1998) *The Feminist Critique of Language: A Reader* (2nd edn). London: Routledge.

Campbell, R. and Wales, R. (1970) The study of language acquisition. In J. Lyon (ed.) *New Horizons in Linguistics*. Harmondsworth: Penguin.

Canagarajah, S. (1999a) On EFL teachers, awareness and agency. *ELT Journal* 53 (3), 207–13.

Canagarajah, S. (1999b) *Resisting Linguistic Imperialism in English Teaching*. Oxford: Oxford University Press.

Césaire, A. (1956) *Cahier d'un Retour au Pays Natale*. Paris: Didier.

Chomsky, N. (1957) *Syntactic Structures*. The Hague: Mouton.

Chomsky, N. (1965) *Aspects of the Theory of Syntax*. Boston, MA: MIT Press.

Chomsky, N. (1986) *Knowledge of Language: Its Nature, Origin and Use*. New York: Praeger.

Clapham, C. (1996) *The Development of IELTS: A Study of the Effect of Background Knowledge on Reading Comprehension* (Studies in Language Testing, Vol. 4). Cambridge: University of Cambridge Local Examinations Syndicate and Cambridge University Press.

Clark, J.L.D. (1977) *The Performance of Native Speakers of English on the Test of English as a Foreign Language* (Research Report). Princeton, NJ: Educational Testing Service.

Clayton, T. (2000) *Education and the Politics of Language: Hegemony and Pragmatism in Cambodia (1979-1989)*. Hong Kong: Hong Kong Comparative Research Centre.

Clyne, M. (1982) *Multilingual Australia*. Melbourne: River Seine.

Cook, G. and Seidlhofer, B. (eds) (1995) *Principle and Practice in Applied Linguistics: Studies in Honour of H.G. Widdowson*. Oxford: Oxford University Press.

Cook, V. (1999b) Going beyond the native speaker in language teaching. *TESOL Quarterly* 33 (2), 185–209.

Cook, V. (2001)Linguistics and second language acquisition: One person with two languages. In M. Aronoff and J. Rees-Miller (eds) *The Handbook of Linguistics* (pp. 488–511). Oxford: Blackwell.

Coppieters, R. (1987) Competence differences between native and near-native speakers. *Language* 63, 544–73.

Corder, S.P. (1981) *Error Analysis and Interlanguage*. Oxford: Oxford University Press.

Coulmas, F. (ed.) (1981) *A Festschrift for Native Speaker*. The Hague: Mouton.

Crewe, W. (ed.) (1977a) *The English Language in Singapore*. Singapore: Eastern Universities Press.

Crewe, W. (1977b) Singapore English as a non-native dialect. In W. Crewe (ed.) *The English Language in Singapore* (pp. 96–119). Singapore: Eastern Universities Press.

Criper, C. and Davies, A. (1988) *ELTS Validation Project Report* (Research Report 1 (1)). London and Cambridge: The British Council and the University of Cambridge Local Examinations Syndicate.

Crowley, T. (1991) *Proper English: Readings in Language, History and Cultural Identity*. London: Routledge.

Crystal, D. (1987) *The Cambridge Encyclopaedia of Language*. Cambridge: Cambridge University Press.

Crystal, D. (1997) *Dictionary of Linguistics and Phonetics* (4th edn). Oxford: Blackwell.

Cummins, J. (1984) *Bilingualism and Special Education: Issues on Assessment and Pedagogy*. Clevedon: Multilingual Matters.

Davidson, F. (1994) Comments and replies. *World Englishes* 13 (1), 119–20.

Davies A. (1984a) Validating three tests of English language proficiency. *Language Testing* 1 (1), 50–69.

Davies A. (1984b) Idealisation in sociolinguistics: The choice of the standard dialect. In D. Schiffrin (ed.) *GURT 84: Meaning, Form and Use in Context: Linguistic Applications* (pp. 229–39). Washington, DC: Georgetown University Press.

Davies A. (1984c) Simple, simplified and simplification: What is authentic ? In J.C.

Alderson and A.H. Urquhart (eds) *Reading in a Foreign Language* (pp. 181–98). London, Longman.

Davies, A. (1984d) ESL expectations in examining: The problem of English as a foreign language and English as a mother tongue. *Language Testing* 1 (1), 82–96.

Davies, A. (1988) Talking in silence: Ministry in Quaker meetings. In N. Coupland (ed.) *Styles of Discourse* (pp. 105–37). London: Croom Helm.

Davies A. (1989a) Is international English an interlanguage? *TESOL Quarterly*, 23 (3), 447–67

Davies, A. (1989b) Communicative competence as language use. *Applied Linguistics* (special issue: Communicative Competence Revisited) 10 (2), 157–70.

Davies, A. (1990a) *Principles of Language Testing*. Oxford: Blackwell.

Davies A. (1990b) The spoken language. In A. Wilkinson *et al.* (eds) *Specifying Spoken English* (pp. 101–11). Milton Keynes: Open University.

Davies, A. (1991) Correctness in English. In M.L. Tickoo (ed.) *Languages and Standards: Issues, Attitudes, Case Studies* (Anthology Series 26) (pp. 510–67). Singapore: SEAMEO Regional Language Centre.

Davies, A. (1991a) *The Native Speaker in Applied Linguistics*. Edinburgh: Edinburgh University Press.

Davies, A. (2000) What second language learners can tell us about the native speaker: Identifying and describing exceptions. In R.L. Cooper, E. Shohamy and J. Walters (eds) *New Perspectives and Issues in Educational Language Policy: A Festschrift for Bernard Spolsky* (pp. 91–112). Amsterdam: Benjamins.

Davies, A. (2001a) Review of T. Bex and R. J. Watts (eds) (1999) *Standard English: The Widening Debate*. In *Applied Linguistics* 22 (2), 302–11.

Davies, A (2001b) Review of Thomas Clayton (2000) *Education and the Politics of Language: Hegemony and Pragmatism in Cambodia, (1979–1989)*. In *Journal of Multilingual and Multicultural Development* 22 (4), 376–9.

Davies, A., Brown, A., Elder, C., Hill, K., Lumley, T. and McNamara, T. (1999) *Dictionary of Language Testing*. Cambridge: UCLES and Cambridge University Press.

Davies, A. and Elder, C. (eds) (in press) *Handbook of Applied Linguistics*. Oxford: Blackwell.

Dawkins, R. (1986) *The Blind Watchmaker*. London: Longman.

De Houwer, A. (1994) The separate development hypothesis: Method and implications. In G. Extra and L. Verhoeven (eds) *The Cross-linguistic Study of Bilingual Development*. Amsterdam: Royal Netherlands Academy of Arts and Sciences.

Department of Education and Science (1988a) *Report of the Committee of Enquiry into the Teaching of English Language* (Kingman Report). London: HMSO.

Department of Education and Science (1988b) *English for Ages 5-11, The First Cox Report*. London: HMSO.

Department of Education and Science (1989) *English for Ages 11-16, The Second Cox Report*. York: National Curriculum Council.

Donaldson, M. (1978) *Children's Minds*. London: Fontana/Collins.

Douglas, D. (2000) *Assessing Language for Specific Purposes*. Cambridge: Cambridge University Press.

Dressler, W. and Wodak-Ledolter, R. (1977) Language preservation and language death in Brittany. *IJSL* 12, 33–44.

Eisenstein, M. and Bodman, J.W. (1986) 'I very appreciate!' expressions of gratitude by native and non-native speakers of American English. *Applied Linguistics* 7 (2), 167–85.

Elder, C. (1994) Are raters' judgements of language teacher effectiveness wholly language based? *Melbourne Papers in Language Testing* 3 (2), 41–61.

Elder, C., Davies, A., Hajek, J., Manwaring, D. and Warren, J. (1997) Is grammar good for you? The relationship between metalinguistic knowledge and success in studying a language at university. *Melbourne Papers in Language Testing* 5 (1), 35–55.

Elder, C., Warren, J., Hajek, J. Manwaring, D. and Davies, A. (1999) Metalinguistic knowledge: How important is it in studying a language at the university? *Australian Review of Applied Linguistics* 22 (1), 81-95.

Ellis, R. (1985) *Understanding Second Language Acquisition.* Oxford: Oxford University Press.

Ellis, R. (in press) Individual differences in second language learning. In A. Davies and C. Elder (eds) *Handbook of Applied Linguistics.* Oxford: Blackwell.

Faerch, C. and Kasper, G. (1989) Internal and external modification in interlanguage request realization. In S. Blum-Kulka, J. House and G. Kasper (eds) *Advances in Discourse Processes Vol. 31: Cross-Cultural Pragmatics: Requests and Apologies* (pp. 221–47). Norwood, NJ: Ablex.

Fasold, R. (1984) *The Sociolinguistics of Society.* Oxford: Basil Blackwell.

Felix, S.W. (1987) *Cognition and Language Growth.* Dordrecht, Holland: Foris.

Ferguson, C. (1959) Diglossia. *Word* 15, 125–40.

Ferguson, C. (1971) Absence of copula and the notion of simplicity: A study of normal speech, baby talk, foreigner talk and pidgins. In D. Hymes (ed.) *Pidginization and Creolization of Languages* (pp. 141–50). Cambridge: Cambridge University Press.

Ferguson, C. (1983) Language planning and language change. In J. Cobarrubias and J. Fishman (eds) *Progress in Language Planning.* Berlin: Mouton.

Fillmore, C.J. (1979) On fluency. In C. J. Fillmore, D. Kempler and W. S.-Y. Wang (eds) *Individual Differences in Language Ability and Language Behavior* (pp. 85–101). New York: Academic Press.

Firth, J. R. (1950) Personality and language in society. *The Sociological Review* xlii (2). Reprinted in J.R. Firth (1957) *Papers in Linguistics 1934-51.* London: Oxford University Press

Firth, J.R. (1957) *Papers in Linguistics 1934-51.* London: Oxford University Press.

Fishman, J. (1967) Bilingualism with and without diglossia; diglossia with and without bilingualism. *Journal of Social Issues* 23 (2), 29–38.

Fishman, J. (1977) Knowing, using and liking English as an additional language. In J. Fishman, R. L. Cooper and A. W. Conrad (eds) *The Spread of English* (pp. 302–10). Rowley, MA: Newbury House.

Fishman J.A., Gertner, M.H., Lowry, E.G. and Milan, W.G. (eds) (1985) *The Rise and Fall of the Ethnic Revival: Perspectives on Language and Ethnicity.* Berlin: Mouton.

Fowler, H.W. (1926) *Modern English Usage.* Oxford: Clarendon Press.

Gardner, R.C. (1985) *Social Psychology and Second Language Learning: The Role of Attitudes and Motivation.* London: Edward Arnold.

Garfinkel, H. (1967) *Studies in Ethnomethodology.* Englewood Cliffs, NJ: Prentice-Hall. Paperback edn: (1984) Cambridge: Polity Press.

Gass, S. M. and Varonis, E.M. (1985) Variation in native speaker speech:

Modification to non-native speakers. *Studies in Second Language Acquisition* 7 (1), 37–57.

Genesee, F. (2001) Bilingual first language acquisition. *Annual Review of Applied Linguistics* 21, 153–68.

Giles, H. (1984) The dynamics of speech accommodation. *International Journal of the Sociology of Language* 46

Giles, H. and Powesland, P.F. (1975) *Speech Style and Social Evaluation.* London: Academic Press.

Gill, S.K. (1999) Standards and emerging linguistic realities in the Malaysian workplace. *World Englishes* 18 (2), 214–31.

Gleitman, L. and Newport, E. (1995) *The Invention of Language by Children: Environmental and Biological Influences on the Acquisition of Language: An Invitation to Cognitive Science.* 2nd edn, ed. L. Gleitman and M. Liberman. Cambridge, MA: MIT Press.

Graddol, D. (1997) *The Future of English.* London: British Council.

Graddol, D. (1999) The decline of the native speaker. In D. Graddol and U.H. Meinhof (eds) *English in a Changing World.* AILA: *The AILA Review* 13, 57–68.

Greenbaum, S. (1985) Commentary on Braj B. Kachru Standards, codification and sociolinguistic realism: The English language in the outer circle. In R. Quirk and H.G. Widdowson (eds) *English in the World: Teaching and Learning the Language and Literatures* (pp. 31–2). Cambridge: Cambridge University Press and the British Council.

Grosjean, F. (1982) *Life with Two Languages: An Introduction to Bilingualism.* Cambridge, MA: Harvard University Press.

Gumperz, J.J. (1964) Linguistics and social interaction in two communities. *American Anthropologist* 66 (6, pt. 2), 137–55.

Gumperz, J.J. (1982) *Discourse Strategies.* Cambridge: Cambridge University Press.

Gumperz, J.J. and Levinson, S.C. (eds) (1996) *Rethinking Linguistic Relativity.* Cambridge: Cambridge University Press.

Halliday, M.A.K. (1975) *Learning How to Mean: Explorations in the Development of Language.* London: Edward Arnold.

Halliday, M.A.K. (1978) *Language as Social Semiotic: The Social Interpretation of Language and Meaning.* London: Edward Arnold.

Hamers, J.F. and Blanc, M.H.A. (1989) *Bilinguality and Bilingualism.* Cambridge: Cambridge University Press.

Hamp-Lyons, L. and Zhang Wen-xia, B. (2000) World Englishes: Issues in and from academic writing assessment. In J. Flowerdew and M. Peacock (eds) *English for Academic Purposes.* Cambridge: Cambridge University Press.

Harley, B. (1986) *Age in Second Language Acquisition.* Clevedon: Multilingual Matters.

Harris, John (1985) *Phonological Variation and Change: Studies in Hiberno-English.* Cambridge: Cambridge University Press.

Harris, R. (1988) *Language, Saussure and Wittgenstein.* London and New York: Routldege.

Harris, R.A. (1993) *The Linguistics Wars.* New York: Oxford University Press.

Harris, R. (1978) *Communication and Language.* Oxford: Oxford University Press. Also excerpted in N. Love (ed.) *Selected Writings of Roy Harris* (pp. 136–50). London: Routledge.

Hatch, E., Flashner, V. and Hunt, L. (1986) The experience model and language teaching. In R.R. Day (ed.) *Talking to Learn (Conversation in Second Language Acquisition)*. Rowley, MA: Newbury House.

Haugen, E. (1966) Dialect, language and nation. *American Anthropologist* 68 (4), 922–34. Also published in J.B. Pride and J. Homes (eds) *Sociolinguistics* (1972) (pp. 97–111). Harmondsworth: Penguin.

Heritage, J. (1984) *Garfinkel and Ethnomethodology*. Cambridge: Polity Press.

Hickey, L. (ed.) (1990) *The Pragmatics of Style*. London: Routledge.

Hill, K. (1996) Who should be the judge? The use of non-native speakers as raters on a test of English as an international language. *Melbourne Papers in Language Testing* 5 (2), 29–50.

Hill, C. and Parry, K. (eds) (1994) *From Testing to Assessment: English as an International Language*. London: Longman.

HMSO (1971) *Census for England, Wales, Scotland*. London, Cardiff, Edinburgh: HMSO.

Holborow, M. (1999) *The Politics of English: A Marxist View of Language*. London: Sage.

Holmes, J. (1988) Doubt and certainty in ESL textbooks. *Applied Linguistics* 9 (1), 21–44.

Honderich, T. (2001) *Philosopher: A Kind of Life*. London: Routledge.

Honey, J. (1985) *Does Accent Matter?* London: Faber and Faber.

Honey, J. (1997) *Language is Power: The Story of Standard English and its Enemies*. London: Faber and Faber.

Hughes, A. (1989) *Testing for Language Teachers*. Cambridge: Cambridge University Press.

Hyltenstam, K. and Abrahamsson, N. (2000) 'Who can become native-like in a second language?' All, some or none? On the maturational constraints controversy in second language acquisition. *Studia Linguistica* 54 (2), 150–66.

Hymes, D.H. (1970) On communicative competence. In J.J. Gumperz and D.H. Hymes (eds) *Directions in Sociolinguistics*. New York: Holt, Rinehart and Winston.

Hymes, D.H. (1989) Postscript. *Applied Linguistics* (Special Issue: Communicative Competence Revisited) 10 (2), 244–50.

Ikome, O. M. (1998) Language 'nativization' in West Africa: Acculturation and acquisition of 'native' speakers in Cameroon. In R. Singh (ed.) *The Native Speaker: Multilingual Perspectives* (pp. 62–78). New Delhi: Sage.

Ioup G., Boustagui, E., Tigri, M.E. and Moselle, M. (1994) Reexamining the critical period hypothesis: A case study of successful adult SLA in a naturalistic environment. *Studies in Second Language Acquisition* 16, 73–98.

Irelé, A. (1964) A defence of négritude: A propos of *Black Orpheus* by J.P. Sartre. *Transition* (Kampala) 3 (13), 9–12.

Janicki, K, (1985) *The Foreigner's Language: A Sociolinguistic Perspective*. Oxford: Pergamon Press.

Jespersen, O. (1922) *Language, its Nature, Development and Origin*. London: Allen and Unwin (Paperback edn, 1969).

Jones, D. (1917) *An English Pronouncing Dictionary, On Strictly Phonetic Principles*. London: Dent

Kachru, B.B. (1985) Standards, codification and sociolinguistic realism: The English language in the outer circle. In R. Quirk and H.G. Widdowson (eds) *English in the*

World: Teaching and Learning the Language and Literatures (pp. 11–30). Cambridge: Cambridge University Press and the British Council.

Kachru, Y.Y. (1988) Language and cultural meaning: Discourse in South Asian English. In B.B. Kachru and L.E. Smith (chairs) *World Englishes: Issues and Challenges of the 1980s*. Colloquium conducted at the 22nd Annual TESOL Convention, Chicago.

Kandiah, T. (1998) Epiphanies of the deathless native user's manifold avatars: A post-colonial perspective on the native speaker. In R. Singh (ed.) *The Native Speaker: Multilingual Perspectives* (pp. 79–110). New Delhi: Sage.

Kaplan, R. (1966) Cultural thought patterns in intercultural education. *Language Learning* 16, 1–20.

Katz, J.J. and Fodor, J.A. (1962) The structure of a semantic theory. *Language* 39, 170–210.

Kenkel, J.M. and Tucker, R.W. (1989) Evaluation of institutionalized varieties of English and its implications for placement and pedagogy. *World Englishes* 8 (2), 201–14.

Kincaid, J. (1988) *A Small Place*. New York: Farra Straus, Giroux.

Klein, W. (1986) *Second Language Acquisition*. Cambridge: Cambridge University Press.

Kramsch, C. (1993) *Context and Culture in Language Teaching*. Oxford: Oxford University Press.

Kramsch, C. (1998) *Language and Culture*. Oxford: Oxford University Press.

Kramsch, C. (2000) The avatars of literature in language study. *The Modern Language Journal* 84 (4), 553–73.

Kramsch, C. (in press) Language, culture and thought. In A. Davies and C. Elder (eds) *Handbook of Applied Linguistics*. Oxford: Blackwell.

Kramsch, C. and Lam, W.S.E. (1999) Textual identities: The importance of being non-native. In G. Braine (ed.) *Non-native Educators in English Language Teaching* (pp. 57–72). Mahwah, NJ: Erlbaum.

Labov, W. (1972) *Language in the Inner City: Studies in the Black English Vernacular*. Philadelphia, PA: University of Philadelphia Press.

Lado, R. (1961) *Language Testing*. London: Longman.

Lambert, R. and Freed, B. (eds) (1982) *The Loss of Language Skills*. Rowley, MA: Newbury House.

Lamming, G. (1960) *The Pleasures of Exile*. London: Michael Joseph.

Le Page, R.B. and Tabouret-Keller, A. (1985) *Acts of Identity*. Cambridge: Cambridge University Press.

Lennerberg, E. (1967) *Biological Foundations of Language*. New York: Wiley.

Leung, C., Harris, R. and Rampton, B. (1997) The idealised native-speaker, reified ethnicities, and classroom realities. Contemporary issues in TESOL. *Working Papers in Urban Language and Literacies* No. 2. London: King's College.

Lo Bianco, J. (1987) *National Policy on Language*. Canberra: Australian Government Public Service.

Long, M. (1981) Input, interaction and second language acquisition. Paper presented at the New York Academy of Sciences Conference on Native and Foreign Language Acquisition.

Long, M. (1983) Linguistic and conversational adjustment to non-native speakers. *Studies in Second Language Acquisition* 5 (2), 177–93.

Long, M. (1990) Maturational constraints on language development. *Studies in Second Language Acquisition* 12 (3), 251–85.

Loveday, L. (1982) *The Sociolinguistics of Learning and Using a Non-Native Language.* Oxford: Pergamon Press.

Lowenberg, P. (1993) Issues of validity in tests of English as a world language: Whose standards? *World Englishes* 12 (1), 95–106.

Lowenberg, P.H. (1995) What do ESL tests test? Issues of cross-cultural norms. In S.K. Gill (ed.) *Intelec '94: International and English Language Education Conference: National and International Challenges and Responses* (pp. 57–65). Kuala Lumpur: Language Centre, Universiti Kebangsaan Malaysia.

McArthur, T. (1998) *The English Languages.* Cambridge: Cambridge University Press.

Malinowski, B. (1923) The problem of meaning in primitive languages. Supplement to C.K. Ogden and I.A. Richards (eds) *The Meaning of Meaning* (pp. 296–336). London: Routledge and Kegan Paul.

Marshall, G. (1994) *The Concise Oxford Dictionary of Sociology.* Oxford: Oxford University Press.

Martin-Jones, M. and Romaine, S. (1986) Semilingualism: A half-baked theory of communicative competence. *Applied Linguistics* 7 (1), 26–38.

Marton, W. and Preston, D.R. (1975) British and American English for Polish university students: Research report and projections. *Glottodidactica* 8, 27–43.

McCawley, J.D. (1986) Review of '*The Native Speaker is Dead!*' by T.M. Paikeday. *Linguistics* 24 (6), 1137–41.

McDonald, M. (1989) The exploitation of linguistic mis-match: Towards an ethnography of customs and manners. In R. Grillo (ed.) *Social Anthropology and the Politics of Language* (pp. 90–105). London: Routledge.

McMorris, J. (2001) *The Warden of English: The Life of H.W. Fowler.* Oxford: Oxford University Press.

McNamara, T.F. (1990) Assessing the second language proficiency of health professionals. Unpublished PhD thesis, University of Melbourne.

Medgyes, P. (1994) *The Non-Native Teacher.* London: Macmillan.

Medgyes, P. (1999) *The Non-native Teacher* (revised 2nd edn). Ismaning, Germany: Hueber.

Meisel, J. (1980) Linguistic simplification: A study of immigrant workers' speech and foreigner talk. In S. Felix (ed.) *Second Language Development: Trends and Issues* (pp. 13–40). Tubingen Narr.

Merton, R.K. (1938) Social structure and anomie. *American Sociological Review* 3 (Jun.), 672–82.

Mitchell, A.G. and Delbridge, A. (1965) *The Pronunciation of English in Australia* (rev. edn). Sydney: Angus and Robertson.

Mohanan, K.P. (1998) On new/non-native Englishes: A quartet: Second response. In R. Singh (ed.) *The Native Speaker: Multilingual Perspectives* (pp. 50–3). New Delhi: Sage.

Morrow, K. (1979) Communicative language testing: Revolution or evolution? In C. Brumfit and K. Johnson (eds) *The Communicative Approach to Language Teaching* (pp. 143–58). Oxford: Oxford University Press.

Mugglestone, L. (1995) *Talking Proper: The Rise of Accent as Social Symbol.* Oxford: Clarendon Press.

Neufeld, G. (1978) A theoretical perspective on the nature of linguistic aptitude. *International Review of Applied Linguistics* 16, 15–26.

wa Thiongo, N. (1986) *Decolonising the Mind: The Politics of Language in African Literature.* London: Heinemann.

Ochs, E. (1982) Talking to children in Western Samoa. *Language in Society* 11, 77–104.

Orru, M. (1987) *Anomie: History and Meanings.* Boston, MA: Allen and Unwin.

Paikeday, T.M. (1985) *The Native Speaker is Dead!* Toronto and New York: Paikeday.

Paradis, M. (1998) Neurolinguistic aspects of the native speaker. In R. Singh (ed.) *The Native Speaker: Multilingual Perspectives* (pp. 205–19). New Delhi: Sage.

Patkowski, M.S. (1980) The sensitive period for the acquisition of syntax in a second language. *Language Learning* 30, 449–72.

Pattanayak, D.P. (1998) Mother tongue: An Indian context. In R. Singh (ed.) *The Native Speaker: Multilingual Perspectives* (pp. 124–47). New Delhi: Sage.

Pawley, A. and Syder, F.H. (1983) Two puzzles for linguistic theory: Naturelike selection and naturelike fluency. In J.C. Richards and R. Schmidt (eds) *Language and Communication.* Harlow: Longman.

Peters, P. (1995) *The Cambridge Australian English Style Guide.* Melbourne: Cambridge University Press.

Phillipson, R. (1992) *Linguistic Imperialism.* Oxford: Oxford University Press.

Phillipson, R., Kellerman, E., Selinker, L., Sharwood-Smith, M. and Swain, M. (eds) (1991) *Foreign/Second Language Pedagogy Research (A Commemorative Volume for Claus Faerch).* Clevedon: Multilingual Matters.

Platt, J. T. (1977) The sub-varieties of Singapore English: Their sociolectal and functional status. In W. Crewe (ed.) *The English Language in Singapore* (pp. 83–95). Singapore: Eastern Universities Press.

Platt, J. and Weber, H. (1980) *English in Singapore and Malaysia: Status, Features, Functions.* Kuala Lumpur: Oxford University Press.

Porter, P.A. (1986) How learners talk to each other: Input and interaction task-centred discussions. In R.R. Day (ed.) *Talking to Learn: Conversations in Second Language Acquisition.* Rowley, MA: Newbury House.

Prabhu, N.S. (1987) *Second Language Pedagogy.* Oxford: Oxford University Press.

Pride, J.B. (ed.) (1985) *Cross-Cultural Encounters (Communication and Mis-Communication).* Melbourne: River Seine.

Punter, D. (2000) *Post-colonial Imaginings.* Edinburgh: Edinburgh University Press.

Quirk, R. (1987) The question of standards in the international use of English. In P.H. Lowenberg (ed.) *Georgetown University Round Table on Languages and Linguistics.* Washington, DC: Georgetown University Press.

Quirk, R. (1990) What is Standard English? R. Quirk and G. Stein (eds) *English in Use* (pp.112–125). London: Longman.

Quirk, R. and Stein, G. (1990) *English in Use.* London: Longman.

Quirk, R. and Widdowson, H.G. (eds) (1985) *English in a Changing World: Teaching and Learning the Language and Literatures.* Cambridge: Cambridge University Press and the British Council.

Rajagopalan, K. (1997) Linguistics and the myth of nativity: Comments on the controversy over 'new/non-native Englishes'. *Journal of Pragmatics* 27, 225–31.

Rajagopalan, K. (1999) Of EFL teachers, conscience and cowardice. *ELT Journal* 53 (3), 200–6.

Rao, R. (1938) *Kanthapura.* Paris.

Richards, J., Platt, J. and Platt, H. (1985/1992) *Longman Dictionary of Language Teaching and Applied Linguistics.* Harlow: Longman..

Rintell, E.M. and Mitchell, C.J. (1989) Studying requests and apologies: An inquiry into method. In S. Blum-Kulka, J. House and G. Kasper (eds) *Advances in Discourse Processes Vol. 31: Cross-Cultural Pragmatics: Requests and Apologies* (pp. 248–72). Norwood, NJ: Ablex.

Romaine, S. (1988) *Pidgin and Creole Languages.* Harlow: Longman.

Romaine, S. (1989) *Bilingualism.* Oxford: Basil Blackwell.

Rosen, H. (1972) *Language and Class: A Critical Look at the Theories of Basil Bernstein.* Bristol: Falling Wall Press.

Rosen, H. and Burgess,T. (1980) *Languages and Dialects of London School Children.* London: Ward Lock.

Ross, J.R. (1979) Where's English? In C.J. Fillmore, D. Kempler and W. S-Y. Wang (eds) *Individual Differences in Language Ability and Language Behavior* (pp. 127–63). New York: Academic Press.

Rutherford, W.E. (1987) *Second Language Grammar: Learning and Teaching.* London: Longman.

Ryan, E.B. and Giles, H. (eds) (1982) *Attitudes Towards Language Variation.* London: Edward Arnold.

Ryan, E.B., Giles, H. and Sebastian, R.J. (1982) An integrative perspective for the study of attitudes towards language variation. In E.B. Ryan and H. Giles (eds) *Attitudes Towards Language Variation* (pp. 1–19). London: Edward Arnold.

Sapir, E. (1931) Conceptual categories in primitive languages. *Science* 74, 578.

de Saussure, F. (1916) *Cours de linguistique générale.* Paris: Payot. (English translation by R. Harris (1984) London: Duckworth.)

de Saussure, F. (1966) *Course in General Linguistics* (trans. W. Baskin). New York: McGraw-Hill.

Scribner, S. and Cole, M. (1981) *The Psychology of Literacy.* Cambridge, MA: Harvard University Press.

Seidlhofer, B. (2000) Mind the gap: English as a mother tongue versus English as a lingua franca. *Views* 9 (1), 51–68. (University of Vienna Department of English)

Seliger, H. (1978) Implications of a multiple critical periods hypothesis for second language learning. In W. Ritchie (ed.)

Singh, S. (1997) *Fermat's Last Theorem.* London: Fourth Estate.

Singh, U. N. (1998) Introduction by the Series Editor. In R. Singh (ed.) *The Native Speaker: Multilingual Perspectives* (pp. 11–25). Delhi: Sage.

Singh, R. (ed.) (1998) *The Native Speaker: Multilingual Perspectives.* New Delhi: Sage.

Singleton, D. (2001) Age and second language acquisition. *Annual Review of Applied Linguistics* 21, 77–89.

Skutnabb-Kangas, T. (1981) *Bilingualism or Not: The Education of Minorities.* Clevedon: Multilingual Matters.

Skutnabb-Kangas,T. and Phillipson, R. (eds) (1994) *Linguistic Human Rights: Overcoming Linguistic Discrimination.* Berlin: Mouton de Gruyter.

Smith, L. (ed.) (1983) *Readings in English as an International Language.* Oxford: Pergamon Press.

Smith, N. and Wilson, D. (1979) *Modern Linguistics.* Harmondsworth: Penguin.

Society for Pure English (1919) *Society for Pure English Tracts* (Vols 1-66). Oxford: Oxford University Press. Reprinted (1979). New York: Garland.

Spolsky, B. (1989) *Conditions for Second Language Learning: Introduction to a General Theory.* Oxford: Oxford University Press.

Spolsky, B. (1993) Testing across cultures: An historical perspective. *World Englishes* 12 (1), 87–93.

Steiner, G. (1968) *Extraterritorial.* London: Faber.

Stern, H.H. (1983) *Fundamental Concepts of Language Teaching.* Oxford: Oxford University Press.

Sutcliffe, D. (1982) *British Black English.* Oxford: Basil Blackwell.

Sutton-Spence, R. and Woll, B. (1999) *The Linguistics of British Sign Language: An Introduction.* Cambridge: Cambridge University Press.

Swain, M. and Lapkin, S. (1982) *Evaluating Bilingual Education: A Canadian Case Study.* Clevedon: Multilingual Matters.

Swales, J. (1984) *Episodes in English for Science and Technology.* Oxford: Pergamon Press.

Swisher, M.V. and McKee, D. (1989) The sociolinguistic situation of natural sign languages. *Applied Linguistics* 10, 294–312.

Taft, R. and Cahill, D. (1989) Mother tongue maintenance in Lebanese immigrant families in Australia. *Journal of Multilingual and Multicultural Development* 10 (2), 129–43. Clevedon: Multilingual Matters

Tajfel, H. (1981) *Human Groups and Social Categories.* Cambridge: Cambridge University Press.

Tannen, D. and Saville-Troike, M. (eds) (1985) *Perspectives on Silence.* Norwood, NJ: Ablex.

Tay, M.W.J. (1982) The uses, users and features of English in Singapore. In J. Pride (ed.) *New Englishes* (pp. 51–70). Rowley, MA: Newbury House.

Taylor, B. (1976) Towards a sociolinguistic analysis of swearing and the language of abuse in Australian English. In M.G. Clyne (ed.) *Australia Talks* (pp. 43–62). Canberra: Pacific Linguistics.

Temple, R. (2000) Comparing learner and native speech production. *Studia Linguistica* 54 (2), 282–297.

Thomas, G. (1991) *Language Purism.* London: Longman.

Thomas, J. (1983) Cross-cultural pragmatic failure. *Applied Linguistics* 4 (2), 91–112.

Tickoo, M. L. (ed.) (1991) *Language and Standards: Issues, Attitudes, Case Studies.* Singapore: RELC/SEAMEO.

Trudgill, P. (1975) *Accent, Dialect and the School.* London: Edward Arnold.

Trudgill, P. (1983) *On Dialect: Social and Geographical Perspectives.* Oxford: Blackwell.

Trudgill, P. (1995) On New/Non-native Englishes. In E.A. Afendras, S. Millar, E.M. Aogain, A. Bamgbose, Y. Kachru, A.P. Saleemi, B. Preisler, P. Trudgill, F. Coulmas and P. Dasgupta *Journal of Pragmatics* 24, 295–321.

Tutuola, A. (1952) *The Palm-wine Drinkard.* London: Faber and Faber.

Tutuola, A. (1953) *My Life in the Bush of Ghosts.* London: Faber and Faber.

van Ek, J.A and Trim, J.L.M. (eds) (1984) *Across the Threshold: Readings from the Modern Languages Projects of the Council of Europe.* Oxford: Pergamon Press (for and on behalf of the Council of Europe).

Van Els, T.J.M. (2000) The European Union, its institutions and its languages: Some language political observations. Final Public lecture University of Nijmegen, The Netherlands, 22 September.

Van Els, T., Bongaerts, T., Extra, G., van Os, C. and Janssen van-Dieten, A. (1977)

(references to English translation, 1984) *Applied Linguistics and the Learning and Teaching of Foreign Languages*. London: Edward Arnold.

Webster, N. (1961) *Webster's Third New International Dictionary*. New York: G&K Merriam.

Webster, N. (1993/4) *Ninth New Collegiate Dictionary of the English Language*. New York: Black Dog and Leventhal.

Wells, G. (1987) Unpublished MSc dissertation in Applied Linguistics, University of Edinburgh.

White, L. and Genesee, F. (1996) How native is near-native? The issue of ultimate attainment in adult SLA. *Second Language Research* 12 (3), 233–65.

Whorf, B.L. (1942) Language, mind and reality. In J.B. Caroll (ed.)

Williams, T. (1985) The nature of mis-communication in the cross-cultural employment interview. In J.B. Pride (ed.) *Cross-Cultural Encounters (Communication and Mis-Communication)* (pp. 165–75). Melbourne: River Seine.

Winitz, H. (ed.) (1981) *Native Language and Foreign Language Acquisition (Annals of New York Academy of Sciences* Vol. 379). New York: Academy of Sciences.

Wittgenstein, L. (1953) *Philosophical Investigations* (trans. G.E.M. Anscombe). New York: Macmillan.

Wolff, H. (1959) Intelligibility and interethnic attitudes. *Anthrop. Ling.* 1 (3), 34–41.

Wolfram, W.A. (1966) The sociolinguistics of glossolalia. Master's Thesis, Hartford Seminary.

Wolfson, N. (1981) Compliments in cross-cultural perspective. *TESOL Quarterly* 15 (2), 117–24.

Wood, R. (1991) *Assessment and Testing*. Cambridge: Cambridge University Press and UCLES.

Wyld, H.C. (1934) *The Best English: A Claim for the Superiority of Received Standard English*. Society for Pure English Tracts No. 39. Oxford: The Clarendon Press. Also excerpted in T. Crowley (1991) *Proper English: Readings in Language, History and Cultural Identity*. London: Routledge.

Yngve, V.H. (1981) The struggle for a theory of Native Speaker. In F. Coulmas (ed.) *A Festschrift for Native Speaker* (pp. 29–49). The Hague: Mouton.

Zuengler, J. (1989) Identity and IL development and use. *Applied Linguistics* 10 (1), 80–96.

Index